SUBMARINE
WARFARE
in the Civil War

Mark K. Ragan

DA CAPO PRESS
A Member of the Perseus Books Group

Set in 11.5-point Bodoni Book by The Perseus Books Group

Cataloging-in-Publication data for this book is available from the Library of Congress.

Originally published as *Union and Confederate Submarine Warfare in the Civil War*
Originally published by Savas Publishing in 2001
First Da Capo Press edition 2002
ISBN 0–306–81197–9

Published by Da Capo Press
A Member of the Perseus Books Group
http://www.dacapopress.com

Da Capo Press books are available at special discounts for bulk purchases in the U.S. by corporations, institutions, and other organizations. For more information, please contact the Special Markets Department at the Perseus Books Group, 11 Cambridge Center, Cambridge, MA 02142, or call (800) 255-1514 or (617) 252-5298, or e-mail j.mccrary@perseusbooks.com.

1 2 3 4 5 6 7 8 9—06 05 04 03

This book is dedicated to my
Great-Great Grandfather's younger brother,
Obadiah Pearce, who was captured at the Battle of Malvern Hill. Copies
of his obituary have been passed down through the generations.

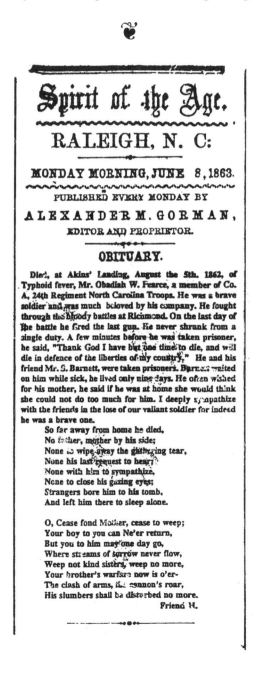

Spirit of the Age.

RALEIGH, N. C:

MONDAY MORNING, JUNE 8, 1863.

PUBLISHED EVERY MONDAY BY

ALEXANDER M. GORMAN,

EDITOR AND PROPRIETOR.

OBITUARY.

Died, at Akins' Landing, August the 5th. 1862, of Typhoid fever, Mr. Obadiah W. Pearce, a member of Co. A, 24th Regiment North Carolina Troops. He was a brave soldier and was much beloved by his company. He fought through the bloody battles at Richmond. On the last day of the battle he fired the last gun. He never shrank from a single duty. A few minutes before he was taken prisoner, he said, "Thank God I have but one time to die, and will die in defence of the liberties of my country," He and his friend Mr. S. Barnett, were taken prisoners. Barnett waited on him while sick, he lived only nine days. He often wished for his mother, he said if he was at home she would think she could not do too much for him. I deeply sympathize with the friends in the lose of our valiant soldier for indeed he was a brave one.

> So far away from home he died,
> No father, mother by his side;
> None to wipe away the gathering tear,
> None his last request to hear;
> None with him to sympathize,
> None to close his gazing eyes;
> Strangers bore him to his tomb,
> And left him there to sleep alone.
>
> O, Cease fond Mother, cease to weep;
> Your boy to you can Ne'er return,
> But you to him may one day go,
> Where streams of sorrow never flow,
> Weep not kind sisters, weep no more,
> Your brother's warfare now is o'er
> The clash of arms, the cannon's roar,
> His slumbers shall be disturbed no more.
>
> Friend H.

Contents

ships from under the surface, but none achieved even remote success. It was not until David Bushnell created his ingenious little *Turtle* during the Revolutionary War that submarines began to be thought of as potential war machines. Although the *Turtle* came within a hair of sinking three British frigates, it failed on both occasions—mostly due to circumstances beyond the vessel's control. But it went down in recorded history as the first vehicle that could navigate in three dimensions, and David Bushnell became the father of underwater warfare. The clever Bushnell also invented floating mines.

Bushnell's vision jump started the concept of designing submerged vessels to destroy surface ships. Robert Fulton of steamboat fame quickly followed with his *Nautilus,* using designs borrowed from Bushnell. Fulton proved the new technology could work by blowing up a barge. Inventors in Holland, France, and Russia began conceiving all manner of submarines. Some worked reasonably well, some were miserable failures. A Dr. Phillips of Buffalo, New York, built at least three submarines that he experimented with in Lake Erie, mounting a cannon on one that could fire from underwater into the hull of a ship above.

The next revelation came with the Confederate submarine *Hunley,* which became the first to finally sink a warship. Its tragic story and other ingenious attempts at submarine warfare during the Civil War are recounted with intriguing detail by Ragan in *Submarine Warfare in the Civil War.* There can be no doubt that Mark's study is the definitive effort on such an important subject. A submariner himself, owning and diving his personal submarine, there can be no better guide into the technology of a bygone era.

No one could have done it better.

Clive Cussler
Telluride, Colorado
June 1998

INTRODUCTION

The American Civil War, like most conflicts throughout history, resembled both the war it followed and those still waiting in the future. In many respects it was the world's first modern war. For the first time since the dawn of man, railroads made it possible to quickly transport large armies hundreds of miles away to distant theaters. Land and underwater mines were laid by the thousands to protect entrenchments, forts, roads, rivers, and harbors. Crude forerunners to the machine gun were built and tested by both sides. For the first time in history, the advent of the telegraph allowed newspapers to report news from the front only hours after an event had transpired. Massive ironclads pounded one another in Hampton Roads and changed naval combat forever.

Of the many technological revolutions spawned during the Civil War, none has received less attention than submarines. Although almost everyone is familiar with the tragic saga of the *CSS Hunley* in Charleston, that boat was but one of a score or more of underwater machines built and deployed by both sides for offensive and defensive use. As strange as that bold statement may sound to students of this well-studied epochal event, it is not fiction. While the submarine was not a new invention, its use in warfare had only been suggested and never attempted with any success anywhere in the world until after the South opened fire on Fort Sumter on April 12, 1861. Why has such a remarkable story been hidden away for so long?

I discovered the answer to that question in the early 1990s, when I began researching the history of the first successful military submarine, the *CSS H. L. Hunley.* The 40' iron boiler with fins and a propeller made the history books on the night of February 17, 1864, when it became the first submarine to sink an enemy vessel during wartime. It did so by attaching a mine to the underside of the Federal sloop *Housatonic,* and detonating it with a lanyard. Compiling together an accurate account of the *Hunley's* operations proved much more difficult than I originally imagined, for surviving records are fragmented and deposited from Alabama to Virginia, and many places in between. Although history recorded that the *Hunley* went down with its victim, strong contemporary evidence suggested otherwise. For example, a shore beacon from Battery Marshall on Sullivan's Island was observed and answered long after the *Housatonic* was resting on the bottom. The exchange of these signals was prearranged between those on shore and the submarine, but thereafter the little boat and her crew of eight were never heard from again. I published my findings in 1995 in a book entitled *The Hunley: Submarines, Sacrifice and Success in the Civil War* (Narwhal). My conclusion that the *Hunley* obviously did not go down with the *Housatonic* was confirmed when a collection of divers and researchers funded by best-selling author Clive Cussler discovered her intact remains a few years ago not far from the site of the sloop's ignominious demise.

It was during the course of my research into the history of the *Hunley* that I unearthed scattered and tantalizing references to other Civil War–era submarines. The more I searched the more documentation I found. To my utter amazement, both sides had pumped substantial resources and energies into the development of underwater boats. Many of them became operational and conducted cruises in search of enemy shipping. The prospects for underwater warfare were taken so seriously that the North formed a commission to analyze and comment on submarine design. The Confederacy issued numerous submarine and related patents and housed much of its documentation on the subject in a "secret archive" that was probably destroyed at war's end. Still, enough contemporary evidence remains to piece together a rich mosaic of the brave adventurers who risked their lives to develop a functional underwater submarine.

The actions of the *CSS Hunley* have been widely reported, but not a single book has been written about these other boats. Contemporary letters, telegrams, factory records, and log books confirm that both large and small submersibles were fabricated and launched across the country. Federal submarines, for example, were built and tested in Newark, New York, and Philadelphia, and utilized in Hampton Roads, the James River, and off Charleston, South Carolina. Much to my surprise, Confederate boats were built and launched in almost every large Southern coastal and river city, from Houston and Galveston, Texas, to Richmond, Virginia. In addition to the *Hunley's* nocturnal assault against the *Housatonic*, Confederate submarine attacks were launched in Hampton Roads, New Orleans, Mobile Bay, and elsewhere. Indeed, in all probability a Richmond-built submarine lies today with her crew near the mouth of the James River after a failed attack against a Federal warship.

Most of these experimental boats failed to meet expectations and several proved fatal to their operators. Some, however, were so advanced in their design they boasted functioning lockout chambers that enabled divers to leave their vessel and operate under the keels of unsuspecting enemy ships. Others experimented with air purification systems, crude periscopes, underwater lights, self-propelled torpedoes, electric batteries, and steam power. Civil War newspapers and magazines North and South provided detailed descriptions of these underwater inventions complete with diagrams and firsthand accounts of their operations. Many of these fascinating blueprints and drawings are reproduced in this study.

I have been interested in the Civil War and underwater adventure since I was a child. In fact, my den is decorated with a mixture of undersea memorabilia and Civil War relics. And across the road, tied to a neighbor's dock, is my own two-man (dry) submarine in which I give weekend piloting classes. It was my passion for small submersibles and the past that led me on my long quest for information on these mid-nineteenth-century iron boats or "infernal machines," as they were often called.

I hope that the reader will find the information presented in this book as fascinating as I do, and worthy of history's attention.

Mark K. Ragan

ACKNOWLEDGMENTS

There are many people who helped make this book a reality, and I would like to take this opportunity to thank them. Their help and encouragement has been invaluable to me. If I overlook someone, I apologize.

First, I would like to extend my sincere appreciation to Clive Cussler, whose NUMA dive team under the direction of divers Ralph Wilbanks, Wes Hall, and Harry Pecorelli discovered the intact hull of the Confederate submarine *H.L. Hunley* on May 3, 1995. Cussler's discovery of the ill-fated iron boat has focused international attention on the little-known story of Civil War submersibles. I also appreciated his willingness to pen a Foreword for this book.

The assistance of Caldwell Delaney, retired head of the Mobile City Museum, was invaluable to me. The museum's collection of files on Alabama–based Civil War submersibles fills a large gap in the historical record.

Charles Peery, M.D., of Charleston, South Carolina, is a maritime collector and Civil War naval historian without peer. Charley was always willing to go "above and beyond the call of duty" to assist me, and I am deeply grateful.

A very special thank you to the archeologist Chris Amer at the South Carolina Institute of Archeology, and Robert Neyland, Richard Wills, and Barbara Volgaris.

A similar hearty thanks is extended to my publisher and chief editor, Theodore P. Savas, of Savas Publishing Company. Ted was involved in the original search for the *Hunley* and has a deep personal interest in Confederate naval history. His advice and guidance in shaping the manuscript were invaluable to me and to the book.

I would also like to thank historians John T. Hunley, Sam Craghead, John H. Friend, Richard Hovis, Richard Sullivan, Sidney H. Schell, Frank Ferman, William C. Schmidt, Jr., Brian Pohanka, Sally Smith, Sen.

Glenn McConnell, James Kloeppel, William Still, Barbara E. Taylor and Charles Torrey of the Mobile City Museum; John Brumgardt, director of the Charleston Museum; Steve Hoffius and Pat Hash of the South Carolina Historical Society; the friendly staff of the Nimitz Library, United States Naval Academy; John M. Coski and Cory Hudgins of the Museum of the Confederacy; Dr. Langley, curator of the Naval History Department, Smithsonian; John E. White, Manuscripts Department, University of North Carolina; the staff of the Valentine Museum; divers Beth Simmons and Greg Cottrell; the staff of the Mobile Historic Preservation Society; George Shroder and George Ewert of the Mobile City Library; the staff of the Library of Congress; Woody West, editor of the *Washington Times;* Caval Cante, curator of the Naval Archives, as well as archivists Michael Musick, Mike Meiers, Becky Livingston, Richard Pizer, Cynthia Middleton, William E. Lind, Mike Pilgrim, and Dianne Blanton; the staff at the Washington Navy Yard; and Ms. Halligan of Houston, Texas.

CHAPTER 1

1861:
ORIGINS

"I propose to you a new arm of war, as formidable as it is economical. Submarine navigation which has been sometimes attempted, but as all know without results, owing to want of suitable opportunities, is now a problematical thing no more."

—*Submarine designer Brutus de Villeroi to President Lincoln, early September 1861*

Although a handful of small and primitive submarines had been constructed and launched prior to the American Civil War, their potential for disrupting and destroying surface vessels was not fully realized until that conflict.

The concept of operating underwater was not new. As early as 400 B.C., ancient sponge divers had used crude diving bells to venture to the bottom of the Aegean Sea. According to Greek philosopher Aristotle, the oxygen within these inverted caldrons was replenished by lowering weighted air-filled animal skins to the working divers below.[1] During the Revolutionary War, an American patriot named David Bushnell built a small one-man submersible in which he conducted history's first recorded underwater attack. On the night of September 6, 1776, Bushnell maneuvered his wooden *Turtle* toward the 64-gun British warship *Eagle*, which was lying at anchor in New York Harbor.[2] Although the tiny *Turtle* failed to destroy the mammoth enemy warship, General George Washington commended Dr. Bushnell for his imaginative efforts and described his amazing underwater invention as an "effort of genius."[3]

Robert Fulton of steamboating fame also dabbled in underwater boats. Fulton built two submarines in the early 1800s and tried to sell them to Napoleon Bonaparte. Even though Fulton was able to sink a

The first known submarine attack was made with David Bushnell's *Turtle* on September 6, 1776. *U. S. Naval Historical Center Diagram*

vessel resting at anchor during an impressive simulation, French officials were (for reasons unknown) not sufficiently impressed and declined Fulton's offer.[4] Another American attack on a British ship was apparently attempted from yet another small wooden submarine during the War of 1812. Although this alleged attack has remained shrouded in mystery, the following account reporting the incident appeared in a Connecticut newspaper during the summer of 1813:

> A gentleman from Norwhich has invented a diving boat, which by means of paddles he can propel underwater. He has been three times under the bottom of the *Ramillies* [a 74-gun British warship] off New London. So great is the alarm and fear on board the *Ramillies* that Commodore Hardy keeps his ships under way at all times.[5]

The exploits of the anonymous operator of the "diving boat" caused such concern amongst the British that Commodore Thomas M. Hardy threatened harsh reprisals against any American found to be involved with underwater weapons. In response to Hardy's threat, the United States Navy officially declared that it deplored torpedo warfare, preferring instead "the more chivalrous method of mowing down crews with grape and canister."[6]

By the beginning of the Civil War in 1861, diving bells and crude underwater breathing equipment (also known as "submarine armor") had been developed in both Europe and the United States. Although the technology enabling man to venture beneath the surface was still in its

1858 photograph of Winan's Cigar Steamer that became an inspiration for several Civil War submariners. It was once suggested that the vessel be used to sink the *CSS Virginia*. *Naval Historical Center*

infancy, several inventors and adventurers recognized the military potential that could be gleaned from a submersible capable of navigating beneath the surface.

On April 19, 1861, just a few days after the capitulation of Fort Sumter in Charleston Harbor, President Abraham Lincoln announced the existence of a blockade of Southern harbors. Since at that time the North had too few ships to effectively close even a single harbor, Lincoln's declaration was little more than a political statement. His threat, however, raised the possibility that at some future time the Confederacy may be isolated from critical and badly needed European munitions and supplies. If an effective blockade was ever imposed, it would eventually strangle the Confederacy and hasten its defeat.

The overwhelming deficiencies in both manpower and manufacturing capabilities relative to the United States, coupled with the fact that the Confederacy would have to be subjugated into submission, dictated primarily a defensive course of action for the South. While generals labored to organize field armies, Secretary of the Navy Stephen R. Mallory

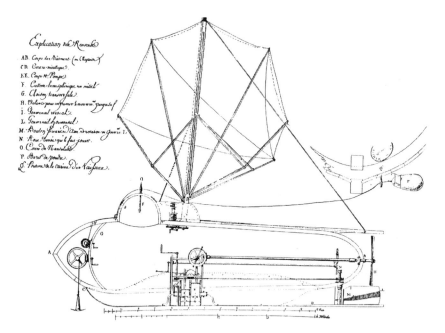

Robert Fulton's *Nautilus* was launched in 1801. *U. S. Naval Historical Center Diagram*

set about defending the Confederacy's shores. Mallory, a Floridian born in Trinidad and former United States senator, had some experience with naval affairs prior to the war and had exhibited a keen interest in ship design and naval innovations. His appointment by Jefferson Davis as naval secretary surprised Mallory, for he had not sought it. Nonetheless, he immediately threw himself into his work.

The difficulties he faced were legion. In the spring of 1861, the newly formed Confederacy had but a handful of vessels from which to form a navy to protect its thousands of miles of vulnerable coastline and inland waterways. Although many Union naval officers of Southern lineage had resigned their commissions and returned to their homes to serve the Confederacy, few ships were waiting for them. In an attempt to alleviate this critical shortage, and forced to utilize any means possible to defend its meandering coastline, the South pressed into service old sailing ships, small tugboats, schooners, and virtually anything that would float. Most of the artillery on these vessels, if they had any at all, were old smoothbore cannons dating as far back as the War of 1812.

Mallory's options to enhance his flotilla were limited: he could either build ships domestically, or have them built overseas. Both alternatives were put into effect. Another idea with merit was the commissioning of privateers to raid Northern commerce on the high seas. Within weeks, privateering commissions from the Confederate government were being awarded to patriotic groups and individuals willing to invest their own capital and ships into the effort. Mallory was willing to try just about anything to defend the several thousand miles of harbors, inlets, and shore-line from attack, and his innovative ideas led to the construction of ironclad ships of war.[7]

◆   ◆   ◆

It was at about this time that the proposed use of small submarines as both offensive and defensive weapons first appear in both Northern and Southern records. In the early months of 1861, an engineer with the Pacific Pearl Company named Julius Kroehl designed a "cigar shaped" submarine boat which he hoped to employ with the Union Navy Department.[8] Kroehl was of the opinion his submarine could be used to enter blockaded Southern harbors and destroy or remove underwater obstructions. Although his first design was never adopted, his later plans won great favor, and a submarine vessel of his conception was actually completed three years later in 1864.[9]

On June 10, 1861, the *Columbia* (Tennessee) *Herald* published what is probably the first account seeking assistance from Southern citizens to build submarines to defend their shores. Its author, Rev. Franklin Smith, was a respected chemist and inventor who owned one of the finest laboratories in the South.[10] It was of sufficient interest to be reprinted in newspapers across the Confederacy:

June, 10, 1861,

SUBMARINE WARFARE,

Excepting our privateers the Confederate States have not a single ship at sea. Throughout our southern seaports, men of a mechanical turn and of the right spirit must go to work, maturing the best plans for the destruction or the capture of every blockading ship.

From the Chesapeake to the mouth of the Rio Grande, our coast is better fitted for submarine warfare than any other in the world. I would have every hostile keel chased from our coast by submarine propellers. The new vessel must be cigar shaped for speed—made of plate iron, joined without external rivet heads; about thirty feet long, with a central section about 4 × 3 feet—driven by a spiral propeller. The new Aneroid barometer made for increased pressure, will enable the adventurer easily to decide his exact distance below the surface.

In closing Rev. Smith stated the following:

I am preparing a detailed memoir on Submarine Warfare, discussing matters not proper to be spoken of here, illustrated with engravings. Copies of the pamphlet will be sent to mayors of southern maritime cities.

Reverend Franklin Smith could well be regarded as the father of the Confederate submarine for his early 1861 article entitled "Submarine Warfare" was copied in newspapers throughout the South. *Photo courtesy of the Athenaeum Rectory Columbia, Tennessee*

It will never be known just how many Southerners acted on Reverend Smith's letter. According to documents in the possession of his decendents, Smith himself is credited with building at least one of the several submarines constructed in Mobile, Alabama, during the war.[11]

◆   ◆   ◆

Within two weeks after the original appearance of Smith's letter, the United States Navy Department in Washington received a troubling communication from someone named E. P. Doer. Rebel engineers, claimed the New York resident, were constructing a submarine boat in New Orleans, and they planned to attack ships at the mouth of the Mississippi River blockading the Crescent City. Doer's letter is the earliest known correspondence addressed to the Navy Department concerning Confederate submarine activity:

Chicago, Ill., June 25, 1861,

Dear Sir:

I am a resident of Buffalo N.Y.; I am here stopping a few days at Tremont House. Yesterday I met a lady belonging in the New England States, who has been engaged for the past three years in teaching school, a little north of New Orleans. She left there a few days (six) since and arrived here yesterday morning. She is a very intelligent, middle-aged woman, full of patriotism for her country, and thankful for her escape from the south.

She tells me that the rebels in New Orleans are constructing an infernal submarine vessel to destroy the *Brooklyn*, or any vessel blockading the mouth of the Mississippi; from her description, she is to be used as a projectile with a sharp iron or steel pointed prow to perforate the bottom of the vessel and then explode. Says that it is being constructed by competent engineers. I put implicit reliance in the correctness of this information.

I am, respectfully, your obedient servant,

E. P. Doer, Buffalo, N.Y.[12]

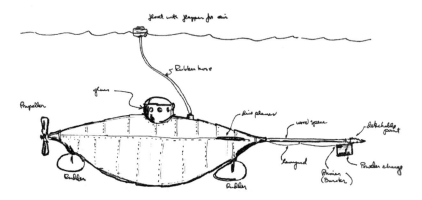

Modern diagram of the New Orleans submarine by historian Sidney H. Schell.

The small submarine described in Doer's correspondence may well be the boat on display today at the Louisiana State Museum in the heart of New Orleans' French Quarter. This mysterious contraption was discovered in 1879 by a diver attached to the dredge boat *Valentine*.[13] Her identity has been the subject of intense speculation ever since. Over the ensuing decades, historians and local news reporters have attempted to identify who designed and built her. Although no one has yet conclusively proven her origins, one objective indicator at least suggests this submarine was the same one written of by Doer in the opening months of the war. Doer's June letter mentions that the submarine then under construction in New Orleans would utilize "a sharp iron or steel pointed prow to perforate the bottom of the vessel," with an explosive device attached to the end. The mystery submarine now on display in New Orleans also utilized a spar arrangement, as can be seen from a hole in her bow designed for that purpose.

The New Orleans mystery boat is well assembled and in remarkably good condition, especially considering it was built more than 130 years ago. The metal plates that make up the hull are attached in a unique fashion, not unlike the early-war New Orleans iron ram *Manassas*. The overlapping iron bands that make up the submarine's hull appear to be attached in the same manner as seen in diagrams of the *Manassas*. Did the same engineers who constructed the submarine boat also put together the *Manassas?* Louis Gennela, a Confederate torpedo boat researcher, first put forth this idea in the early 1960s. Lacking other

No records of who built this early-war submarine have been found. Historian Louis Gennela has theorized that it may have been fabricated by the same group that built the privateer iron ram *Manassas*. The illustration of the *Manassas* shows that both vessels looked very much alike. *Naval Historical Center*

The *CSS Manassas* from *Harper's Weekly*

evidence, Gennela's theory is as good as any as to who constructed the New Orleans submersible.

Whoever constructed it knew what they were doing, for the excellent workmanship was the result of competent and innovative engineers. This was a time when ships were built almost exclusively out of wood, and little was known regarding the use of iron in the manufacture of a hull—a fact that makes their accomplishment that much more amazing. Some answers as to how it was constructed, powered, and operated are contained within the hull, which is where John Hunley, perhaps the leading expert on the New Orleans submarine, ventured in the 1970s. Hunley's survey of the vessel's cramped interior resulted in meticulously recorded measurements and notes regarding the vessel's construction. Although much of the internal machinery had been removed, his examination uncovered a plethora of fascinating detail.

The boat is 19' 6" from bow to stern and has a 6' high pressure hull displacing about four tons of seawater. The small Confederate submarine carried a crew of only three men. Two sat on a wooden plank located on the port side of an iron crankshaft that was in turn attached to a four-blade stern propeller. At the base of the crankshaft (within the pressure hull) directly in front of this propeller was a differential gear that enabled the external propeller to revolve much faster than the shaft being turned by the two crewmen. The skipper, or pilot of the vessel, probably operated the diving planes, which were located on either side of the boat's narrow bow. This was accomplished with a lever attached to rods that penetrated the iron hull through stuffing boxes. A hole in the top of the submarine appears to have once supported a small conning tower that has long since been lost. The earliest known photographs of this vessel show that the observation tower—which probably was about a foot or two high with small glass windows and a metal hatch—was removed long ago. Small rudders at each end of the submarine enabled the vessel to maneuver to port or starboard, while an internal ballast tank allowed the vessel to sink whenever seawater was allowed to enter. A simple hand pump attached to the outside of this ballast compartment expelled the water, thus allowing the vessel to rise to the surface when desired. Two lifting eyes are bolted to the top of the hull, which allowed it to be hoisted in and out of the water by crane. (It is interesting to note

Frances J. Wehner, a former officer in the 5th Louisiana Infantry, claimed to have helped construct the New Orleans submarine during the early months of the war. In 1924, at the age of 81, he posed for this photograph alongside what then remained of the vessel. *Alabama Archives*

that small modern submarines have this same arrangement.) An opening in front of the entry (conning tower) hole appears to have once held a snorkel assembly of some kind, and probably supported a flexible tube attached to a flotation device that drifted on the surface and allowed oxygen to enter the boat. Regardless of how well the New Orleans boat was constructed or how innovative her design, we will probably never know whether she was used during the early stages of the war. Other than the cryptic and incomplete June 25, 1861, letter from E. P. Doer to the Federal Navy Department, no records regarding the boat have been found.

Although no contemporary Confederate documentation has thus far come to light, in 1924, an 81-year-old ex-lieutenant from the 5th Louisiana Infantry named Frances J. Wehner, stated in a newspaper interview that he had helped build the vessel in New Orleans during the early months of the war. A review of Lt. Wehner's war record at the National Archives revealed that he had indeed joined the 5th Louisiana at New Orleans on May 10, 1861, and had apparently remained in the vicinity of the city for several months following his induction. Wehner was later wounded at the battle of Payne's Farm, Va., on November 27,

1863, returned to service several months later, only to be captured at the Battle of the Wilderness in May of 1864. Unfortunately Wehner never revealed any information as to where the submarine had been constructed in his postwar interview, or for that mater, the names of the engineers who had designed her. A sad fact that may remain unanswered for the foreseeable future. From regimental documentation Lt. Wehner appears to have been an honorable man with a distinguished war record, whose statements regarding his early war involvement with the submarine in question, in light of his known credentials, are hard to dispute. [14]

For several years following the discovery of this small submarine, her rusting hull lay in the weeds near where it had been found. In 1909, she was transported to the Confederate Veterans Home, where she was on display for many years.[15] All that is known for sure is that she was built during the early days of the Civil War by competent engineers dedicated to breaking the blockade in a most unusual way. Since New Orleans was captured in April 1862, and the submarine most likely scuttled shortly before or after, we can say with some certainty that the only time she may have been in service was from the summer of 1861 through the early months of 1862.

◆   ◆   ◆

Although history has accorded the unique New Orleans boat some notoriety, there appears to have been other submarines operating at the same time in other parts of the country. While the Crescent City's unknown builders worked on their boat, a curious contraption was being examined by United States naval officers some 1,200 miles away at the Philadelphia Navy Yard. On the evening of May 16, 1861, an iron vessel was observed moving down the Delaware River near Smith's Island. With the Philadelphia harbor police in hot pursuit, the partially submerged craft ran aground on the lower end of the island and was boarded by her pursuers. The four men arrested on board revealed to the suspicious officers that the mysterious vessel was in fact a submarine boat. Within hours, word of its discovery was sent clicking over the eastern seaboard's telegraph lines.

Diagram of Brutus de Villeroi's submarine, from *Frank Leslie's Illustrated Newspaper*, May 25, 1861. *U. S. Naval Historical Center*

The next day, the following (and remarkably detailed) story appeared in the *Philadelphia Evening Bulletin:*

Never since the first flash of the bombardment of Fort Sumter, has there been an excitement in the city equal to that which was caused by the capture of a mysterious vessel which was said to be an infernal machine, which was to be used for all sorts of treasonable purposes, including the trifling pastime of scuttling and blowing up government men-of-war. For a few days past the police have had their attention directed to the movements, not of a 'long, low, black schooner,' but of an iron submarine boat, to which very extraordinary abilities and infernal propensities were attributed.

Externally it had the appearance of a section of boiler about 20 feet long, with tapered ends, presenting the shape and appearance of an enormous cigar with a boiler iron wrapper. The after end was furnished with a propeller, which had a contrivance for protecting it from coming in contact with external objects. The forward end was sharkish in appearance as only the ridge of the back was above water, while the tail and snout were submerged.

Near the forward end was a hatchway or 'manhole,' through which egress and ingress were obtained. This hole was covered with a heavy iron flap, which was made airtight, and which was secured in its place by numerous powerful screws and hooks. Two tiers of glass bull's eyes (view ports) along each side of the submarine monster completed its external features, afforded light to the inside, and gave it a particularly wideawake appearance.[16]

On the same day that the Philadelphia paper ran its story, the *New York Herald* printed an account substantiating the former article and adding additional details:

Capture of a Submarine Boat. Philadelphia, May 17, 1861.

Quite an excitement was created in the upper part of the city this morning by the seizure of a submarine boat, the invention of De Villeroi, a Frenchman. It was going down the river and struck on an island. Four men were found on board. Villeroi says he was about taking it to the Navy Yard to test; but the officers of the yard disclaim any knowledge of him. The boat was constructed some time since for raising wrecks and other submarine work, but was never put in active use. It is Cigar shaped and made of iron, thirty feet long. It supplies its own air, and will be useful in running under a fleet.[17]

The day after its discovery, a Philadelphia reporter was allowed to enter the contraption and take notes. The following excerpts are taken from the story he penned for his readers later that evening:

After dropping from a high wharf into a skiff and then jumping a few feet, we found ourselves upon the back of the iron mystery. The top of the manhole was lifted off, and divesting ourselves of our coats and hats, we squeezed into the machine.

We suddenly found ourselves squatting inside a cigar shaped iron vessel, about four feet in diameter. There was a crank for the purpose of operating upon the propeller already described, apparatus for steering rods, connected with fins outside, which could be moved at pleasure, and which had something to do with steadying and sinking the craft. There were pumps, brass faucets, pigs of ballast lead, and numerous other things, which might be intended for infernal or humane purposes for aught we know. The interior was abundantly lighted by means of the double tiers of bull's eyes (View ports) we have described.[18]

Soon after examining the "iron mystery," the same reporter visited two of the incarcerated crewmen. The submarine, they informed him, was the invention of Brutus de Villeroi, a French inventor who had come to the United States in 1859 to build a vessel in which he hoped to salvage shipwrecks off the American coast. Thirty years earlier, de Villeroi had built his first three-man submarine vessel in his native village of Nantes, France. On August 12, 1832, a demonstration of his invention was conducted at a French dock, from which the following remarkable account was written:

> There we saw M. de Villeroi enter into a boat made of iron, having the shape and appearance of a fish, ten feet long, three feet wide, which boat was manned by three men, the inventor included. M. de Villeroi, began operations at 3 P.M.
>
> After several evolutions on the surface of the water, he began to navigate about one foot beneath the surface of the water, till thirty-five minutes past three; then descended near the bottom of the water, but in a different direction, in order to deceive the boats which were following him on the surface. At forty-five minutes past three o'clock he returned near the surface of the water, where, after ten minutes of different evolutions in various directions, he came up on the surface and opened his safety door. At fifty-five minutes past three he made his appearance out of his boat, cheered by all present, having remained with his companions inside of that boat fifty-five minutes without any communication with the exterior atmosphere, and maneuvering his boat with the greatest facility.[19]

It is interesting to speculate whether another Nantes native, six-year-old Jules Verne, was among those present at the demonstration that day. A generation later, Verne would thrill the world with his underwater adventure novel, *Twenty Thousand Leagues Under the Sea.*[20]

Within days after the capture of his Delaware River submarine boat, de Villeroi gave an astonishing interview before numerous reporters and other interested parties. His submarine, claimed the Frenchman, not only had the ability to remain submerged for several hours, but a diver could exit the vessel and work outside. He also claimed he had invented an air purifying device—perhaps some form of crude scrubber that re-moved carbon dioxide—that supplied air to the crew while submerged. In closing, he informed his audience that he had brought his invention to the navy yard so as to allow naval officers to examine his boat and gain support from the War Department for using his vessel against Con-federate shipping.[21]

De Villeroi's publicity stunt, if it was one, worked well. Two weeks following the vessel's capture, Capt. Samuel F. Du Pont, Commandant of the Philadelphia Navy Yard, ordered three of his engineering officers to examine the vessel and make a full report as to their findings. The study submitted on July 7, 1861, described de Villeroi's submarine as "An iron cylinder about 33 feet in length, four feet at its greatest diameter. It is propelled by means of a screw at the stern." The report went on to state the following:

> First. De Villeroi's machine could remain submerged for a consider-able time without communication with the surface and without fa-tigue or exhaustion to her crew;
>
> Second. That the boat could be sunk or raised at the will of her commander;
>
> Third. That her crew could leave or return to her without coming to the surface;
>
> Fourth. That a man could leave the boat and live for an appreciable time by means of tubes attached to the boat;
>
> Fifth. That with a larger vessel capable of housing a larger crew the vessel could be navigated at a speed of one mile per hour;
>
> Sixth. That it would be possible for a diver using a boat like this for his base to attach some 'engine of destruction' to the hull of a hostile vessel, and return in safety to his boat; and that the boat could be used for the examination of the bottoms of lakes or harbors, and the raising of cargos of sunken vessels."

In closing, the three naval officers made the following recommenda-tion: "We therefore consider that the services of the distinguished French engineer would be very valuable to the Government and that the possession of his invention would be of the greatest importance."

Within a matter of days, the report was forwarded to Secretary of the Navy Gideon Welles, in Washington, D.C.[22]

De Villeroi was not a patient man, and by the following month was exhibiting some anxiety about the navy's inability to come to a decision as to whether or how it would employ his services. On September 4, he wrote a fascinating letter directly to President Abraham Lincoln outlining the reasons for his concern. "The grave circumstances which threaten the union of this glorious country," he counseled, demand that any means for beating the enemy must be utilized. "I propose to you a new arm of war, as formidable as it is economical," he continued. "Submarine navigation which has been sometimes attempted, but as all know without results, owing to want of suitable opportunities, is now a problematical thing no more." De Villeroi reminded the president of the experiments conducted at New Castle and Marcus Hook in the Delaware River, trials which "demonstrated positively that with a submarine boat like mine, well constructed and properly equipped, it becomes an easy matter to reconnaissance the enemy's coast, to land men, ammunition, etc. at any given point, to enter harbors, to keep up intelligence, and to carry explosive bombs under the very keels of the enemy's vessels and that without being seen." The stunning advance in technology, claimed the French inventor, would render large enemy fleets obsolete. The model "I have experimented with is 32 feet in length. It is built of iron and is furnished with a screw propeller. It can be made to go on the surface of the water or at any depth almost below, and without communication whatever with the external atmosphere." When under water, he continued, "the men can go out of the boat to perform any work, to remove any object from the bottom . . . and come in again without the least difficulty."

The incredible ramifications of de Villeroi's correspondence certainly were not lost on Lincoln, who appreciated innovative thinking and often tried out new weapons and inventions himself. "Sir," de Villeroi concluded, confident he had furnished the president with enough information to convince him of the boat's military merits, "should you judge my services to be profitable to the Union I could place myself at your disposal with my boat and a well practiced crew. And should several such boats be deemed necessary I could have them properly built and their respective crews could be made to practice in the original one during the construction of the others."[23]

Attached to the back of this letter was an undated lengthy news article from the *Philadelphia North American* describing de Villeroi's submarine vessel. It is likely that Lincoln himself read it:

> We saw the curious boat which is above described, into which, in our presence, M. Villeroi, with five men entered; and then with all on board, descended into the water, remaining beneath the surface one hour and a quarter, during all of which time the boat had no communication with the external atmosphere. Incredible and impracticable as this may seem, it is nevertheless true, as those who were on the shore can testify.
>
> We saw also M. Villeroi's men (sailors) plunge into the water and disappear, and after entering the boat, reappear on the surface, thus testing the power to enter and exit the boat while she was underwater. By what wonderful new invention in science this was achieved we cannot say, and indeed the principle is undoubtedly the most extraordinary discovery of the age.[24]

Lincoln's initial reaction to de Villeroi's letter, or whether he personally made any recommendations regarding the submarine, is not known. Shortly after the president received this intriguing communication—which he likely sent off to the War Department for further consideration—Confederate naval officers 100 miles south of Washington in Richmond, Virginia, were nearing completion of a small iron submarine boat of their own.

◆   ◆   ◆

The Southern submarine in question was the product of an underwater explosives designer named William Cheeney, who worked with the Confederate Navy Department at Richmond, Virginia. By the time Lincoln received his letter from de Villeroi that September, the Confederate Navy had already contracted for the three-man Rebel submarine. In fact, it was well under construction and perhaps nearing completion at the Tredegar Iron Works on the banks of the James River.[25]

A view of the famous Tredegar Iron Works on the banks of the James River, Virginia. During the war this foundry built over 1000 cannons and carriages, ironclad armor, and at least two submarines. *National Archives*

While records regarding this particular early war boat are scarce, enough documentation has been uncovered to sketch out its obscure history with reasonable certainty. The submarine was designed by Southern naval engineers to be operated by a crew of only two men. A third crewman provided with diving gear—known as "submarine armor"—was apparently stationed at the bow of the vessel in some sort of compartment or lockout chamber. A floating camouflaged hose attached to an air pump within the vessel provided oxygen to both the occupants and the diver outside. While operating submerged, the diver rode in a small compartment at the bow. When the target ship came within reach of the diver, he would exit the craft and attach an explosive device to the bottom of the enemy ship, returning thereafter to the submarine. The boat would then withdraw a safe distance and detonate the device, either by a lanyard or timing mechanism.[26] A diagram captured later in the war that may have been drawn by one of the designers of this vessel demonstrated in stark black and white terms the underwater craft's

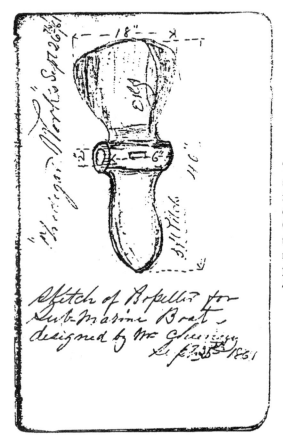

This submarine propeller sketch was drawn by Confederate William Cheeney on September 25, 1861. Cheeney designed at least two James River submarines during the first year of the war. *Virginia State Library*

ingenious design, which may have been a very formidable weapon in the hands of an experienced diver and well-practiced crew.[27]

While this Confederate diving machine seems at first blush too technologically advanced for her time, the observations of a Union spy lends substantial credence to the archival documentation of the boat's design and existence. The agent actually watched a demonstration of the little submarine's capabilities in the James River in the autumn of 1861. Her observations and subsequent reports about this Rebel "infernal machine" would soon send shock waves through the Federal blockading fleet anchored near Hampton Roads at the mouth of the James.

Specific details about the submarine's origins are lacking. Exactly when this first submarine boat, which was built on the banks of the James River, was actually completed may never be known. The earliest reference to this Richmond-based submarine comes in the form of a sketch drawn by its designer, William Cheeney. Dated September 25, 1861, Cheeney's schematic includes the dimensions of the vessel's rather large propeller, which from top to bottom measured 46". A propeller of that length meant that the diving machine was a formidable craft, as opposed to a small boat. Several other references detailing the boat's construction are contained in a ledger receipt book from the Tredegar Iron Works. An entry dated October 1861, for example, certifies that Cheeney paid a bill for $6.00 for "a box (air pump)," and purchased other "articles for diving bells. $60.00."[28]

At about the same time that Cheeney and his staff of naval engineers were putting the finishing touches on their submarine, Allan Pinkerton, a government-employed detective who organized the Federal Secret Service in Washington, was being briefed as to the existence of the Rebel boat then under construction at the Confederate capital. Just how Pinkerton first received news of this Rebel submarine has not come to light. His involvement with Cheeney's vessel, however, is contained in Pinkerton's postwar memoir, *The Spy of the Rebellion: A True History of the Spy System of the United States Army During the Late Rebellion.* One of its chapters, "The Discovery and Destruction of the Submarine Battery," sheds considerable light on the existence and circumstances surrounding the boat's operations.

Besides the *Merrimac* (ironclad *CSS Virginia*), explained Pinkerton, the Confederacy had developed a "great many ingenious machines in the shape of torpedoes and submarine batteries," all for the purpose of "blowing up the Union vessels that blockaded the Southern ports." It was through the efforts of one of his operatives, explained Pinkerton, "that the existence of one of these submarine batteries was discovered, and that, too, just in a nick of time to save the Federal blockading fleet at the mouth of the James River from probable destruction." According to Pinkerton, he dispatched a female spy to Richmond "for the purpose of ascertaining as much information as possible about these torpedoes and infernal machines, which I had good reason to believe were constructed at the rebel capital." The woman's name was "Mrs. E. H. Baker," who had been in his employ for some time and who had at one time lived in Richmond.

Pinkerton's operative was acquainted with (or struck up a friendship with) a family named Atwater, who lived in Richmond. She arranged to stay with them during her undercover operations in the Southern city. As luck or good planning would have it, the head of the household, "Captain Atwater," held a position at the Tredegar Iron Works and was completely unaware of Mrs. Baker's connections with the United States Secret Service. "Mrs. Baker found herself comfortably situated beneath the Captain's hospitable roof," recalled Pinkerton, "and nearly a week was passed in viewing Richmond and the strange sites it then offered." The unsuspecting officer apparently escorted her wherever she wanted to go. One of her journeys included a trip to "the earthworks and fortifications around Richmond," where she "gained many valuable points of information in regard to their number and extent." One evening the guest-spy casually remarked that "she desired very much to visit the Tredegar Iron Works." Initially Atwater had no objection to showing her the facility, but after a few moments retracted his offer when he remembered he was slated to witness a test of the new submarine battery the following morning. With this unbelievable stroke of good luck, Mrs. Baker tactfully asked if she and Mrs. Atwater could accompany the captain to the demonstration the following day. Atwater agreed. From a cloak and dagger point of view, the visit to the banks of the James River could not have been more successful.

Pinkerton's detailed account of the event reads as follows:

> Arriving at the appointed spot, they found quite a large number of military men, many of them accompanied by ladies, assembled to witness the testing of the machine, from which so much was expected.
>
> A large scow had been towed to the middle of the river, and the submarine vessel was to approach it and attach a magazine, containing nearly a half a bushel of powder, to which was attached several deadly projectiles, and this was to be fired by a peculiarly constructed fuse, connected to a long wire coiled on board the submarine vessel.

At a given signal the boat was sunk in the river, about half a mile below the scow, and shortly afterwards it began to make its way under the water towards it. The only visible sign of its existence was a large float that rested on the surface of the water, and which was connected with the vessel below, designed to supply the men that operated it with air. This float was painted a dark green, to imitate the color of the water, and could only be noticed by the most careful observer.

"As my operative listened to a full explanation of the machine and its workings," continued Pinkerton, "she could scarcely control her emotions of fear for the safety of the Federal boats, in the event of its successful operation, and provided the government was not speedily warned of its existence." Part of the intelligence gathered indicated that the submarine conducting the trials "was but a small working model of a much larger one, that was now nearly completed, and would then be taken to the mouth of the James River, to operate on the war vessels guarding that port." Mrs. Baker informed her employer that, "Two or three men who operate the boat were provided with submarine diving armor, which enabled them to work under the water and attach the magazine to the ship intended to blow up. They then had only to quickly move away to a safe distance, fire the fuse, and the work is done."

The demonstration, much to the hidden dismay of Mrs. Baker, was a complete success:

> While they were talking, my operative was closely watching, by the aid of her glass, the movements of the boat, and she now noticed that having approached to within a few rods of the scow, it stopped, and the water 'float' which indicated the position remained motionless. After remaining in this position for a few minutes, it slowly began to recede from the scow, in the direction from whence it came.
>
> It moved steadily away for some hundreds of yards, and Mrs. Baker was wondering at the seemingly long delay, then suddenly, and without any previous warning whatever, there was a terrific explosion, and the scow seemed to be lifted bodily out of the water and thrown high into the air. Her destruction was complete, and there was no longer any doubt that the submarine battery could be used with deadly and

Short note from William Cheeney reminding the iron works to pay bills and charge them to the account of the "submarine boat." *National Archives*

telling effect on the ships constituting the Federal blockading squadron.

Mrs. Baker looked on with a heavy heart as she reflected upon the terrible consequences of the workings of this machine, and at once felt the urgent necessity of taking steps to inform me of what she had witnessed.

After their return home that evening, she made copious notes of what she had learned and witnessed, which she safely secreted about her person. The next day, in company with the Captain, she visited the Tredegar Iron Works, and inspected the boat that was being built. It was truly a formidable-looking engine of destruction.

The next day, she bade farewell to her host and amiable spouse, and left Richmond for Fredericksburg. From there she made her way to Washington, and lost no time in reporting to me the success of her trip.[29]

Mrs. Baker's account, as related by Pinkerton, is too credible to dismiss. Her careful observations, together with documents from the Tredegar Iron Works and William Cheeney, confirm the existence of an early war James River submarine. It is also interesting to note the remarkable similarities between the descriptions of the boat trials Baker witnessed and the technology employed by de Villeroi's submarine in the Delaware River.

◆   ◆   ◆

There is overwhelming evidence that the small experimental submarine observed and reported on by Mrs. Baker was transported to Hampton Roads, at the mouth of the James River, soon after her departure
from Richmond. On October 12, 1861, a correspondent with the *New
York Herald* stationed at the tip of the Virginia peninsula at Fort Monroe, penned a remarkable article for his newspaper—a reporting coup
ignored or previously unseen by historians. The article documents, for
the first time, a legitimate attempt to sink a ship by a submarine during
the Civil War. The intended victim was the *USS Minnesota*, part of the
North Atlantic Blockading Squadron and Flag Officer Louis M. Goldsborough's flagship. The lengthy piece ran three days later in the October 15 edition, and is reprinted below in full:

Fortress Monroe, October 12, 1861.

Last evening a flag of truce came down, bringing sixty persons;
among the number was a gentleman who brings the following intelligence: On Wednesday evening last an infernal machine was sent
down from Seawall's Point for the purpose of blowing up the flag-ship.
She came down to the ship without any difficulty, but she caught in
the grappling always hanging from the jib-boom of the ship. This was
taken by those inside for the chain cable, and when they thought they
were under the bottom of the ship they made preparations for screwing
the torpedo on the bilge, but, to their surprise, they found they were
sadly mistaken, and they came near losing their lives as well as the
machine. They, however, escaped, and worked themselves on shore on
rebel ground, and the machine was carted back to Norfolk, to try the
experiment at some future time.

From the gentleman who made the statement I learn the following
particulars in relation to the machine. He states that it is built of iron, of
a similar shape to the Ross Winan's cigar boat, of a sufficient capacity to
accommodate two persons, who work it ahead by means of a small screw
propeller. It is guided by a rudder, and it is ballasted by means of water,
let in and forced out by means of a pump. A compass guides them, and

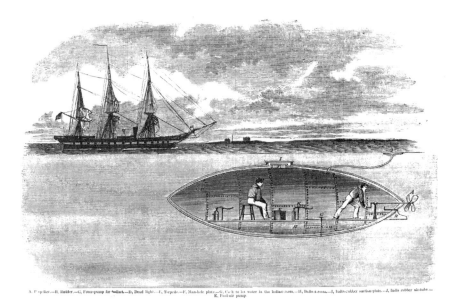

A, Propeller.—B, Rudder.—C, Force-pump for ballast.—D, Dead light.—E, Torpedo.—F, Man-hole plate.—G, Cock to let water in the ballast-room.—H, Ballast-room.—I, India-rubber suction-plate.—J, India-rubber air-tube.—K, Fresh-air pump.

Page from the November 2 edition of *Harper's Weekly* showing a diagram of the *"Rebel Infernal Machine"* suspected to be prowling the waters near Norfolk, Virginia.

a velocimeter shows how great a distance is run each moment. Bearings and courses are given the men, and they go out on a hazardous voyage, with a large chance of accomplishment. An India-rubber tube, which is floated on the surface, furnishes them with fresh air.

On arriving at the place desired, a grapple catches the cable of a vessel, and the machine is veered away until it is supposed to be near one of the magazines; the water ballast is then pumped out, and the machine floats up under the ship's bottom. By means of an India-rubber sucking-plate this machine is attached to the bottom of the ship, while a man-hole plate is opened and the torpedo is screwed into the vessel. It is fired by means of a time fuse. As soon as this is set in motion the men inside place a prepared sheet of rubber over the man-hole, and while one lets the water into the compartment to sink the machine, the other person screws up the plate, the grapple is let go, and the infernal machine is left to explode, while the machine is worked in shore out of harm's way.[30]

Flag Officer Goldsborough was a former superintendent of the Naval Academy and too experienced an officer to ignore what was transpiring around him. From his flagship *USS Minnesota* in Hampton Roads on October 27, he notified the rest of the ships in his squadron to be on the alert for "submarine infernal machines." The Confederates, or "insurgents at Norfolk," as he disparagingly called them, "are said to possess one calculated to be used underwater, and thus to attach a torpedo with a time fuse to a ship's bottom. It is, I understand, to be first towed tolerably near a ship by means of a tug, or else by boats with muffled oars, then to be submerged and so navigate to the vessel against which it is to operate."[31]

◆　◆　◆

At about the same time that a submarine was apparently operating against Goldsborough's fleet in Hampton Roads, a bright young Confederate private belonging to Maj. Gen. Thomas J. "Stonewall" Jackson's Brigade was putting onto paper ideas of his own regarding underwater warfare. Charles P. Leavitt, a 19-year-old former machinist in Company K, 2nd Virginia Infantry, penned his ideas from his camp near Centerville, Virginia, on October 21, and boldly sent them directly to Confederate Secretary of War Judah P. Benjamin.[32]

"I have so far succeeded in my own mind as to induce me to write to you on the subject," he concluded. Leavitt's plan called for a submarine gunboat he thought would be effective in breaking the Federal blockade. "I have invented an instrument of war which for a better name I have called a submarine gunboat," explained the young private. "In many of its details I have not hesitated to adopt the plans of others, being far better to use machinery that has been found to be useful than to try to make a perfectly novel boat. I have thus greatly reduced the chance of failure." My plan, he continued,

is simple. A vessel is built of boiler iron of about fifty tons burden, similar to Winan's cigar steamer, but made of an oval form with the propeller behind. The boilers are so constructed as to generate steam without a supply of air. The air for respiration is kept in a fit condition for breathing by the gradual addition of oxygen, while the carbonic acid is absorbed by a shower of lime water. This I conceive is far better than taking down a large supply of compressed air.

I propose to tow out my gun-boat to sea and when within range of the enemy's guns it sinks below the water's surface so as to leave no trace on the surface of its approach, a self-acting apparatus keeping it at any depth required. When within a few rods of the enemy it leaps to the surface and the two vessels come in contact before the enemy can fire a gun. Placed in the bow of the gun-boat is a small mortar containing a self-exploding shell. As it strikes the enemy the shell explodes and blows in the ships sides; then the engines are reversed, the gun-boat sinks below the surface and goes noiselessly on its way towards another ship. After a few ships are sunk the enemy can scarcely have the temerity to remain in our waters.

I need not enumerate to you the advantages of such a weapon when England is looking elsewhere for cotton. I have written you on this subject in order to obtain an opportunity to draft out my invention, which with the means at command in Richmond can be done in a week at most.

Leavitt closed his epistle by apologizing for not having drafted a suitable drawing for the secretary's examination. "As for making the drawings in the army with accuracy it is almost impossible," he explained, "since neither paper, instruments, nor necessary tables can be procured."[33]

The private's cogent idea impressed Lt. Colonel Josiah Gorgas, the Confederacy's brilliant chief of ordnance. With remarkable speed for a bureaucracy, the letter wound its way into Gorgas' hands within days. On October 26, he endorsed the reverse of Leavitt's letter, recommending "that this man be granted furlough to come on here and in this office or that of the Chief Engineer's [to] draw out his plans." The young private was probably shocked when he received a direct response to his proposal from Judah Benjamin himself. "Your letter of 21st Oct has been received," wrote the secretary of war on October 28. "The Chief of Ordnance to whom your letter has been referred, has been so far pleased with your design, that at his request, I desire you to request a furlough of your commanding officer, for the purpose of constructing and explaining your drawing here. On your arrival in Richmond, you will at once report to Lt. Col. Gorgas, Chief of Ordnance for this purpose."[34]

Private Leavitt was a remarkable enlisted man. He possessed substantial (and surprising) knowledge about some of the problems associated with undersea craft, especially oxygen depletion and carbon dioxide build-up within a confined area. It has been generally accepted by modern historians and researchers that these early submarine pioneers (and mid-nineteenth-century science in general) were unaware of such things as the presence of carbon dioxide and its effects on the human body. While other similar submersibles of the period utilized a snorkel assembly attached to air pumps, Private Leavitt concluded that by adding oxygen and absorbing the "carbonic acid" (carbon dioxide) with a shower of lime water (also known as beryllium, a chemical used in many small submersibles for absorbing carbon dioxide), snorkels were unnecessary.[35] Another interesting idea that Leavitt may have originated was the use of steam for powering his craft. Just how he planned to supply the fires with air and expel the smoke was not revealed in his letter to the secretary of war. Given his careful and thoughtful reasoning on other issues, however, it is likely he had a plausible (and practical) application in mind. Other Southerners, however, also suggested the use of steam engines in submarines, and some may have actually implemented the idea. As it turned out, it wasn't Leavitt's idea of an underwater boat, but his notion on how to conduct an underwater attack—he wanted to utilize a cannon of some variety as opposed to a spar with an explosive—that intrigued Richmond officials the most.[36]

Exactly when Private Leavitt was granted his furlough to visit Gorgas in the Confederate capital is not known, for Leavitt's compiled service record does not record any absence from his unit in the fall of 1861. A letter from the private addressed to Secretary of War Benjamin in early February 1862, however, confirms that he had indeed visited Richmond in December of 1861, where his sketches and ideas regarding a new submarine gunboat were met with great enthusiasm.[37]

On December 2, 1861, Leavitt was released from military service. His discharge papers note simply that "His labor [is] required for other important Government work."[38] Thereafter, Leavitt's duties and connection with submarines remain largely a mystery. On February 4, 1862, he wrote to the secretary of war from his new address in Richmond, where he apparently was laboring on "important Government work," and inquired as to the status of his design submission. "The drawings were left in the charge of one of your clerks to be given to you," he informed Benjamin, "as they were universally approved by very practical men that saw them before they went to you. I can not think it possible you can consider them unworthy of your consideration."[39]

Private Leavitt's letter confirms that as of the second month of 1862, his duties did not involve the construction of his submarine gunboat. While the exact nature of his responsibilities remain obscure, his obvious acumen in naval design and innovation, coupled with his reassignment to "government work," indicate Southern officials intended to put his talents to good use. It is entirely possible he was working during this period with Acting Master Cheeney and other naval personnel on the Tredegar (James River) submarines heretofore described. Unfortunately, records setting forth the names of those involved with these boats have not come to light.

◆　　◆　　◆

While Leavitt was peddling his idea in Richmond, and Goldsborough and his officers pondered methods to foil an attack by an "insurgent infernal machine," a navy circular in Washington concerning the Frenchman de Villeroi's invention docked at the Philadelphia Navy Yard was making the rounds. "For many years the ingenuity of man has been taxed to invent means of destroying an enemy vessel by attaching explosive machines to their bottoms," it began, "but such means have not [yet] . . . proved successful. There is difficulty in holding on whilst attaching the instrument of destruction to the vessel, when the operator cannot touch the bottom." If the submarine boat proposed by de Villeroi, however, could be "propelled at a rate of three miles per hour and the persons working it can detach themselves from it and operate outside it returning to it in safety," claimed the report, "the invention might prove useful against vessels in an enemy port." The drafters of the document concluded that extended tests were required with a boat "built under the direction of the inventor, the cost of which . . . will not exceed $14,000, and men employed who are trained to work it." If successful, the submersible "could be used for war purposes as well as for general submarine explorations." De Villeroi, who was anxious to execute a contract and move into production, proposed "to enter into contract with the government for a given sum to destroy the vessels in the port of Norfolk without pay in the event of failure." His terms were generous and offered the United States virtually no downside risk. "This would be a safe experiment for the government," concluded Navy Department officials, "and probably the most satisfactory to both parties provided the price to be paid is limited to the amount of damage inflicted on the enemy."[40]

Although there were several Southern vessels in the port of Norfolk, the primary target of interest for the Navy Department was the nearly completed Confederate ironclad *Merrimac (CSS Virginia)*. The iron behemoth was being constructed from the hull and engines of the *USS Merrimac*, a frigate that had been burned to the waterline and abandoned when Federal forces vacated the Norfolk Navy Yard three days after Virginia seceded from the Union. The fact that the Confederates were building a formidable ironclad to defeat Federal warships and break the blockade of the James River was a poorly kept secret. In fact, the ship's construction was so widely known that *Harper's Weekly* published a sketch of the vessel on the front page of one of its 1861 editions.[41] Federal officials lived in fear that when the *Virginia* was finished, she would disperse any flotilla sent to oppose her and steam up the Potomac and shell the capital. With this menacing new warship nearing completion and with so many rumors circulating around the fleet concerning Rebel submarine boats, the United States Navy Department enthusiastically entered into a contract with de Villeroi for a submarine vessel of their own.[42]

The contract between Brutus de Villeroi and the Federal government provided that "one iron submarine" was to be ready "within forty days" at a cost not to exceed $14,000. De Villeroi was to supervise construction of the vessel. On November 1, 1861, the contract was formally executed between de Villeroi and the Philadelphia shipbuilding firm of

Neafle & Levy. On the same day that the terms of the contract were agreed upon, Commodore Joseph Smith, the chief of the Bureau of Yards and Docks, memorialized specific aspects of the agreement with de Villeroi. After confirming that the "Iron Submarine Propeller" project was under the charge of its inventor, Smith reiterated that de Villeroi was to handpick the crew. "Your pay," continued the bureau chief, "will be at the rate of $2000 per annum for the time you shall be employed by the Navy Department, to be paid monthly." De Villeroi, directed Smith, must "employ only such men for the crew of the vessel as may be absolutely necessary for your purposes, and the Navy Department will furnish more men when you require them." "Be particular in the construction," Smith admonished, "that no mistake be made, and see that it be well provided, according to contract in all respect, for immediate action in the service intended, of which you have been informed." Brutus de Villeroi's contribution to the Union war effort was on its way to becoming a reality. Commodore Smith had also recently made a noteworthy contribution to the Union cause. The career naval officer had sat on an examining board to determine the feasibility of constructing a new type of warship. When the evidence was presented, he voted in favor of authorizing the construction of the ironclad *USS Monitor*.[43]

While de Villeroi and shipyard engineers poured over the diagrams for the new submarine boat, William Smith, the captain of the powerful frigate *USS Congress* anchored 200 miles away in Newport News, devised a method for defending against the submarine boat suspected to be prowling the waters nearby. On November 4, Smith wrote to Flag Officer Goldsborough and advised him of his preparations "against fire craft, torpedoes, infernal machines, etc." The captain theorized that "any of these things with which the rebels may attack us will be towed and placed directly ahead and as near the ship as they can safely come, so that when let loose they will drift with the tide to the ship." Smith's plan to defend against such an event consisted of preparing a sort of trap to either capture or ward off the infernal device:

> We have made with spars a frame in the shape of the letter A, which we suspended by the crosspiece from the bowsprit cap; the ends reach aft to the lower booms, resting on the water, and are secured by tackles

to the ship's sides to steady them. Suspended from the Jib boom and under the above frame is a spar athwartship, some 30 feet long, to which is attached on its whole length a strong netting 14 feet deep and kept in a vertical position by weights at the bottom.

Should such a machine as the one that attacked the *Minnesota* approach us and come near the cable, it must be caught in the net and held there until we relieve it. Or should it pass outside the net, the tube which floats on the surface to supply the inmates with fresh air would be caught in the A spars, and the supply of fresh air be cut off, causing suffocation, and if it should pass outside of the spars it would go entirely clear of the ship, doing no harm. I think this arrangement will secure us against such torpedoes.

Smith concluded his communication with a reference to the Southern ironclad under construction in Norfolk. "I have not yet devised any plan to defend us against the *Merrimac* (*CSS Virginia*), unless it be with hard knocks." As it turned out, "hard knocks" would not suffice, for on March 8, 1862, the *USS Congress* was shelled and burned by the *CSS Virginia* with great loss of life.[44]

As the use of nets and other devices described by Captain Smith to thwart an attack were instituted squadron-wide in the Hampton Roads area, the submarine threat was carried into the homes of the general public. The illustrated pages of *Harper's Weekly,* widely considered the cutting-edge publication of its time, included a diagram of the "Submarine Infernal machine" then suspected to be operating in the waters near Norfolk.[45]

Captain Smith's reference to the attack on the *USS Minnesota* is one more piece in the historical puzzle confirming that an underwater assault actually took place. Unfortunately, the event is shrouded in mystery and has been largely ignored or misunderstood by historians. On October 19, 1861, seven days after a reporter with the *New York Herald* broke the story about an aborted attempt by a submersible to sink the vaunted flagship, the same Fortress Monroe correspondent filed another related report. This time, the article quoted a Southern deserter who confirmed that a small submarine was indeed at the Norfolk Navy Yard preparing to attack the Union fleet.[46]

Page 1212 from the Tredegar Iron Works account book for 1861, itemizing materials used in constructing the Confederate Navy's submarine boat. *Virginia State Library*

The November *Harper's Weekly* diagram of the machine outlined how the vessel functioned and was remarkably similar to the description of the James River boat submitted by Mrs. Baker, Allan Pinkerton's operative. Records from the Tredegar Iron Works provide additional evidence that support the submarine attack in Hampton Roads. An accounting invoice addressed to the Confederate Navy Department and dated November 23, 1861, several weeks after news of the submarine first appeared in the *New York Herald,* reads as follows:

> W. G. Cheeney for Confederate States Navy Department 'One Submarine Boat' as follows . . . Boiler Plate . . . $892.87, Castings . . . $1,206.45, Painting . . . $17.70, Labor . . . $3,318.50, Bolts . . . $327.63, Brass Castings . . . $149.40, Cloth 26 Yards [Probably used to pack the stuffing boxes that kept water from leaking into the hull] . . . $5.20, Hauling . . . $290.00, Building house over boat to conceal it . . . $200.00.[47]

The entry of importance impacting this issue is easily overlooked: "Hauling . . . $290.00." Where, exactly, was the James River submarine "hauled," i.e., transported, to justify a bill to the Confederate Navy of $290? Given the mosaic of information developed thus far, common sense leads to the conclusion that the submarine boat witnessed by Mrs. Baker in the early fall of 1861 was transported to Norfolk, about sixty miles away, and then returned to the Tredegar Iron Works for modifications after its unsuccessful attack on the *Minnesota*. We will probably never know for certain. Most Confederate records concerning submarines and underwater contact mines were intentionally burned at the end of the war to keep the identities of those involved in such activities secret.[48] In fact, most activities concerning submarine boats and underwater mines were conducted by members of the Confederate Secret Service, a branch from which few records survived.[49]

During the mid-nineteenth century, many people considered unconventional methods of killing, i.e., land mines (torpedoes), underwater mines, submarines, and so forth, to be beyond the boundaries of civilized warfare. These types of military hardware were branded inhumane in their method of attack largely because they denied their victims a reasonable opportunity to defend themselves. In other words, they were not "honorable" or "chivalrous" weapons. In many cases concerning Civil War submarines, all that is known about them is an obscure line in a dispatch or a paragraph in a letter. So little is known about some of these underwater projects that the very existence of some boats may never be discovered.

A good example of this paucity of information is found in the closing paragraphs of Allan Pinkerton's narrative concerning the James River submarine reported on by Mrs. Baker:

> I immediately laid my information before General McClellan and the Secretary of the Navy, who at once transmitted the intelligence to the commanders of the squadron, instructing them to keep a sharp look out for the 'water colored surface float,' and to drag the water for the purpose of securing possession of the air tubes connecting the float with the vessel below.
>
> Nothing was heard from this for about three weeks, but about that time I was informed that one of the vessels of the blockading fleet off the mouth of the James River had discovered the float, and putting out her drag-rope, had caught the air tubes and thus effectually disabled

the vessel from doing any harm, and no doubt drowning all who were on board of her.

This incident, and the peculiarity of the machine, was duly discussed in the newspapers at the time, who stated that 'by a mere accident the Federal fleet off James River had been saved from destruction'—but I knew much better, and that the real credit of discovery was due to a lady of my own force.[50]

The Tredegar Iron Works' records document the existence of a James River submarine boat whose fate is unaccounted for. Read and appreciated in context with Pinkerton's account, it is more probable than not that a small Confederate submersible and her crew now lie buried beneath the shifting sands at the mouth of the James River. It is also apparent, as Pinkerton alluded, that the destruction of the submarine was not reported in the press. In fact, the topic was only lightly touched upon in official circles, if Flag Officer Goldsborough's confidential dispatch to Gideon Welles is referencing the same event. The only naval document found describing a probable submarine attack on Goldsborough's squadron was sent on October 17, 1861. "On the 9th," wrote Goldsborough, "an attempt, no doubt, was made by the insurgence to get an infernal machine among our shipping here [Hampton Roads], but was happily foiled by the alertness of the *Lockwood,* which they tried to cut off with their two tugs engaged in the nefarious business."[51] Unfortunately, the only remaining log books from the *U.S.S. John L. Lockwood* begin in December of 1861, two months after the alleged attack.[52]

But what of the other James River submarine boat? According to Pinkerton, Mrs. Baker's account allowed for the existence and construction of two submersibles in Richmond. More than two months after the apparent demise of one of these submarines in Hampton Roads, another was either being built or modified at Tredegar. A brief note penned by Acting Master Cheeney in the Southern capital on December 15, 1861, reads as follows: "J. R. Anderson and Company: [another name for the Tredegar Iron Works] Please pay written bills $199.00 and charge to account of Submarine boat. W. G. Cheeney."[53] The career and fate of this second submersible is unknown. Unfortunately, Cheeney's instruction is the final bit of evidence concerning the Tredegar Iron Works and its relations to submarines. With so little documentation available, it may never be known just how extensive those efforts were. But as we shall see shortly, submarine activity (both Union and Confederate) in the James River was still very much in its infancy in the fall of 1861.

◆   ◆   ◆

Ironically, despite the large sums of money and energy spent constructing boats just a handful of miles from the hive of naval activity hovering about Norfolk, it was a submarine venture taking shape in New Orleans that would eventually capture the imagination of the public and historians thereafter. The Crescent City project eventually produced the world's first submarine privateering vessel. It also led to a more ambitious effort that would cost the lives of most of those who volunteered their services, and in the end, awkwardly usher in history's first successful underwater attack.

The two men responsible for this early-war Louisiana submarine were steam gauge manufacturers named James McClintock and Baxter Watson. They hoped to construct a boat to use as a privateering vessel

James R. McClintock designed the privateering submarine *Pioneer* during the late summer or early fall of 1861. *U. S. Naval Historical Center*

against the Union fleet anchored at the mouth of the Mississippi. Few records of their earliest efforts have been found. Its keel was laid at the Leeds Foundry in the late autumn of 1861. A description of the craft provided at the time of its commissioning as a privateering vessel recorded that its hull was painted black and measured 34' in length, with its bow and stern terminating with round conical (cigar-shaped) ends. James McClintock, one of the few people closely associated with the project to survive the war, explained in a postwar letter that the small submarine was designed to be crewed by three men, two of whom turned a crank attached to the propeller, and a third who piloted the craft.[54]

◆   ◆   ◆

As 1861 waned, it looked as though the largely agrarian Southern Confederacy enjoyed a remarkable advantage over its Northern counterpart in underwater technology. McClintock and Watson were hard at work on a boat in New Orleans, Charles P. Leavitt had taken leave from his unit and was acquainting himself with his new duties in the Confederate capital, and Acting Master William Cheeney and the Tredegar Iron Works had launched at least one and possibly a pair of submarines in the James River. Union naval officers at the Philadelphia Navy Yard, on the other hand, were growing impatient with the slow progress being made in the construction of their own submarine vessel. More than two months had come and gone since the contract with de Villeroi had been entered into for delivery of an iron submarine boat. The Frenchman was to have delivered the craft "within forty days" of November 1, 1861. An inspection of the progress of the vessel (or lack thereof) by Navy Department personnel prompted them to extend de Villeroi's deadline. They had little choice. They needed de Villeroi's invention to combat the Southern ironclad *Merrimac* (soon to be renamed *CSS Virginia*), which was nearing completion in Norfolk. It was their hope that the submarine would be finished and towed to the mouth of the James River before the Rebels could launch the ironclad and wreak havoc on the ships blockading the river near Hampton Roads.[55]

While de Villeroi and his engineers continued their work on the submarine's cold and still dry iron hull through the Pennsylvania winter,

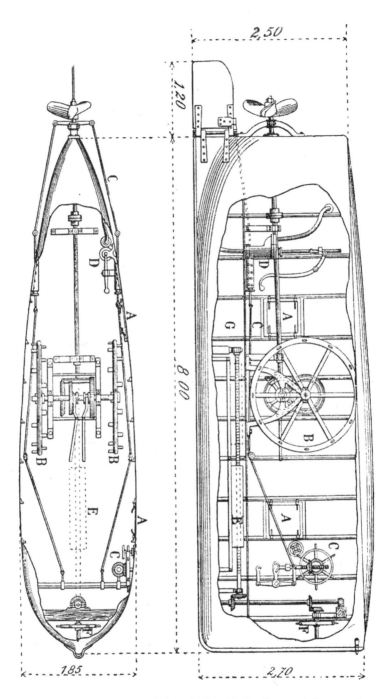

Diagram of Bauer's submarine vessel described in Mr. Biedermann's letter to the
Union Secretary of the Navy. *Z Files, U. S. Naval Historical Center*

E. Biedermann, an American living in London, posted a letter on December 30 to Navy Secretary Gideon Welles. Unaware of the submarine then under construction at the Philadelphia Navy Yard, Biedermann wrote to inform Welles of an invention that had been used six years earlier during the Crimean War. "I beg to submit to your honor a description of a submarine boat intended for the purpose of sinking vessels either by boring holes, from underwater through the bottom of such vessels, or by attaching explosive machines thereto," he explained. The plan for the boat "was laid before the late Prince Consort, who entertained a very favorable opinion of it, and by whose recommendation it was brought before the Lords of the Admiralty, who however declined entering into it for the reason that they did not consider it necessary to adapt such novel means for the prosecution of the war." Undaunted, the boat's designer, known only as "Mr. Bauer," submitted his plan "to the Duke Constantine, and by his special order built such a boat with which he made, accompanied by several workmen, over one hundred successful trips near St. Petersburg, remaining underwater from 6 to 8 hours, fully proving the practicability of his invention." Biedermann, who apparently furnished additional specifications (and possibly drawings) in his communication to Welles, concluded, "I have no doubt a practical engineer should have no difficulty in carrying out this plan."[56]

The Biedermann letter is interesting in its own right, but it is also historically significant. On the upper corner of this communication, apparently in Welles' own handwriting, is the following endorsement: "This propeller for submarine work is similar to one now under contract by the Navy Department [de Villeroi's boat]. This novel mode of warfare we consider legitimate since the enemy has inaugurated it against us."[57]

Unbeknownst to the Union and Confederate soldiers shivering within the shanties of their respective winter quarters, bold projects in underwater warfare were diligently underway, ushering in a new era of warfare.

CHAPTER 2

1862:
TRIAL & ERROR

"As far as practicable, you will keep secret the movements of the submarine
propeller recently from Philadelphia, and take into consideration the propriety of her
being used on the Appomattox River to operate against the Petersburg Bridge."

—*Gideon Welles to Flag Officer Louis M. Goldsborough*

By the dawn of 1862, inventors in several cities across the South were
experimenting with submarine boats. In addition to Richmond and
New Orleans, inventors in Mobile, Alabama, and Savannah, Georgia,
had also planned and built boats during the latter months of 1861. Unfortunately, the two submersibles constructed amongst the palmetto trees
and shallow marshes of these cities remain shrouded in mystery.

The existence of the first of these two mysterious vessels, the Mobile-
based boat, was discovered in a letter dated January 5, 1862, and sent to
Confederate Colonel Danville Leadbetter, an engineering officer examining Mobile's defenses. The fascinating passage in question describes an
event that took place on the Mobile River some days earlier: "The submarine apparatus in the river was boarded and sunk by some reprobate
(scoundrel) during some night of last week."[1] Although several submarines were built and launched in the Mobile area during the war
years, this is the earliest reference found regarding an operational boat.

Just when this inaugural Alabama submarine was completed and who
its builders were will probably never be known with certainty. There is,
however, some evidence suggesting that Reverend Franklin Smith may
have been responsible for fabricating the vessel. Smith had advocated
submarine construction—"cigar shaped for speed"—as early as June of

1861. His letter compelling "Men of a mechanical turn and of the right spirit" to build such undersea vessels was copied in several newspapers throughout the Confederacy. Papers belonging to the Smith family clearly state that construction on Reverend Smith's design for a submarine boat was acted upon and completed in Mobile, Alabama, during the opening months of the war. Additional evidence that Smith may have financed and fabricated this boat comes from an 1862 Confederate Patent book now on file at the Museum of the Confederacy. Under the heading "Navigation and Maritime Implements," in "Report of the Commissioner of Patents for 1862" comes the following entry: "Patent Number 61, Invention— Submarine Battery, Patentee—F. Smith, Residence—Memphis, Tennessee, date January 8, 1862." Certainly the evidence is circumstantial only, but interesting to contemplate. No one knows whether the boat was raised or abandoned. Perhaps more information will someday surface pertaining to this early Alabama submarine sunk in the Mobile River by "some reprobate" in early January 1862.[2]

At about the same time that Confederate engineering officers in Mobile were likely discussing the retrieval of the submarine apparatus resting at the bottom of the Mobile River, two Georgia adventurers 300 miles east were nearing completion of a small privateering submarine vessel of their own. The existence of this small early war Georgia boat was first discovered by historian James Kloeppel during his research for his excellent book *Danger Beneath the Waves*. During the first few weeks of 1862, two men living in Savannah, Georgia, Charles G. Wilkinson and Charlie Carroll, were almost finished constructing a small submersible.[3] Very little is known about the boat other than it was designed with a flawed valve that proved fatal to Wilkinson. On the morning of February 23, 1862, he and Carroll set out to test their undersea invention in Savannah harbor. The boat was taken "down to the foot of Montgomery Street," where the men "got into it, to try it, and one of the air valves would not work. The poor old man [Wilkinson] was caught some way and was drowned before they could do anything for him. When the boat was raised they found him dead in the bottom. Mr. Carroll had to creep out of a very small hole."[4]

The tragic accident was covered the following day in the *Savannah Daily Morning News:*

This 1844 wood-cut engraving shows the type of diving gear in common use during the nineteenth century.

Lamentable Accident. Yesterday an experiment that was being tried for the benefit of the Confederacy, and which two brave men, Dr. Wilkinson and Mr. Charles Carroll, had experimented, resulted in a misfortune, in which one of the gentleman engaged lost his life. The chain of a crane upon which the instrument was suspended gave way, and Dr. Wilkinson, the inventor, lost his life. Mr. Carroll miraculously escaped, after having urged Dr. Wilkinson to make his escape. We commend to the Confederacy the patriotism of these men, who were doing nothing for profit, but simply for the benefit of the cause in which they were engaged, and we are proud to state that they were both Irishmen. Dr. Wilkinson leaves an only daughter, and we hope and trust that the people of the Confederacy will not allow her to suffer in a pecuniary point, although we know that nothing can replace an honored, loving, and devoted father. At some future period we shall explain more fully everything relating to this sad occurrence.[5]

Unfortunately, the Savannah paper did not "explain more fully" this fascinating and historically significant news story. In fact, nothing more is known of the event or the fate of the boat. However, the evidence is the first confirmed fatality of the neophyte, if unofficial, Confederate submarine service. Sadly, the 49-year-old Dr. Charles G. Wilkinson was but the first of many who would be killed during submarine testing and operations during the Civil War.

◆   ◆   ◆

While Wilkinson's and Carroll's experiment ended in tragic failure in Savannah, another experiment on a grander scale was approaching success. At the Norfolk Navy Yard, Confederate naval personnel were feverishly trying to complete their iron monster, the *CSS Virginia.* Throughout the frigid days and nights of late February and early March, nearly 100 blacksmiths, iron workers, and sailors had worked overtime, without pay, to complete the armored and still dry-docked ram. Just as the construction of the *Virginia* was an open secret, so too was the construction of the Union ironclad *Monitor,* which had recently been launched. Some Southerners feared that the Yankee "steel-clad battery" was even then steaming in Chesapeake Bay on her way to Norfolk to destroy the *Virginia* before it could be launched. The *Monitor,* it seemed, and not Brutus de Villeroi's "iron submarine boat," would engage the new Norfolk ironclad.[6]

The delays encountered in finishing the Frenchman's boat frustrated Navy Secretary Gideon Welles. On the first of February 1862, Welles sent an urgent communication to the Philadelphia shipbuilding firm of Neafle & Levy ordering them to have de Villeroi's submarine boat ready for service at Hampton Roads no later than February 10.[7] Welles knew better than most that the Southern ironclad was almost complete and that the *Monitor* was not quite ready for her (in fact, many did not believe the small Union ironclad would be a match for the larger enemy vessel). His letter, however, did not bring about the completion of the submarine. More than three weeks later, on February 27, a second letter, almost certainly with Welles' blessing, was sent to Neafie & Levy, this time from the Bureau of Yards and Docks: "If the contractor will deliver the boat to Fortress Monroe [Hampton Roads] within ten days complete and ready for operations, payment will be made for her at the contract price. Until there is a compliance with these terms, the Department will take no further order in the matter, and will consider the bargain as closed." Ten days passed without the appearance of de Villeroi's boat, and the bargain was considered "closed."[8]

The ironclad *Monitor* had also encountered delays and mechanical problems both while under construction and once she was launched. Fortunately for the Union, she made her appearance in Hampton Roads with only hours to spare. On the morning of March 8, 1862, the *CSS Virginia* steamed from the narrow mouth of the Elizabeth River and into the waiting arms of several Federal warships. By the end of that memorable day, both the 50-gun frigate *Congress* and 24-gun *Cumberland* were destroyed by the innovative Southern engine of war. That evening, while the once-mighty *Congress* burned in the Virginia moonlight, news of the history-making event was sent clicking over telegraph lines from Bangor, Maine, to Houston, Texas. By a strange twist of fate, the *Monitor* arrived at Hampton Roads that very night, its newly painted black iron hull and turret glistening in the firelight within sight of the burning *Congress*.

At sunrise the following day, the *Virginia* again ventured forth, only this time the cards had been evenly dealt. The pair of iron ships met and hammered one another throughout the morning while thousands of Union and Confederate soldiers and civilians watched the spectacle from shore. The lumbering *Virginia*, slow and cumbersome, could not catch and ram the more nimble *Monitor*, which more than held her own against the larger vessel. In the end, neither ship could batter the other into submission, and both limped away claiming victory.[9]

While the *Monitor's* gallant effort was lauded across the North, her inability to destroy her opponent outraged at least one man—not because

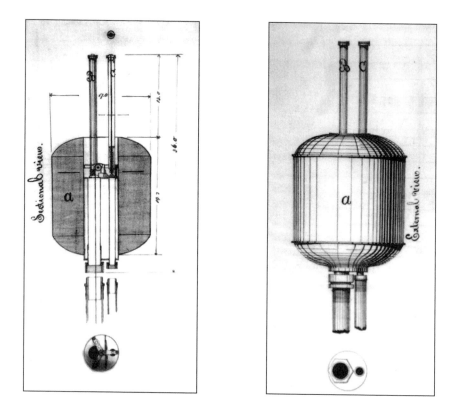

Diagrams of a captured device simply labeled "Rebel Apparatus for supplying air to a person under water." Just where this strange Confederate invention originated from, or how it may have functioned, remains a mystery. *Navy Subject File, National Archives*

the *Monitor* was ill-handled, but because de Villeroi's boat was not there to assist. Louis Hennet, a self-described engineer attached to the submarine project in Philadelphia, sent a blistering letter to the *Philadelphia Public Ledger* complaining bitterly about the constant delays on the Frenchman's boat. "It is almost certain that if the submarine propeller that for the last two months has been lying at the factory of Neafle & Levy, Philadelphia, had been in service at its destination," lamented Hennet, "things would have gone differently. The *Merrimac* [*CSS Vir-*

ginia] would have been destroyed, or at least rendered harmless."[10] Brutus de Villeroi was also probably as disgusted by the delays as Hennet, although perhaps for a less laudable reason: de Villeroi claimed in a postwar letter to Gideon Welles that the sum of $75,000 was agreed upon to be paid he and his crew following the destruction of "The famous *Merrimac.*" Needless to say, de Villeroi never collected his prize money.[11]

Others, however, were more than willing to step into the void left by de Villeroi's failed submarine project. Less than two weeks after the historic ironclad encounter, the Union War Department received an interesting proposition from a New York submersible designer named J. B. Morrell. "Having communicated my views to the Sec of Navy, some days since, I thought it proper to represent the subject for your consideration," explained the New Yorker:

> Being the inventor of a submarine battery submerged to any depth in the water, propelling itself two hours at a speed of four miles per hour, having offered the same to the former Secretary of War without reply, I am induced to make this proposition, to blow the Merrimac beyond 'Davy Jones Locker' for Three Hundred Thousand Dollars, and for each of their other vessels, one Hundred Thousand Dollars.

Transportation for both his submarine battery and himself to Fortress Monroe would be required, advised Morrell, and he would need at least one flat-top barge for use as a base of operations. He went on to state that if he failed to sink the *Virginia*, no payment would be sought for his services. Morrell, apparently, was in possession of a working submarine docked somewhere near New York Harbor. Unfortunately nothing more is known about Morrell or his mysterious invention, and the question as to how much attention was paid to his offer by the War Department may never be known.[12]

On March 29, just eight days after Morrell offered his services to the War Department, President Abraham Lincoln received an apologetic letter from de Villeroi outlining the reasons why his submarine had not been ready for her intended rendezvous with the *CSS Virginia:*

His Excellency Abraham Lincoln, President of the United States,

Sir,

A letter from the Secretary [Welles] dated February 1st, ordered to have the propeller and crew ready to go to the Fortress Monroe on the 10th of February at the very latest. Thus it was very well understood that the crew was to be kept in readiness up to that time. Every thing was ready for the projected expedition for some time, but the contractor Mr. Martin Thomas, for reasons that we do not wish to detail, persisted in refusing certain articles needed in the machine, which this inventor considered indispensable.

This refusal stopped every thing and caused that the expedition was missed. The Government had granted a sum of 14,000 dollars to complete the propeller [the boat itself]. The expenses including every thing do not amount to 11,000 dollars. The following are the positive orders of the Navy Department in that respect. 'The contractor should furnish you with all you require, or give up the enterprize at once.' Nothing has changed our determination to serve the cause of the Union.

De Villeroi,
superintendent and commander of the submarine vessel.[13]

Although de Villeroi's letter at first appears to be nothing more than an excuse-filled document, and not a particularly persuasive one at that, there was a foundation of truth to his story and a reason for his anger. A letter from an officer with the Bureau of Yards and Docks written on February 17, 1862, reported that the "certain articles needed in the machine" not provided by the contractor were costly chemicals required for the air purifying system, something the naval chemists considered "unnecessary." De Villeroi would not risk the lives of himself and his crew without them. If the bureaucratically minded chemists had not delayed completion of the submersible, perhaps history's first successful submarine attack would have taken place at Hampton Roads in the early spring of 1862, instead of Charleston Harbor almost two years later.[14]

◆   ◆   ◆

The news of the sinking of two of the Union's most powerful warships boosted morale across the Confederacy. It was during this period of jubilation that Baxter Watson and James McClintock, the two Louisiana steam gauge manufacturers from New Orleans, prepared to launch their three-man submarine. On March 12, 1862, just seventy-two hours after the fierce duel between the *Virginia* and *Monitor* had been fought to a draw, the 30' black iron hull of the soon to be christened *Pioneer* slid down wooden ramps into the muddy waters of the New Basin Canal.[15]

At some point during the construction of this small submarine, another Louisiana man had eagerly joined Watson and McClintock in their daring underwater venture. The newcomer, Horace L. Hunley, was a wealthy lawyer and Assistant Customs Agent at the New Orleans Customs House. At the outbreak of the war, Hunley had led an expedition to Cuba to obtain arms and munitions for the Southern war effort. "On our outward voyage, we saw but one vessel before reaching the coast of Yucatan, and returning we saw but one till we reached the coast of Louisiana," Hunley reported to his supervisor, F. H. Hatch. "I am confident that any quantity of arms could be safely introduced into Louisiana over this course, in a small light draft steamer, with very little danger. There are numerous deep Bayous along this coast protected by bars having a depth of six to seven feet and from which arms could be conveyed by the Opelousas Railroad to New Orleans." The Louisiana attorney possessed significant seafaring knowledge and was dedicated to the idea of an independent Southern Confederacy. Just when the adventurous Horace Hunley joined Watson and McClintock in their submarine experiments may never be known. All that is known for sure is that from the time he joined the two Louisiana manufacturers until his death in 1863, Hunley remained intimately involved with the construction of the three submarines the trio of partners would build during the war years.[16]

As mentioned above, the Louisianians' inaugural project was the *Pioneer*, a remarkably seaworthy submarine which required only minor modifications to stop the leaks that trickled into the dark interior of her narrow hull. After her leaks were plugged, the tiny submersible was towed down the canal to Lake Pontchartrain to continue testing. James McClintock, in a postwar letter to ex-Confederate scientist Matthew

Fontaine Maury, filled in some of the blanks regarding the testing of the *Pioneer:*

> In the years 1861, 62, and 63, I in connection with others was engaged in inventing and constructing a submarine boat or boat for running under the water at any required depth from the surface. At New Orleans in 1862 we built [completed] the first boat, she was made of iron 1/4 inch thick. The boat was of a cigar shape 30 feet long and 4 feet in diameter. This boat demonstrated to us the fact that we could construct a boat that would move at will in any direction desired, and at any distance from the surface. As we were unable to see objects after passing under the water, the boat was steered by a compass, which at times acted so slow, that the boat would at times alter her course for one or two minutes before it would be discovered, thus losing the direct course and so compel the operator to come to the top of the water more frequently than he otherwise would.[17]

James McClintock was interviewed in 1872 by an officer of the British Navy, which wished to build a submarine boat of its own. The engrossing report of this discussion, which is still on file with the British Admiralty in London, provides fascinating detail about early submarine efforts in the Confederacy. McClintock offered information on a variety of issues.

On the subject of air supply:

> He (McClintock) supposed on good authority, that the boat he was then using could not contain a supply of air for himself and an assistant for more than 15 minutes, increased confidence came with increased experience and they gradually prolonged the time during which they remained submerged until they found they were able to remain below for a period of two hours without suffering any serious inconvenience.

On monitoring depth when submerged:

> The depth was constantly indicated on an ordinary mercurial system gauge fixed immediately opposite the pilot—one end of which was

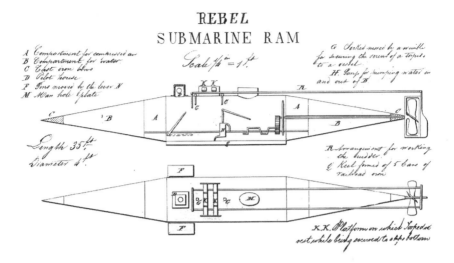

REBEL
SUBMARINE RAM

This is a previously unpublished diagram of the *CSS Pioneer*, drawn by engineer William Shock of the *USS Pensacola* soon after the fall of New Orleans. Until now, no one knew what the *Pioneer* looked like. *National Archives*

open to the outside water. Each 1/2 inch of Mercury represents about one foot of immersion.

On monitoring the speed of the vessel while submerged:

> McClintock states that when under weigh beneath the surface, it is quite impossible to ascertain whether the vessel is progressing as there are no passing objects by which to recognize the fact of motion; on several occasions when experimenting with his boat they continued working the crank when all the time the boat was hard and fast in the mud.[18]

Despite these apparent shortcomings, the owners and backers applied for and were granted a Letter of Marque (a privateering commission) from the Confederate government on March 31, 1862. Their invention, officially called "A Submarine Propeller," was armed with a "Magazine of Powder." The boat measured 34' from bow to stern, and was 4' in diameter with round conical ends (cigar shaped). The boat's narrow hull was painted black to help conceal the craft while running beneath the surface.[19]

From the Letter of Marque sent to Richmond on March 29, 1862, we know that the submarine's skipper was a man named John K. Scott, a fellow employee of the Customs House with Horace Hunley. Scott and his crew of two were granted a commission to cruise the high seas, bays, rivers, and estuaries in the name of the Confederate States of America, and were entitled to a share of every vessel destroyed or captured in the name of the Confederacy.[20]

Although a substantial amount of information is known about the physical characteristics of the little *Pioneer,* her short career as a privateer is a virtual blank slate. From the time of her commissioning as the world's first submarine privateer until the fall of New Orleans, barely a month passed. During that period, David G. Farragut, the flag officer of the West Gulf Blockading Squadron, concentrated his fleet at the mouth of the Mississippi, pushed northward past Forts Jackson and St. Philip, and captured the Crescent City on April 25, 1862. No information exists as to whether the small submarine was deployed against Farragut's ships in defense of the city. Some historians have suggested, with some objective evidence to the contrary, that the *Pioneer* was prepared to engage the enemy in conjunction with the steam-powered ironclad ram *Manassas* and other privateering vessels known to have taken part in the engagement. Unfortunately the only bit of evidence regarding the boat during this period is a message announcing her demise, a sentence from the postwar McClintock letter to Matthew F. Maury stating, "The evacuation of New Orleans lost the boat before our experiments were completed."[21]

The catastrophic capitulation of one of the most important cities in the Confederacy caused the retreating Southerners to destroy anything of value that could be used by the victorious Yankees. "The river and shore were one blaze, and the sounds of explosions were terrific," remembered one Union naval officer who witnessed the physical carnage.[22] While smoke from thousands of burning cotton bales filled the skies, Hunley, Watson, and McClintock followed the example set by their retreating army and hastily scuttled their unique invention in the New Basin Canal. With the city in panic, the three partners returned to their shop on Front Street, gathered together whatever diagrams and notes they could carry, and joined the mob of refugees clogging the roads leading away from the doomed Crescent City.

The sudden collapse of the city sent shock waves throughout the Confederacy. The loss of the seaport of New Orleans meant both the loss of valuable commodities from abroad for the South, and access up the waterway for the Federal deep-water navy. Shortly after the stars and stripes had once again been unfurled over City Hall, the scuttled *Pioneer* was discovered by Union sailors and dragged to shore. The discovery of the derelict submarine caused some concern amongst the sailors in the fleet, and officers from the Engineering Department were summoned to examine the machinery aboard this strange Rebel contraption. G. W. Baird, a young engineer's assistant, accompanied his superiors on an inspection of the craft. Commander Baird later wrote a detailed and long-ignored assessment of his historic inspection for the U.S. Naval Institute. "When a third assistant aboard the *Pensacola* during the Civil War," remembered Baird, "I had the pleasure of assisting Second Assistant Engineer Alfred Colin in the measurements and drawings of a submarine torpedo boat which had been fished out of the canal near the 'New Basin' between New Orleans and the Lake Pontchartrain. Mr. Colin's drawing was sent by the Fleet Engineer [William H. Shock] to the Navy Department."

The boat, Baird recalled,

> was built of iron cut from old boilers, and was designed and built by Mr. McClintock, in his machine shop in the city of New Orleans. She was thirty feet in length; the middle body was cylindrical, ten feet long, and the ends were conical. She had a little conning tower with a manhole in the top, and small, circular, glass windows in its sides. She was propelled by a screw, which was operated by one man. She had vanes, the functions of which were those of the pectoral fins of a fish. The torpedo was of a clockwork type, and was intended to be screwed into the bottom of the enemy's ship. It was carried on top of the boat, and the screws employed were gimlet-pointed and tempered steel.
>
> Mr. McClintock (whom I met after the Civil War had ended) informed me that he had made several descents in his boat, in the lake, and succeeded in destroying a small schooner and several rafts. He stated that

the U.S. Steamers *New London* and *Calhoun* had been a menace on the lake, and this gave rise to the torpedo boat; but before an attack was made the fleet of Farragut had captured New Orleans, and his boat was sunk to prevent her from falling into the hands of the enemy.[23]

Fortunately, a search in the National Archives turned up the diagram Fleet Engineer William Shock drafted of McClintock's scuttled New Orleans submarine. An informative letter to Gustavus Fox, the Assistant Secretary of the Navy, accompanied the detailed drawing of the "Rebel Submarine Ram." Shock wrote the letter from the flagship *Pensacola* of the West Gulf Blockading Squadron off New Orleans. Given its historical significance, and since no one apparently has seen it for more than a century, it is worth reprinting in its entirety:

Dear Sir:

Some few weeks since I had some duty calling me to a place known as the 'New Basin' where I discovered a Submarine Machine. I embraced the first favorable opportunity and examined it, got its history and had a drawing made of it, a tracing of which I send you as a curiosity.

The history of the machine is simply this. In the early part of Admiral Farragut's operations here the gun boat *New London* was a perfect terror to the Rebels on the lake, so it occurred to them if they could get a Machine that would move underwater, they could succeed in securing a Torpedo to the bottom of the ship, move off, touch the wires, and thus terminate her existence. They finally got the thing done, made a good job of it, got it overboard and put two men in it, they were smothered to death. The thing was a failure and a monument to badly expended talents.[24]

Shock's letter is the first indication that two men were killed attempting to sink a Federal warship on Lake Ponchartrain. McClintock never mentioned it, and no other information on the subject has come to light. Shock's hasty dismissal of the Southerners' attempts at submarine operations, "badly expended talents," as he called them, is peculiar— especially since he himself was an engineer.

Shock's extraordinarily detailed diagram of the boat, however, provides a wealth of information on early submarine construction and operation in general, and detailed intelligence on the *Pioneer* in particular. It is especially valuable since nothing other than a brief description of the *Pioneer* had been found prior to the discovery of Shock's illustration. The plans demonstrate that the finished vessel was a menacing looking engine of war, simple in concept and yet surprisingly complex, and quite striking in appearance. A small forward box-shaped observation tower allowed the pilot to maneuver the vessel beneath a ship and screw in the torpedo that rode in the rack bolted to the top of the black iron hull. With a large differential gear placed at the base of the propeller shaft, two men could have easily provided the necessary power to propel the vessel either above or below the surface. If Shock's diagram is accurate, McClintock and company affixed the forward diving plans too low, a construction defect that might have caused the *Pioneer* to experience stability problems while diving. Experimentation seems to have corrected this problem, for on later projects these fins were moved higher and placed on the horizontal axis.

Despite the obvious historical value of the small boat, the little *Pioneer* was sold as metal scrap soon after the close of the war. According to an auction announcement in the February 15, 1868, issue of the *New Orleans Picayune,*

> A torpedo boat, which was built in the city or hereabouts during the war, and which is now lying on the banks of the New Canal, near Claiborne Street, is to be sold at public auction to-day, by the United States authorities, at 12 o'clock, at the canal street entrance of the Custom House. The boat in question, which is built of iron and weighs about two tons, was sunk in the Canal about the time of the occupation of the city by the Federal forces, in 1862. It was built as an experiment, and was never fully perfected, and is only valuable now for the machinery and iron which is in and about it.

Later that day, a brief statement appeared in the afternoon edition of the same paper: "The torpedo boat, of which we made mention this morning, was sold at public auction to-day at noon, for forty-three dollars. It cost, originally, twenty-six hundred." The saga of the little privateer *Pioneer* had come to an inglorious end.[25]

But a minor mystery lingered. For a number of years, many people believed that the small submarine now on display at the State Museum in the heart of New Orleans' French Quarter was the *Pioneer*. There is no dispute that the submarine at the museum, however, was not discovered until 1879—almost ten years after the 30' submarine was auctioned off for scrap on the banks of the New Basin Canal. If the prominently displayed boat is not the *Pioneer*, what boat is she? While we may never know with certainty, she may well be the same submarine described in E. P. Doer's June 1861 letter to the Union Secretary of the Navy. Mr. Doer, it will be recalled, was a resident of Buffalo, New York, who had information that a submarine was being constructed in New Orleans long before the *Pioneer* came into existence.[26]

◆   ◆   ◆

In any case, the *Pioneer* by no means represented the end of underwater expermentation by McClintock, Watson, and Hunley. The three disappointed inventors ended up in Mobile, Alabama, where they rekindled their hopes of building a second and more formidable submarine vessel. On April 30, 1862, Maj. Gen. Benjamin Butler moved his army into the defeated city of New Orleans and placed its citizens under marshal law. That same day hundreds of miles away in Pennsylvania, the long-awaited launching of Brutus de Villeroi's "iron submarine boat" was taking place in front of a cheering crowd at a Philadelphia dock.[27]

Although one would think the navy would want to keep the existence of a new submarine secret, the launching of de Villeroi's boat was anything but a closed-door affair. According to the May 2, 1862, morning edition of the *Philadelphia Inquirer,*

> the Launch of the Government Submarine Vessel . . . at Messrs. NEAFLE & LEVY'S Works took place contrary to first arrangements, on Wednesday afternoon, between four and five o'clock. Ropes were fastened around her as she lay on the wharf, and she was then raised

by means of shears, and lowered easily into the water. No one was within her, but Mr. Levy, one of the firm which constructed her, stood upon the top during the launch.

When fairly in the water she lay half submerged, her iron guards being almost level with the surface. Two men went into the interior, and tried the effect of the oars or paddles. Although but two or three were moved at once, the vessel obeyed them readily, and when the whole sixteen or eighteen are put in motion, it is believed that she can be propelled with considerable velocity. She will be entirely submerged, when necessary, by means of lead or other ballasting; and it is believed that, when this is accomplished, a very slight variation in weight will suffice to lower her to the bottom, or raise her to the surface. When entirely submerged, the glazed aperture in her roof will keep her lighted.

She was yesterday afternoon to be towed to the Navy Yard. The present position in which she lies will be her natural one; she will only be sunk when necessary to conceal her operations. With her gothic arched back, and conical bow, she looks not unlike a big sturgeon.[28]

The article's description is the first reference we have that de Villeroi's boat had oars or paddles and an arched hull. Although no diagrams of his submarine are known to exist, an excellent description of the vessel—the most thorough and detailed that I have thus far seen—appeared in the *Philadelphia Inquirer* under the heading "The Government Submarine Vessel":

She is 40 feet in length, about 6 feet deep, and 4 feet 6 inches in breadth. In shape and appearance she is very much like an iron boiler with a tapering or conical end, and a rounded stern. A sheet iron horizontal guard runs around the outside of the vessel, under which the hand paddles, 8 on a side, are attached. These are two-leaved, and the leaves close on a hinge on the upward or back stroke, to avoid the resistance of the water. Their handles, to which the paddles are at right angles, pass through the iron sides of the vessel, and are moved by the rower, the iron rod or handle acting as a hinge.

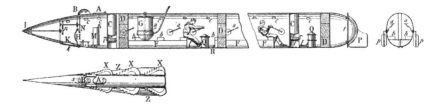

A nineteenth-century French diagram of the U.S. Navy submarine boat *Alligator*. *LA Navigation Sous Marine*

Inside she looks somewhat like a bomb-proof man-of-war barge, with white painted iron thwarts crossing at regular intervals, and her arched iron roof perforated with small glazed apertures (windows).

On her conical bow is a water tight compartment, connected by a small door with the main interior space, and having in the bottom a little round door, called a 'man hole,' through which a diver in submarine armor may descend to the bottom of the water and carry on his destructive work at leisure and unobserved. There is a fan like rudder of a crescent shape, hinged on the stern, fastened at its horns to the top and bottom of the end. The vessel contains pumps, an air-condenser, anchors, and is entered by a man hole on top by the bow. Mr. Villeroi, a French gentleman, is the inventor.[29]

The "submarine armor" or diving gear was probably quite different from the standard deep sea diving gear of the period. Instead of walking about the bottom in heavy lead boots like other divers of the era, the diver attached to the submarine had to have the capability to swim freely and rise off the sea floor at will in order to attach an explosive device to the bottom of an enemy ship. How the diver in the "water tight compartment" in the bow of the vessel was supplied with air is unknown, but it must have been a revolutionary design, perhaps involving the use of a hose connected to an interior compressed air tank (which were already in use during the Victorian period). Since the hull of the submarine vessel was self-contained—it did not have a snorkel assembly—it would have been impossible to supply the outside diver with air by means of a pump within the craft. Compressed air stored within the pressure hull of the vessel may have been the answer. One of the several intriguing details contained in the article was the description of a device labled an "air condenser"; its function and design are unknown.

The *Philadelphia Inquirer* article clearly stated that the remarkable submarine, whose appearance must have caused quite a stir to those who witnessed her baptism, "was yesterday afternoon to be towed to the Navy Yard." There, the boat was to be evaluated and tested by Union naval personnel. A communication sent by the Bureau of Yards and Docks just five days later confirms the boat's arrival at the yard, where it was placed under the charge of a naval engineer named William L. Hunt. The engineer's responsibilites were important ones: "He [Hunt] is instructed at once to carry out the orders of the Navy Department and to prepare, man, and report the boat ready for service."[30]

Although no documents have surfaced concerning Hunt's secret underwater tests of de Villeroi's submarine, we can say with some certainty that they must have been successful, for within a month and a half after being launched at Philadelphia, the boat and her volunteer crew of underwater adventurers were ordered into action at Hampton Roads at the mouth of the James River.

At the time of the submarine's launching, it was hoped by many in the North that the novel underwater invention might still strike a death blow against the battleworn but still threatening *CSS Virginia*, which had recently returned to dry dock at the Norfolk Navy Yard. On the day following the historic duel between the two innovative ironclads, John L. Worden, the wounded commander of the Federal *Monitor*, had informed President Lincoln that his vessel was extremely vulnerable if attacked by a determined boarding party of Rebel sailors. Worden's evaluation immediately prompted orders from Washington which severely restricted the movements of the *Monitor*. The danger rested with the turret, which could be wedged with iron spikes to prevent it from turning, and seawater could be poured down the smokestack to extinguish the ship's fires. It was finally decided that the little ironclad, with its two formidable guns, should be held in reserve and not engage the *Virginia* except on the best of terms and as a last resort.[31]

While sailors on Union picket boats strained their eyes for a glimpse of the hourly expected Rebel ironclad, the *Virginia* remained in dry dock for much needed repairs and improvements. Her performance had been somewhat disappointing. She proved tediously slow, difficult to steer, leaked badly, and drew too much water. In addition, she was a larger target and thus easier to hit than her smaller and faster opponent. Additional armor was placed below her waterline, and a heavier iron ram was attached to her bow. Thick metal doors were added to the gun ports and additional ballast was placed in her keel, which increased her draft to twenty-three feet.[32]

On the morning of April 11, 1862, the refitted *Virginia,* accompanied by six small Confederate gunboats, once again steamed down the Elizabeth River into Hampton Roads looking for a fight. At her helm and steering for the Federal ironclad *Monitor* was Capt. Josiah Tattnall, who had taken command from Franklin Buchanan.Worden's discussion with Lincoln was prescient, for Tattnall's plan was to capture the *Monitor* by drawing her out into the open, boarding her, wedging the turret, and throwing small explosives through her open gun ports. Although the hidden Confederate boarding party was poised and ready to strike, the ironclad remained under the protective guns of Fortress Monroe, immobilized by her orders to avoid an engagement. While the crew of the *Monitor* watched helplessly from inside the gunports, one of the Rebel gunboats accompanying the *Virginia* easily captured three sailing vessels and towed them back to Norfolk as prizes.[33]

Following the nonengagement of April 11 in Hampton Roads, the *Virginia* was once again returned to dry dock to repair her overtaxed steam engines. It was during this period that the "Government Submarine Propeller" was launched in Philadelphia some 200 miles away. It was hoped by all concerned that the testing of the little submarine would be completed swiftly and that the vessel could then be towed down the Chesapeake Bay to the mouth of the James River before the massive Rebel ironclad once more put to sea. It was not to be.

On May 3, 1862, just hours after de Villeroi's submarine boat had been launched in Pennsylvania, the Confederate Navy Department issued orders for the abandonment of Norfolk. All the stores and machinery that could not be shipped to the navy yards at Richmond were to be

destroyed. The evacuation was prompted by the movement of Union
General George McClellan's Army of the Potomac, which had landed on
the tip of the Virginia Peninsula between the York and the James
Rivers, and was marching against nearby Yorktown. On May 8, the *Virginia* once more left her mooring and limped to the mouth of the James
River to cover the Confederate navy's escape to Richmond. When the
Federal ships caught sight of Captain Tattnall's battle-worn ironclad,
"they retired with all speed under the protection of the guns of the
fortress [Monroe] . . . "[34]

Unfortunately for the Rebels, the *Virginia's* draft was over twenty
feet, and she was unable to follow her smaller sister ships over the
Jamestown Flats. When all hope of floating the ironclad's heavy hull
into the shallow mouth of the James River was abandoned, she was run
aground on Craney Island and set ablaze at 3:00 a.m. on May 11. Two
hours later, while hundreds of Union sailors watched her thick armor
glow red from the blaze, fire reached the *Virginia's* magazine and she
was blown out of existence. As the mighty ironclad disappeared into the
dark waters at the mouth of the Elizabeth River, Union sailors cheered
the death of the hated Rebel monster from the decks of their ships anchored in nearby Hampton Roads. On New Year's Eve seven months
later, the *USS Monitor* shared a similar fate when she was lost in a gale
while being towed off the coast of North Carolina.[35]

◆   ◆   ◆

While large pieces of the iron skin from the scuttled *Virginia* cooled in
the waters near Norfolk, William G. Cheeney, the designer of the James
River submarine boats, was preparing to test a new and improved undersea weapon in the cold and muddy waters of the James River in
Richmond. On May 13, only forty-eight hours after the iron hull of the
Virginia had vanished beneath the waves, Acting Master Cheeney and
his staff of underwater visionaries took delivery of a modified submarine
boat at the Tredegar Iron Works.[36]

Disappointingly, like most other Civil War submarines, no diagrams
or drawings are known to exist of this vessel. Detailed lists itemizing her
fabrication costs and materials purchased during construction, however,

Tredegar Iron Works,

Confederate States Navy
Richmond, May 13th 1862

P. W. G. Cheney

Bought of J. R. ANDERSON & CO.,

TERMS:
MANUFACTURERS of BAR and GUIDE IRON, CHAIRS and SPIKES, BRIDGE BOLTS, LOCOMOTIVES, CARS, TRUCKS, WHEELS and AXLES, MARINE, STATIONARY and PORTABLE ENGINES, SUGAR MILLS, SAW and GRIST MILLS, &c., CANNON and PROJECTILES, IRON and BRASS CASTINGS, STEEL, &c., &c.

Bars.	Bdls.	Size.	Weight.	Price.	Amount.
1861					
Dec 11		To Cash for R O Haskins for 2 double blocks			24 00
"		" " " S M Price & Co for Cotton Goods			6 44
"		" " " R I Denny for 1-60 ft Tape Line			1 35
"		" 2 Tons Pig Iron		35	70 00
"		" Hauling same			2 00
1862		For alterations to Submarine Boat			
May 13th		" False Bows put on Boat	2235	15	
		" Boilermakers work on same in shop Pat Ready day	13th	3 50	457 63
		Hauling same to Boat & Handling			5 00
		Bolts & Hinges	328	25	82 00
		Pattern Makers making Patters for			
		Propeller & castings for gas furnace day 18¼	3 50	63 88	
		1 Chain for Rudder of Boat	18	15	2 70
		Hooks & Ring Put in Same	8	25	2 00
		Safety Spring in Hook			1 00
		Splicing Handle			75
		One Oil Cup with Cock			1 75
		4½ lb Putty		25	1 13
		Machinist fitting work	days 15	3 50	52 50
		Do Turning Do	" 10¼	6 00	61 50
		6 Pieces Brass Casting for air Pump 36			
		1 Brass Pump	63		
		16 Couplings	16		
		1 Guard for Pumps	6		
		1 Pipe for Do	19		
		1 Casting for Propeller	32	193 75	144 75
		Paint used in Painting Boat			35 35
		Painters Painting Boat	days 5½	3 50	19 25
		Grinding Glass for Light			10 00
		Drayage 2 board to Boat			1 00
		1 wrought furnace for making gas			
		Brass Bolts & fixtures for same	561	961 20	961 20

Page one of a three-page Tredegar Iron Works invoice for "Alterations to Submarine Boat." Some of the more interesting entries include casting the propeller, fitting air pumps, and grinding four glass panes for viewing. *Confederate Navy Subject File, National Archives* have been recently located. Amongst the thousands of entries scribbled into the account books kept at the Tredegar Iron Works are several faded pages detailing work performed by Tredegar's iron workers and machinists. Listed under the heading "Alterations to Submarine Boat" are a small handful of the fascinating and somewhat baffling entries describing work performed within some of the Tredegar's numerous shops:

> False Bow put on boat . . . $342.75, Boiler makers work on same in shop . . . 130 days . . . $457.63, Pattern makers making patterns for propeller . . . 18 days . . . $63.88, One door plate [Hatch?] . . . $101.85, making and fitting 4 valves to air pumps . . . $8.00, Grinding 4 glass plates for sight . . . $10.00, 2 brass stop cocks . . . $5.00, 1 glass globe lantern . . . $1.50, cord for trailing torpedoes . . . $14.00, paint used in painting boat . . . $25.25, painters painting boat . . . 5 1/2 days . . . $19.25.[37]

It is probable that the items modified or made were for the larger submarine vessel reported on by Union spy "Mrs. Baker," who claimed the boat was nearing completion at the Tredegar Iron Works during her undercover operations in the Confederate capital in the fall of 1861. There are several pieces of evidence upon which to base this conclusion. Mrs. Baker related that the new submarine carried a man "provided with submarine diving armor." Cheeney's new boat was fitted with a "false bow," likely a modification to the forward compartment in which the diver was carried (recall the description of de Villeroi's submarines, for example). The entry describing the "fitting of four valves to air pumps" indicates that a snorkel assembly of some kind, as described by Mrs. Baker, was still being used. The "four glass plates for sight" and "one door plate" is evidence that the small submarine probably had a single hatch or conning tower pierced by four view ports located fore, aft, port, and starboard in the conning tower's trunk. The "glass globe lantern" appearing on the list was certainly the means by which the submarine's interior was illuminated when running submerged. Evidence that the craft was rather large may be concluded from the entry, "painters painting boat . . . 5 1/2 days." This probably included both the interior and exterior in order to justify a cost of $25.25 for "paint

This small flat-decked "Submarine Torpedo Boat" was drawn by General Gabriel Rain, head of the Confederate Torpedo Bureau. No information regarding this vessel has thus far come to light. *Brockenbrough Library, Museum of the Confederacy*

used in painting boat." The $14.00 "cord for trailing torpedoes" is something of a mystery. Why should a tow rope cost the equivalent of a month's pay for a Confederate private? Perhaps this "cord" was in fact not a rope or line at all, but instead some sort of insulated wire.

As will soon be related, Acting Master Cheeny was well acquainted with, and was perhaps a pioneer in, electrically detonated underwater explosives. The $14.00 "cord" recorded in the Tredegar ledgers could be evidence that Cheeney's submarine boat was employing an electric charge to detonate the trailing torpedo. If so, the charge may have been stored in a crude galvanic battery placed within the submarine's hull. Although there is no hard proof to back up this theory, it is offered for the reader's consideration. As it turns out, others besides Cheeney proposed using electricity in a Civil War submarine.

Speculation aside as to the boat's identity, it is known for certain that on May 13, 1862, while McClellan was slowly moving his army up the peninsula toward Richmond, Acting Master William G. Cheeney, on behalf of the Confederate States Navy Department, took delivery of a modified submarine vessel that had been under construction for some time ("Boiler makers work on same in shop . . . 130 days").

◆   ◆   ◆

At about the same time that Cheeney and his staff were taking delivery of their modified submarine boat, tests were being conducted in the James River on an unconventional invention known from requisitions as simply "The Submarine Cannon."[38] On the same day alterations to the submarine boat were charged, an interesting entry in the Tredegar Iron Works' sales book was inserted: "Charge to C. S. Navy Dept. for shot and shell for submarine batteries, and Sundry shot and shell for crews taught Submarine Gun." Additional documentation on this project, recently discovered in the National Archives, reads as follows: "May 30, 1862. The Confederate States Navy Department to George Leonhardt, Office of Appropriations for Submarine Batteries. For making a working pattern or model of the Submarine Cannon . . . $50.00." The mechanism was clearly at the testing stage, as evidenced by the following document: "May 30, 1862. The Confederate States Navy Department to John Messier, Office of Appropriations for Submarine batteries. $10.00 for repair of lighter [a flat bottom barge] borrowed from Canal Company and injured in testing Submarine Cannon." Was Private Charles Leavitt's invention of a submarine gunboat finally coming to fruition?[39]

Perhaps we will never know. Once again, no diagrams or sketches of the "Submarine Cannon" memorialized by these puzzling documents are known to exist. The weapon may have been intended for use with Cheeney's large submarine. Almost certainly it had something to do with Leavitt's design, an idea that had so impressed Secretary of War Judah Benjamin and Ordnance Chief Josiah Gorgas, they arranged for Leavitt's "discharge from military service. His labor being required for other important government work."

Acting Master Cheeney took delivery of his modified submarine boat at a most inopportune time. Within forty-eight hours after taking possession, Union warships were pounding fortifications along the James River just south of Richmond. With orders to "Shell the place [Richmond] into surrender," the USS Monitor and several other Federal warships had steamed up the James virtually unopposed. At Drewry's Bluff, a mere eight miles downriver from the capital, the small armada halted due to powerful obstructions that had been placed in the river following the smaller Rebel navy's retreat from Norfolk. Unfortunately for the Confederates, these obstructions of sunken ships, barges, large crates of stones, and old scrap iron were to be as much a barrier to them as to the enemy.[40]

The danger to Richmond's very existence was a real one. With Federal naval forces battling below the city and George McClellan's Army of the Potomac approaching by land up the peninsula, it's highly unlikely that an underwater explosives expert like Acting Master Cheeney would be tinkering with a newly painted and untested submarine boat during such a crisis. In fact, within days after accepting delivery of his modified submersible boat, Cheeney was several miles south of Richmond at Chaffin's Bluff planting and maintaining electrically detonated underwater mines.[41]

Cheeney's service during this time, recorded Matthew F. Maury, was on the James River,

> ... [which] is mined with 15 tanks below the iron battery at Chaffin's Bluff. They are to be exploded by means of electricity. Four of the tanks contain 160 pounds of powder; the 11 others hold 70 pounds each. All are made of boiler plate. There is a quantity of admirably insulated wire, a number of shells for anchors or torpedoes, and a sufficient quantity of chains for the wires remaining.
>
> The galvanic batteries, viz, 21 Wollaston's and 1 Cruikshank (the latter loaned by Dr. Maupin from the University of Virginia), with spare acids, are at Chaffin's Bluff in charge of Acting Master Cheeney. He has also in jugs sufficient quantity mixed to work the batteries, and ready to be poured in for use.[42]

Cheeney's obvious expertise with electric explosives and galvanic batteries may well explain his expensive submarine "cord" heretofore discussed.

The intended base of operations for the James River submarine is unknown, but given its large size it was probably unfit for operations on its namesake waterway. In all likelihood it was intended to operate out of Norfolk and the Chesapeake Bay. The abandonment of the Norfolk Navy Yard and subsequent scuttling of the *CSS Virginia*, however, effectively sealed the James River off from Hampton Roads and virtually the entire Norfolk fleet was bottled up on a few miles of river below Richmond. So was Cheeney's submarine. Whether it was transported by railroad to another location is unknown, and no record exists that it ever left Richmond. The only available information on what can only be described as a remarkable submarine is contained in a few pages of invoices found within ledgers kept at the Tredegar Iron Works, and faded bills to Acting Master Cheeney and the Confederate Navy Department. Whatever else was committed to paper relative to this unique invention was probably consumed in the fires that raged through the collapsed Confederate capital at the end of the war in April of 1865. With the Union Navy now in control of the river and threatening Richmond, perhaps Cheeney and his staff turned their attentions away from submarine boats and concentrated their unique skills on perfecting electrically detonated underwater mines.

If so, Acting Master William G. Cheeney's new engagement was short-lived. Within a few weeks he became disillusioned with the Confederate cause. During the late summer of 1862, Cheeney abandoned his efforts along the James River (he probably deserted) and made his way to Washington, D.C., under the assumed name of William L. Walker. From a prison cell in Missouri in 1864, he swore in a deposition that he took with him "information [for] President Lincoln of great importance." This information, undoubtedly intelligence about the South's capacity for submarine warfare, "was reduced to writing and handed to the porter at the White House about the 1st of September, 186[2]." Failing to get an answer from the White House, Cheeney returned to his home state of New York and worked in the printing business before traveling to Missouri, where he started a lead smelting operation. He was suspected of being a member of the Order of American Knights, an organization whose purpose was the overthrow of the Lincoln Administration and an end to the war, and was arrested in June of 1864. His fate thereafter is unknown.[43]

◆   ◆   ◆

During the chaotic months of May and June, while Cheeney and his assistants anchored their electrical mines on the muddy bottom of the James River, Brutus de Villeroi's "submarine propeller," which had been launched in Philadelphia some weeks earlier, was preparing to join Flag Officer Louis M. Goldsborough's fleet at Hampton Roads. Testing on the arch-backed submersible was finished, and it was deemed serviceable and ready for action. Although the *CSS Virginia* was no longer in existence, the Navy Department still hoped de Villeroi's underwater invention could be put to good use in the James River. On June 13, Gideon Welles notified Goldsborough that "The Submarine Boat, 47 feet in length, at Philadelphia, is all ready to be sent to James River, and you will send one of your small and swift steamers to that port to tow her down."[44]

Two days later, Goldsborough ordered Acting Master Amos P. Foster, commanding the steamer *USS Satellite*, to "proceed to Philadelphia, via the Delaware and Chesapeake Canal . . . for the purpose of towing to this place the submarine boat which has been prepared there for this station." You will bring her here, the flag officer admonished, "with as little delay as possible." Four days later, Foster's steamer had arrived at the naval yard and was ready to begin the operation.[45]

"The submarine propeller under contract with Mr. Martin Thomas will leave Philadelphia at 11 o'clock a.m. this day for Hampton Roads, via the Chesapeake and Delaware Canal," Goldsborough was advised by Welles on June 19. "The boat is under charge of Mr. Samuel Eakins. Mr. Thomas goes to Fortress Monroe with the boat, which is, or should be, manned with twenty men, including the master, who receive $40 per month each, including subsistence. If the crew is not full, you can supply deficiencies." The large boat was "prepared for operation with two torpedoes [mines] and all apparatus for submarine work," whatever that might have entailed. If Goldsborough was wondering exactly how to utilize his new charge, the Navy Secretary's telegram offered him only vague suggestions. De Villeroi's submersible, instructed Welles, will be employed "for clearing obstructions in James River, or any other submarine work you may think proper, and supply the powder on government account." Welles was leaving its use up to Goldsborough's discretion. "Please report when the propeller arrives, and also when and where she shall operate. The obstructions in the Elizabeth River, and also the *Merrimack* [*CSS Virginia*] and other sunken wrecks may perhaps be looked at," he concluded.[46]

As Welles noted in passing in his instructions to Goldsborough, the boat would be under the charge of Samuel Eakins. Virtually nothing is known about the man or how he came to be involved with the project. Perhaps he was associated with Brutus de Villeroi (who unfortunately disappears from the historical record), or possibly Eakins was engaged with the boat's design and/or construction. The earliest reference to Eakins is found in the payroll books of the USS *Princeton*, a receiving ship at Philadelphia. Its faded pages record that he was appointed superintendent of the submarine boat on June 1, 1862, at a monthly salary of $125 dollars. The earliest dispatch or order containing his name is dated within twenty-four hours of Welles' departure orders to Goldsborough (discussed above). On June 18, the day before the boat departed with the *Satellite* for Hampton Roads, the Commandant of the U.S. Navy Yard informed Eakins that he would "proceed with her through the Delaware and Chesapeake Canal to Hampton Roads, where you will report your arrival to Flag-Officer Goldsborough for further instructions." Since some of the crew had not yet signed the required oath, explained the Commandant, "I have enclosed blank forms. . . . The crew are to be enlisted for a time, not to exceed one year, at the pleasure of the Department."[47]

At 11:00 a.m. on the morning of June 19, 1862, the United States Navy's first combat submarine parted her mooring at the Philadelphia Navy Yard. The strange contraption trailing behind the stern of an unnamed tug and accompanied by Foster's *Satellite* was guided by Samuel Eakins, who carefully monitored the long tow lines that would haul his boat throughout its long journey to Hampton Roads. In the hot and dimly lit engine room below the tug's deck, soot-stained sailors shoveled coal onto the hot fires as its over-taxed engines strained under the increased weight of the partially submerged vessel in tow. One can only wonder what thoughts possessed the submarine's daring crew and divers as they waved farewells to the crowd that lined the docks.

Oddly, the submarine was still officially nameless. She was still referenced in dispatches and orders as "the submarine propeller," or "submarine boat." Perhaps the chaotic rush to get her tested and into action at Hampton Roads was the reason a formal name had not yet been adopted. Within two months after her departure from the Philadelphia Navy Yard, however, she had a name: *Alligator*. Just when she formally received this appropriate appellation has not yet come to light. The name she has come to be known by is *The United States Submarine Propeller U.S.S. Alligator.*[48]

Secretary of the Navy Gideon Welles had high hopes for the submarine boat on its way to rendezvous with the Federal fleet at the mouth of the James River. On June 21, he instructed Goldsborough to, "as far as practicable . . . keep secret the movements of the submarine propeller recently from Philadelphia, and take into consideration the propriety of her being used on the Appomattox River to operate against the Petersburg Bridge." The structure was an important logistical lifeline and carried supplies and troops into and out of the capital of the Confederacy. Goldsborough either viewed the telegram as an order or believed the idea meritorious, for within hours he dispatched confidential orders from his flagship *Minnesota* to Commander J. P. Gillis of the *USS Wachusett* on the James River. Gillis was to return to Norfolk with his ship, "without delay," and turn over papers relating to the management of affairs on the river to Commander John Rodgers of the *USS Galena*. "Say to Commander Rodgers," wrote Goldsborough, "that the President of the United States is especially anxious to have the railroad bridge at Petersburg destroyed, if possible, and that I wish him to accomplish the object, if it can be done." The flag officer then offered the means to accomplish the feat: "A submarine propeller for clearing the obstructions, etc., in the James River will be sent to Commander Rodgers the moment it arrives here from Philadelphia. She is now hourly expected, and she, perhaps, may be used to great advantage in destroying the bridges in view." Exhort Rodgers, Goldsborough urged Gillis, "to lose no time in getting the work [this order] bespeaks done. It is of the utmost importance that it should be accomplished before the next fight comes off between General McClellan and the rebel army."[49]

Thus a plan to find a way to destroy the railroad bridge was already in the works before the *Alligator* even reached Hampton Roads. While Samuel Eakins and his crew watched the long tow line strain under the weight of their heavy submarine, strategies for arming and deploying the new secret weapon, deep within enemy territory, were already being acted on by Goldsborough and his subordinate officers. Eakins and his crew of untested volunteers faced a dangerous assignment.

While still in route to Hampton Roads, a June 21 letter was sent to Eakins by the Navy Department:

You are placed in command of the submarine propeller. It is a trust of considerable importance, requiring skill and good judgement on your part. So as soon as you have fully tested the boat, you will report to the Secretary of the Navy her description. The length, breadth, depth, amount of ballast, what apparatus you have on and in her of all kinds, how she moves submerged, and at what speed, how she steers, how long it takes to depress her in five fathoms of water, and how long to elevate her, how far and with what distinctness an object can be seen through the glass globe on the top of the boat, how the divers operate outside the boat at a depth of forty feet, and how well they are supplied with air from the boat, and generally, her completeness for service and the objects for which she was designed. You will of course act under the orders of Flag-Officer Goldsborough.[50]

In addition to impressing Eakins with the importance of his assignment, Secretary Welles was anxious to discover how the boat operated in the waters off Norfolk. She was, after all, the first of her kind; the success or failure of underwater warfare for the North depended to a large degree on the *Alligator's* performance and Eakins' report thereof.

As it turned out, an attack on the bridge spanning the Appomattox River at Petersburg was out of the question—at least according to Commander Rodgers. "The subject has already engaged my attention," the commander of the *Galena* explained, "and I met the following difficulties":

The gunboats can not send a boat on shore without danger of an ambush. Every movement is carefully watched by armed rebels. The Appomattox, scarcely wider than a canal, has its channel obstructed by vessels and lighters sunk in the bottom of the river. We can not approach by steamers, and rowboats would be destroyed.

When I last heard from Petersburg, about a month ago, by two deserters, there were some 6,000 or 7,000 troops there under General

[Benjamin] Huger. If I see any opportunity of carrying out the subject of your letter, I shall zealously do so.[51]

Goldsborough ordered a copy made and sent to Washington. "I appreciate the difficulties of which he speaks," agreed Goldsborough in an endorsement to Rodgers' dispatch. "The submarine propeller, when just awash, draws six feet of water, and in order to get the men out of her bottom it ought to go no nearer the ground than 18 inches or two feet. Hence," concluded the flag officer, "operating even in as much as eight feet of water, her upper surface will be in sight and exposed." Even night work, he informed the Navy Secretary, would be hazardous, and there may not be "light enough" to navigate. "The Appomattox, after ascending it some five miles, becomes very narrow and shoal, and the tide is frequently rapid. We will do our best. This is all I can at present promise."[52]

It is unlikely that the crew of the *Alligator* could have imagined the hazardous inaugural operation waiting for them. It was obvious interior river work was completely unsuited to the large submarine—she was, after all, 47' long. Still, Goldsborough intended to send her deep into enemy territory, possibly under cover of darkness, to destroy a heavily guarded railroad bridge in the shallow and twisting Appomattox. The *Alligator* was designed to operate upon the hulls of ships anchored in deep harbors, such as the port of Norfolk—not on shallow twisting waterways. Goldsborough's decision demonstrated an utter lack of understanding of the boat's capabilities.

Although she was expected "hourly" on June 21, Eakins' submarine was towed into Hampton Roads on June 23, four days after leaving Philadelphia. As the tug dropped anchor in the deep waters near Fortress Monroe, stunned Union sailors stared in disbelief at the partially submerged contraption floating behind her. Within hours after setting eyes on the immense fleet of supply ships, hospital barges, and warships supporting General McClellan's Army of the Potomac's drive on Richmond, Samuel Eakins received his first order from Flag Officer Louis Goldsborough. "Proceed up the James River, with the submarine propeller and the tug which towed her from Philadelphia under your charge," he instructed, "and report yourself to Commander John

Rodgers, commanding the *U.S.S. Galena*, who will inform you what services are to be performed by that propeller." The *Satellite* was ordered to accompany the *Alligator*, and Goldsborough ordered the steamer's commander to "afford you and your men every accommodation in his power. Commander Poor, Naval Ordnance Officer at Fortress Monroe, will furnish you with 20 barrels of powder, which is to be taken on board the *Satellite* and kept there for your use as you may require it." The *Satellite*, added the flag officer, "is to remain in company with the submarine propeller as long as may be necessary."[53]

On the same day Eakins was ordered to proceed up the James River, the *Satellite's* Acting Master Amos Foster received instructions of his own after the officers from each vessel met with Goldsborough. Presumably the mission was discussed in some detail, although no record of their conversation exists. When it was discovered that "No arrangement had been made to provision" the *Alligator's* crew, "at the request of the parties, [Goldsborough] agreed to let each one have a ration per day, the value of which to be deducted from the monthly pay allowed." Foster thus was ordered to "receive on board the officers and crew of the submarine propeller . . . you will ration this crew while it remains with you."[54]

The speed with which orders were dispatched to Eakins did not allow him much time for the additional trials and tests regarding the submarine's diving characteristics that Gideon Welles desired. In fact, it is doubtful that they were performed, for there is no evidence that the report Welles directed Eakins to prepare was ever submitted. The only mention of any type of "test" of the vessel after her arrival comes from Goldsborough himself, on the day of the submarine's departure up the James River. The submarine, he informed the Navy Secretary, arrived safely. "She is not prepared for operation with any torpedoes," he continued, and "required a lot of whisky barrels, twenty barrels of powder, and a steamer to accompany her and the little tug, in order to accomodate powder, men, etc., all of which were promptly furnished." Goldsborough continued his assessment of the situation to Welles:

To-day she leaves for the James River, accompanied by the tug that brought her from Philadelphia and by the *Satellite*. Owing to the very light draft of the tug, and for other reasons, it is well to retain her services for the present, and I have given orders accordingly. I have directed Commander Rodgers to use her first in the Appomattox, if she can possibly be applied there to any advantage whatever in the destruction of the bridge at Petersburg, and next in removing the obstructions at Fort Darling.

"I saw this contrivance yesterday," was how Goldsborough, the lifelong sailor, first broached the subject to his superior. He was not impressed. "I hope it may be of service to the Government, but my impression is that it is next to a very useless concern." Thus far, he added, "no experiments have been made with it of any consequence," although the prejudiced naval man failed to explain what trials or tests the boat could conduct that would rise to the level of "consequence" in his mind. "Some men went down in it and remained underwater three-quarters of an hour, but this they easily could have done in an ordinary diving bell. Beyond this no other experiment has been attempted, as I am informed by Mr. Eakins."[55]

On the overcast afternoon of June 24, *Alligator*, in tow by the steam tug *Fred Kopp*, hoisted anchor and slowly followed the *Satellite* up the James River. Although no one realized it, the day was one for the history books. Confederate Acting Master William G. Cheeney, it will be recalled, had taken possession some six weeks earlier of a Tredegar-built and modified boat just a handful of miles up the river behind the obstructions at Drewry's Bluff. While we know the Southern submarine was in existence at this time, we do not know exactly what her service during this period entailed. Perhaps she was undergoing tests or even prowling the waters behind the water barricades. Either way, it can be stated with some confidence that June 24, 1862, was the first time in history that opposing naval forces had functioning submarines operating in the same theater.[56]

The following day at 3:00 p.m., the *Alligator* and her two support ships "came to anchor near the *Galena* at City Point," located at the confluence of the James and Appomattox Rivers. A skiff was launched to Commander Rodger's vessel bearing instructions penned by Flag Officer Goldsborough forty-eight hours earlier. "I send you the submarine propeller, in charge of Samuel Eakins," he informed Rodgers. If Louis Goldsborough knew the submarine's name, he refused or forgot to use it. "The *Satellite* has twenty barrels of powder on board for the use of the submarine propeller. This contrivance, as I have already intimated to you," Goldsborough added somewhat sarcastically, "should be employed at once up the Appomattox, if it can be of any service whatever there in destroying the railroad bridge at Petersburg, or removing obstructions in our way. It afterwards may be employed to remove the obstructions abreast of Fort Darling. Make it as useful in every way as you can." Goldsborough was faithfully executing his orders and attempting to find gainful employment for the submarine, but he obviously had little faith that the effort would produce worthwhile results.[57]

The *Alligator's* arrival at City Point coincided with the beginning of the Seven Days Battles, a series of actions designed by Confederate General Robert E. Lee to turn General McClellan's army away from Richmond and destroy it. While McClellan was in the middle of dealing with Lee—the battle was probably within earshot of the *Alligator's* crew—Commander Rodgers sent the general a situational report about the prospects his small armada of Federal ships had in destroying a bridge over Swift Creek, a waterway flowing into the Appomattox River several miles downriver from Petersburg. The bridge supported the Richmond and Petersburg Railroad, one of the most important lines in the Confederacy. Rodgers did not believe the task easily accomplished. "Four thousand troops in vicinity of Petersburg, and pickets everywhere," he wrote. "Positive official information showing bridge 250 feet long . . . from 50 to 80 (about 50) feet high. The banks above," he lamented, "command our decks." Soldiers "screened by trees, fire and disappear before we can reply. An intolerable annoyance. Horse artillery put nine shots through the *Jacob Bell* and got off before assistance could arrive. We can fight when needed, but we can not be in the narrow part of the river idle." As if to make matters worse, a Southern battery located "on [the] right or west bank of river, has heavy guns. Both sides," he concluded, "must be taken before we can work at removing obstructions."[58]

The land war interrupted any plans Rodgers may have had to employ the *Alligator.* Lee's attacks against McClellan continued, forcing back the Army of the Potomac, which the Federal general decided should withdraw to Harrison's Landing on the James River. Every war-ship available might be needed to help assist McClellan against the vastly superior numbers he erroneously believed he was facing. The un-expected development at the very gates of Richmond presented Rodgers with a dilemma. Should he still attempt to utilize the submarine boat, or send her back to Norfolk? He debated the issue for several days, during which time Eakins' *Alligator* remained with Rodgers' small fleet.

Although nothing is known of her actions during this time, it is probable she was not employed at all. On the night of June 27, immedi-ately following a bloody tactical defeat at Gaines' Mill, McClellan sent a telegram to Flag Officer Goldsborough outlining his current situation. After asking for specific assistance in the form of gunboats, "Little Mac" informed the navy officer that he was "obliged to fall back between the Chickahominy and the James. I look to you to give me all the support you can in covering my flank, as well as in giving protection to my sup-plies afloat in the James."[59]

Commander Rodgers had his hands full and his ships and crews were needed elsewhere. Turning his attention away from destroying ob-structions with the submarine boat, he instead focused his energies on assisting the beleaguered Federal army. The advancing enemy, however, concerned Commander Rodgers considerably, for he feared the *Alliga-tor* might fall into Confederate hands or be destroyed. As a result, he hastily made plans for her evacuation downriver. On June 29, Rodgers filed a report with Goldsborough informing him of his decision.

"I send back to Fortress Monroe for further orders the machine for blowing up obstructions in the James River," he began. "Rebel pickets observe every movement. Her presence here is doubtless known." In addition, Rodgers did not believe the submarine's efforts against the type of obstructions he found would be beneficial. "If she were to blow up the stones filling the lighters sunk in the James River," he explained, "they would sink again. While the lighters remain whole, there is a bare chance of moving them bodily with tugs to one side of the channel, and by all means I would recommend this before the craft containing these stones are broken to pieces."[60]

Rodgers' lengthy and meticulous report detailed other reasons why he decided to pull the craft out of harm's way:

In going up the Appomattox to Petersburg the machine will show above water, since on the bars there is not depth to submerge her. Regiments and field artillery will fire at her. Should she escape these, as the rebels are badly off for food, and fish with nets very diligently, some poor negro fisherman will drag her to shore. She is, in the present posture of our affairs here, and from physical causes, utterly powerless to help our cause, but in the hands of our enemies, destruction to us. She might be used to blow up the *Monitor, Galena, Minnesota,* or whatever vessel should be advanced either in position or importance.[61]

Rodgers clearly parted company with Goldsborough in his opinion of the potential for advantage offered by the *Alligator*. In fairness to the flag officer, Rodgers had spent considerably more time with the submarine and likely discussed her possibilities indepth with Eakins and other crew members. "The machine," he continued in his report,

is so terrible an engine, if employed against us, that if I retain her I must keep a strong force to guard her. It is simpler to send her back for further orders.

We are in rifle shot of the shore, and horse artillery can give us annoyance or even damage and retreat before any reply can be made. We are already more crowded in the narrow channel than quite comports with free movement. . . . The west or right bank of the James River is entirely in the hands of the rebels. Nearly the whole power of the Southern Confederacy is within a few miles of us. . . . This is no place for unarmed vessels, except their presence be necessary and their use immediate. . . . Vessels which can not [defend themselves] had better not be sent here.[62]

It is clear the *Alligator* arrived at her theater of operations at the most inopportune moment imaginable. Since the beginning of the war, nothing like McClellan's Peninsula Campaign had been experienced. The timing, especially for Eakins and his crew, was simply unfortunate. With the submarine's shortcomings obvious to all concerned, she was once again tied behind her steam-powered support vessel and towed back to the mouth of the James.

While the submarine propeller slowly made its way back down the river, General McClellan's bloodied army was steadily retreating in the direction of Harrison's Landing. On July 1, a portion of his army took up a defensive position on Malvern Hill, a powerful plateau perfectly situated for defensive operations. With Federal artillery dominating the position, Lee's infantry marched into the teeth of McClellan's alignment and were slaughtered. Wave after wave fell before the Federal iron rain.[63]

While soldiers from both armies searched Malvern Hill's sloping fields for survivors, the *Alligator* at far away Fortress Monroe rocked gently behind her support vessel, safe but unable to contribute to the Federal war effort. Now that the submarine was out of harm's way, Goldsborough pondered the future of this strange contraption that had been placed under his command. With General McClellan's army in need of support, Goldsborough wasted little time in reaching a decision that undoubtedly pleased him. "Commander Rodgers, as you will perceive by copies of communications from him which I forward by the mail of to-day," the flag officer wrote to Navy Secretary Gideon Welles, "has, on finding the submarine propeller of no use to him, and for other reasons, sent it to Fortress Monroe. Had I not better send it to Washington for safe keeping? At best it can only operate successfully in clear and tolerably deep water." In an effort to convince Welles to take the thing off his hands, Goldsborough tried another tack: "All the experiments required by the Chief of the Bureau of Yards and Docks can be much better conducted at Washington than here," he insisted, "particularly at this very critical conjuncture of our affairs hereabouts." Goldsborough wanted nothing more to do with the arched-back and oar-encrusted *Alligator*.[64]

While awaiting a reply from Washington, the submarine's tug support vessel was dispatched to other duty. Her place was taken by Benjamin J. Totten's storeship *Brandywine*. Totten, as it turned out, had grave reservations about his new assignment. "I do not think that this submarine vessel is safe alongside this vessel," he wrote his superior Goldsborough on July 2, the day following the Battle of Malvern Hill. "In rough weather, as to-day, she labors and pitches terribly. The only place to secure her by, a shackle forward, is not trustworthy. If she breaks adrift, which I look for in a heavy sea, we have no means of saving her." Offering an alternative, Totten wisely suggested that the craft be "taken into smooth water in the cove [where] she would be safe."[65]

Ben Totten was in luck. Within twenty-four hours the wary commander was relieved of his nerve-racking task when Goldsborough's earlier offer to Gideon Welles to rid himself of the iron submersible was accepted. "Send the submarine boat to the Washington Navy Yard," instructed the Navy Secretary. The directive undoubtedly brought a smile to the flag officer's face and a thankful sigh from the *Brandywine's* commander.[66]

On the morning of July 4, 1862,[67] the country's 86th birthday, some of the crew of the *Alligator* readied their unique vessel for a long tow to the Washington Navy Yard. Eakins and several others, for reasons not readily apparent, were not with the submarine. "I send the submarine propeller to the Washington Navy Yard in tow of the tug *Fred Kopp*," Goldsborough informed Gideon Welles on July 5, "The tug is the same one that brought the machine from Philadelphia." Turning to more important matters, the flag officer informed the secretary that "Both Messrs. Thomas and Eakins took upon themselves to leave, if not abandon, the submarine propeller up James River, and went off to indulge their curiosity. I can hear nothing of either of them, although I wrote to Commander Rodgers a number of days ago that I wanted them here." Their absence incensed and perplexed the lifelong career naval officer, who surely viewed their departure as a form of desertion. "The course of these gentlemen has been most singular," he fumed, "They have, as far as I can learn, several of the hands with them employed for the propeller at $40.00 a month, and what they are doing with them is more than I can derive." Goldsborough added, "Mr. Eakins told me he had a list of the men showing the time they had entered service, but he never gave it to me. Nor am I formally informed of the terms upon which the tug *Kopp* was employed. Her Captain has acted in good faith and done his part well." Happy to be done with the entire affair, the flag officer concluded, "As I shall not need the service of the *Kopp* any longer I suppose she may be paid off at Washington upon information from Philadelphia. Mr. Thomas mentioned to me in conversation that she was to have $400 for bringing the machine to Hampton Roads, and then $45 per day afterwards as long as she remained in government employment."[68]

With the Federal "submarine propeller" safely in tow and heading up the Chesapeake Canal, the United States Navy's first submarine expedition into an active war zone officially came to an end.

◆   ◆   ◆

Within days after the April 30, 1862, launching of the *Alligator* in far away Philadelphia, Horace Hunley, Baxter Watson, and James McClintock, the three New Orleans inventors who had built the Confederate privateering submarine *Pioneer*, arrived in the besieged city of Mobile with hopes of building a second more formidable submarine. With their diagrams and ideas in tow and a privateering commission from the Confederate government in hand, the three men were granted an audience with Mobile's commanding general, Dabney Maury, the nephew of the underwater explosives scientist Matthew Fontaine Maury.

General Maury was impressed with the trio's proposal to construct an underwater weapon. Within weeks after their arrival in the city, construction of a second and somewhat larger submarine boat was well underway at the dockside machine shop of Park and Lyons. "We built a second boat at Mobile," McClintock wrote after the war, "and to obtain room for machinery and persons, she was made 36 feet long, three feet wide and four feet high. Twelve feet of each end was built tapering or molded, to make her easy to pass through the water." Delays were encountered, however, for this boat was intended to be special—very special. According to McClintock, "There was much time and money lost in efforts to build an *electro-magnetic engine* [emphasis added] for propelling the boat."[69]

The implications of McClintock's statement are breathtaking, and provide striking evidence as to how far ahead of their time these Southern underwater visionaries were actually thinking and laboring. The idea of powering their new submarine with an electric motor can only be viewed as ingenious considering the era in which they were working. A late-war letter sent by Baxter Watson to the Confederate War Department claimed that an engine of "electro-magnetism" capable of powering a small submarine could in fact be purchased in New York City at a cost of $5,000. Watson volunteered to travel to New York (risking possible death if captured) and purchase the engine if the government would furnish him the funds.[70]

General Dabney H. Maury was the Confederate military commander of Mobile, Alabama. Maury took a great interest in underwater boats. *U. S. Library of Congress*

In the middle of 1862, however, the three inventors were laboring themselves to develop the electric motor they required. Unfortunately, explained McClintock after the war, we were "unable to get sufficient power to be useful" (perhaps due to the scarcity of materials in wartime Mobile). McClintock did not mention whether any open water tests were actually conducted in Mobile Bay with an electric submersible. When it became apparent that a strong enough electric motor would not be forthcoming within the time frame necessary, the partners turned to a more conventional means of propulsion: a small custom-built steam engine.[71]

One's first impression is that a steam engine would not be compatible for use in a vessel that traveled beneath the surface of the water. How could the fires burn without an external air supply, and where would the smoke go? Unfortunately, none of the men left behind the

This old building at the corner of Water and State Streets in Mobile, Alabama, is the former Park and Lyons machine shop where the Confederate submarine torpedo boat *H. L. Hunley* was built in 1863. It was still serving as a machine shop in 1961. *U.S. Naval Historical Center*

answers. McClintock and Watson, however, had been steam gauge manufacturers before the war, and they understood the mechanics of steam power and pressure. Perhaps the compact steam engine was designed to build up a tremendous amount of pressure within its boiler while running on the surface. The crew would then extinguish the fire just before submerging, and run on the remaining pressure. The Mobile trio were by no means the last to attempt to utilize steam power in a Civil War submarine.

Although their luck designing a workable electric engine had not been particularly good, McClintock, Watson, and Hunley struck gold when their paths converged with William Alexander. The sandy-bearded mechanical engineer was an English immigrant who had arrived in Mobile, Alabama, barely two years before the war began. Besides Horace Hunley (whose reason for lasting fame will be discussed later), Alexander is perhaps the most famous Civil War submariner. His postwar lectures, newspaper articles, and letters are the most in-depth writings on the subject found to date. At the start of hostilities, Alexander enlisted in the 21st Alabama Volunteers, a Mobile

Horace L. Hunley helped build at least three submarines during the war, the last of which bore his name. He is perhaps the war's best-known submariner. *Naval Historical Center*

unit well-stocked with machinists, mechanics, and engineers. Throughout his first year of service, the 24-year-old Englishman had been in charge of constructing works at Fort Morgan at the mouth of Mobile Bay. By early spring of 1862, he had been reassigned to supervise musket conversions at the Park and Lyons machine shop on Water Street—the same facility at which the three New Orleans inventors would set up shop to build their second submarine.[72]

The troika of inventors needed assistance in their endeavor, and Lieutenant Alexander's superiors ordered him and his men to place the musket conversions on hold and give their full attention to the plans submitted by the three strangers. The shop's company must have been flabbergasted by the proposed project. Few people in 1862 dared dream that such inventions were possible. With the full backing of the military, Watson, Hunley, and McClintock unrolled their diagrams and began work.

William Alexander was involved throughout the fabrication process of the second diving machine. He may have even contributed to the design and manufacture of the failed electro-magnetic motor. The submarine's pressure hull and ballast system were completed about the same time that the Federal *Alligator* was operating at Hampton Roads. The submarine itself was completed shortly thereafter, although work with her propulsion system was still undergoing experimentation. McClintock's statement to Matthew Maury after the war that the "electro-magnetic engine was unable to get sufficient power to be useful," suggests that the small group of inventors may have installed the device and quietly experimented with it soon after the sub's completion. They also experimented with a small steam engine, which was assembled after the failure of the electric motor. That mode of propulsion, too, was unsuccessful, and was soon disassembled and removed from the submarine after testing. The days passed quickly, and the hot Deep South summer of 1862 was consumed with the designing and redesigning of the submarine's unique propulsion system.[73]

◆   ◆   ◆

While the disappointed Louisiana inventors poured over their submarine diagrams with Alexander in the sweltering heat of the Park and Lyons machine shop, the depleted crew of Philadelphia submariners, some 1,200 miles away, were busy acquainting themselves with the many sights in wartime Washington. By a strange twist of fate, at the same time the little *Alligator's* crew received orders to report to Washington, events transpiring on the James River resulted in an immediate call for the submarine's redeployment back to Hampton Roads.

On the humid afternoon of July 4, 1862, while the *Alligator* was being prepared for her tow up the Chesapeake to Washington, a small Confederate gunboat laying underwater mines was surprised by the patrolling Union gunboat *Maratanza* near Turkey Bend on the James River. After a short engagement, the crew of the *CSS Teaser* abandoned their vessel and fled into nearby woods. A search of the captured gunboat discovered detailed maps showing the exact locations of Acting Master William G. Cheeney's electrically detonated underwater mines, as well as other war-related documents invaluable to Union intelligence.[74]

One of the more interesting articles found aboard *Teaser* was a large Confederate observation balloon fashioned from old silk dresses donated by patriotic Southern ladies. Among the numerous letters, requisitions, and documents discovered aboard the captured vessel were detailed drawings and diagrams of a new ironclad ram, *Virginia II*, which was under construction at the navy yard in the Confederate capital. Within a few weeks *Harper's Weekly* acquired copies and printed them in one of their July issues. From all over the North crackpot ideas flooded the Navy Department outlining plans that might be utilized for destroying this new threat to the Union fleet. One of strangest schemes called for lashing two gunboats together with a pair of huge spring tongs fastened between them. The two vessels could then seize the *Virginia II* and push her to shore. Needless to say, nothing ever came of this fanciful idea.[75]

Fearing another near-disaster on the scale of the first ironclad *Virginia*, Assistant Secretary of the Navy Gustavus Fox devised a daring plan to send the *USS Alligator* back up the James River to destroy *Virginia II* at her Richmond dock before she could be launched. The *Alligator's* civilian crew, however, had just returned from that war-torn region and wanted nothing to do with the hazardous scheme. With Samuel Eakins gone and the submarine team in tatters, it appeared that Eakins' fill-in, Masters Mate John McMillan, was unequal to the task. A search was launched for a new commander. Within a few weeks Lt. Thomas O. Selfridge, a bold and experienced naval officer who had himself just returned from Hampton Roads, was given command.

The 27-year-old naval lieutenant was a graduate of the Naval Academy who had recently been assigned to the Washington Navy Yard. For two of Selfridge's eight years in the navy he had served in the Pacific fleet on a ship commanded by Josiah Tattnall, the same officer who took the *Virginia* into battle against the *Monitor* at Hampton Roads. Selfridge had demonstrated courage and leadership abilities while stationed on the *USS Cumberland*, where he commanded the frigate's forward battery. After being rammed by the *Virginia* on March 8, 1862, Selfridge climbed the masthead and retrieved the ship's colors as the 24-gun frigate sank beneath him. By early July 1862, Selfridge was hoping for a command of his own. His desires would be satisfied, although certainly the vessel he was to receive surprised him. Summoned to the office of Assistant Naval Secretary Gustavus Fox, Selfridge was offered command of the "submarine propeller" with the following words: "Mr. Selfridge, if you will take

A postwar photograph of Thomas Selfridge, who commanded the Union submarine *Alligator* for several weeks during the summer of 1862. *U. S. Naval Historical Center*

the *Alligator* up the James River and destroy the *Virginia II*, I will make you a Captain."[76]

The offer came as a disappointment to the eager young officer. "I declined the offer," he later wrote, "renewing my request for the command of a ship holding out a better prospect for effective work. None such being available, at my request I was granted leave and visited my mother in Vermont." What did he know about commanding a submarine? he must have thought. Reflection made him realize that he may have damaged his chances for promotion. "I became conscience-stricken over a possible lack of patriotism," was how he explained it, "and telegraphed my acceptance to Mr. Fox, who replied with telegraphic directions to report in Washington."[77]

If Lieutenant Selfridge was not overly thrilled with his new assignment, his first impression of the submarine did little to stoke the fires of excitement. "My preliminary inspection of the *Alligator*, then lying at the Washington Navy Yard, was disappointing," he remembered long after the war. "She was little more than a cigar-shaped hull with crude man power propulsion machinery inside." The boat had gone through some minor revisions since its first trip to Hampton Roads and beyond. "A very crude mechanism was provided for attaching a mine to an enemy vessel, after reaching a position under her bottom," Selfridge explained. Apparently the torpedo delivery system no longer required a diver to implement the explosive charge. Unfortunately, Selfridge failed to describe the new system. He also failed to elaborate on his intriguing description of "wire cutting fins" and "two small cannons" that according to some sources were then in the design and testing phase.[78]

Selfridge could certainly have used de Villeroi's assistance, for as the officer explained it, the air purifying system so important for long submerged operations in enemy territory was nonexistent. "The Frenchman," as Selfridge put it, "had disappeared, leaving no information as to his secret process of air purification." Just where de Villeroi disappeared to will probably remain a mystery. Since the completion of his invention in the early spring of 1862, no mention of him, or his whereabouts, appears in any naval documents during this period. Without a functioning scrubber—a system involving the use of a carbon dioxide–absorbing chemical called beryllium—submerged operations would be greatly minimized and perhaps reduced to no more than an hour or two.

In spite of her apparent shortcomings and obvious mortal dangers to her own crew, Lieutenant Selfridge reluctantly accepted command of the strange contraption and reported to Assistant Secretary Fox with a request for men to man her. Within days after this meeting, Selfridge found himself in New York Harbor being ferried out to the receiving ship *USS North Carolina*. Shortly after presenting his orders to the vessel's captain, the entire ship's company was called to quarters and stood at attention while Selfridge outlined the secret operation to destroy *Virginia II*, which Federal authorities believed was nearing completion at Richmond.[79]

After explaining that the submarine would enter the James River and venture underwater to the very capital of the Confederacy, Selfridge ended his speech and perhaps waited for the snickers and catcalls sure to follow such an outrageous proposal. Instead of being met with a barrage of heckling, "About half the whole ship's company responded, so that there was little difficulty in picking out fourteen promising looking men to take back to Washington." The *Alligator's* new volunteers boarded a Washington-bound train and set off for their base of operations far to the south. Shortly after the crew's arrival in the nation's capital, Lieutenant Selfridge led his weary command through the busy streets to the Washington Navy Yard, located eight blocks south of the domeless Capitol building. The missing Samuel Eakins had turned up in the interim, and though he was still associated with the boat, his title was now superintendent instead of commander.[80]

With the *Alligator* now in the hands of an experienced naval officer and military crew, it was time to put the boat through sea trials to determine its capabilities. "The first experiment was made by putting all the crew and myself inside the *Alligator*, closing the manhole, and sinking the vessel by the admission of water, as provided in her design," remembered its commander, Thomas Selfridge. "We remained on the bottom for about five minutes and successfully came to the surface again by pumping out the water; the precaution of attaching lines, with which, on signal, she could be raised in the event of difficulty, proving superfluous." For several days Selfridge and his crew continued to test the novel invention in the murky waters of the Potomac River. With whispers circulating that the *Virginia II* was nearing completion at Richmond, Assistant Navy Secretary Gustavus Fox hoped that training of this new crew would be completed swiftly, and that his bold plan for destroying the new Rebel ironclad could be acted upon before she steamed down the James River.[81]

Selfridge's experimentation with the submarine continued apace, although his inaugural cruise on August 4 was almost his last. After a simple submersion and surfacing, "the next venture was to make a short cruise down the river." Selfridge "remained on deck to con the boat while below the crew worked the crankshafts, each of which was attached to an external paddle, feathered during the forward stroke by closing like a book." It was difficult work, "Since the feathering was only partial, however, much power was lost and great exertions were required to make even a very low speed." It was inevitable that the new submersible's crew would encounter a difficulty, and it arrived after the *Alligator* "had proceeded but a short distance." Without warning, the bow of the boat suddenly dropped beneath the surface of the river, "notwithstanding a forward water-tight air compartment." Selfridge stole a glance down the conning tower hatch and discovered "a rush being made by the men to get out, and then the seriousness of a lack of air supply became strikingly evident." The cool young commander "cautioned [his men] to be careful, to come up one at a time, or the transfer of their weight to the forward end of the ship would sink her." Following his lead, everyone reached the safety of the deck, "though a few were too much exhausted to gain the deck without assistance." With the bow of the *Alligator* down at a steep angle and the arched deck sticking up into the air, the submarine "drifted helpless down the river [until] a nearby schooner was hailed, a small boat borrowed from her, and the new-fangled submarine towed back above water to the Navy Yard by the old fashioned propulsion of oars."[82]

The boat's "new" superintendent, Samuel Eakins," filed a report three days later in which he avoided mentioning the near-fatal accident. Eakins, who had some experience with the submarine, was more concerned with her diving capabilities than her inadequate propulsion system. The result's of Selfridge's test were not encouraging. "A full crew of eighteen men were on board the boat but were unable to overcome the tide current of the river near the Washington Navy Yard said to be one and half miles per hour," explained Selfridge. "This trial continued some hour and half and was ended by the complete exhaustion of the crew." Selfridge had taken the boat out again on August 5 with an engineer on board to examine the propulsion system "without a more favorable result." The next morning, August 6, reported Eakins, "in company with Lieutenant Selfridge and crew of eighteen men I submerged the boat in eighteen feet of water and remained without communication with the outer air twenty seven minutes. No inconvenience was felt by those enclosed, and the time might have been extended without hurt to those in the boat."[83]

Lieutenant Selfridge filed his own unflattering report outlining several of the boat's drawbacks. They were significant, and Selfridge was patently distressed about the condition of his new command:

> This submarine boat, as I understand, was to have possessed the following properties:

1st. Facilities of Emulsion and Emersion.

2nd. Self propulsion above and below water.

3rd. Capability of remaining with her crew a long time underwater, by purifying the air contained in her.

4th. To be able to operate underwater, and to permit a person to pass in and out at pleasure.

Most of these properties she does not possess to a practical degree. Her apparatus for sinking and rising is good, and sufficient for the purpose. She is incapable however of being suspended in the water, but must sink when once immersed to the bottom, therefore she could only operate in such depth of water, that a person standing on her could reach the vessel above him.

Propulsion above and below water: She is in this particular, very defective, being totally incapable of stemming an ordinary tide of the velocity of 1 1/2 knots, and she is from her low rate of speed and length, difficult to manage with any exactness with the helm.

Capability of remaining underwater: She has no means known to me of purifying and replenishing the retired air other than forcing it through lime water. This though it would absorb much of the Carbonic acid would be of little practical use with her crew of twenty two persons, it would not be safe to remain more than an hour under the surface. By means of an air chamber, which is filled with compressed air, a person can get in and out of her. But there is no means of supplying that person with air, other than a common tube connecting with the mouth.

Selfridge went on to describe the submarine's propulsion system as an "inherent defect," that absolutely had to be remedied for the boat to be utilized as envisioned by her builders. "If her speed were greatly increased, and steering apparatus improved," he continued, "she could perhaps be made effective." Further trials, however, should only be attempted *after* these "improvements" had been made.[84]

Although he did not specifically come out and say it, Selfridge's report spelled the doom of Gustavus Fox's plan for a daring underwater raid: an attempt to destroy the *Virginia II* with the underpowered and unwieldly *Alligator* was out of the question. Without a suitable air purification system, it would have been impossible to remain submerged throughout the long journey up the James River. In addition, the vessel was incapable of navigating against even the weakest current. Fox's plan was scrapped, and the navy's energies were turned toward improving the submarine's propulsion system.

And on that inglorious note, Lt. Thomas O. Selfridge's association with the United States Navy's first commissioned submarine came to a speedy end. As plans for a new propeller and other design modifications progressed, Selfridge and his crew were relieved from further duty with the *Alligator*. Just four days after the filing of his critical report, Gideon Welles ordered ". . . the eighteen men now on board the USS '*Alligator*,' to be conveyed to Cairo, Illinois." Selfridge was ordered to accompany them. The gallant young officer was yet to be heard from. He was given command of the gunboat *USS Cairo*. On December 12, 1862, exactly four months after being ordered west, Selfridge and the former crew members of the *Alligator* enjoyed the dubious distinction of being in command of the first Union vessel sunk by a Confederate mine. While patrolling the Yazoo River in Mississippi, the ironclad gunboat struck a submerged torpedo and sank within a few minutes. Although no lives were lost, news of the successful sinking of a Union warship added a spark to Southern production and deployment of underwater "infernal machines."[85]

While Selfridge and his crew prepared to head west for their ill-fated command in far-off Illinois, Samuel Eakins remained behind and helped oversee the submarine's improvements. On August 18, Eakins was ordered to travel to Philadelphia to examine a new propeller being prepared for the boat. Whether Eakins had a hand in designing this new propeller is not known. However, he was actively engaged with the refitting of the vessel for continued service. Although he was asked to report on the matter when he returned to Washington, no record of his report has been found. Since the propeller was nearing completion by the end of August, it is logical to assume that about that time the *Alligator* was removed from the water and placed in a dry dock for her much needed improvements.[86]

The chief problem associated with the submarine boat was its reliance on a system of oars (or paddles). Why the *Alligator's* inventor and chief designer, Brutus de Villeroi, incorporated these rows of opening and closing paddles for his propulsion system may never be known. Navy reports filed in 1861 reagarding his original 30' submarine make it clear that a hand-turned prop, located at the stern of the vessel, was capable of producing sufficient propulsion. Adding extra bodies to essentially pull on oars was simply ineffective, and as Selfridge later pointed out, "great exertions were required to make even a very slow speed." To the commander stationed near the forward hatch of the dimly lit vessel, these sailors must have looked very much like a Viking crew rowing an ancient longboat.[87]

◆   ◆   ◆

Issues relating to submarine development and advances continued to move forward behind Confederate lines. On October 14, 1862, a patent for a "submarine battery" was granted to a Jas G. Patton of Petersburg, Virginia. Unfortunately few Confederate patent diagrams survived the fires that raged through Richmond in April 1865, and it must be assumed that Mr. Patton's plans for a submarine boat were destroyed at that time. Although no diagrams of this boat are known to exist, a 10-inch metal patent model of a steam-powered submarine survived the fires and is now in the possession of a Washington, D.C., Civil War maritime collector. Whether this Confederate patent model was submitted by Jas Patton is unclear, for no other documentation other than its being from the ruins of the Confederate patent office are known to exist. Whose submarine was it?

The question is difficult to answer. Although Richmond Patent Office books on file at the Museum of the Confederacy are woefully incomplete, at least four submarine patents were granted by the Confederate government between 1861 and 1865. (By way of comparison, not a single one was issued by the United States Patent Office during the war years.) The first such Confederate patent was granted to "Mr. F. Smith" of Tennessee in early 1862, while the second was awarded to Jas G. Patton on October 14, 1862. The last two (known) patents were issued to "Mr. C. Williams," a founding partner of a Richmond-based submarine venture (to be discussed in the next chapter). Since Reverend Smith's early war submarine was to be powered by hand, and since both of the

Photograph of a ten-inch model steam-powered submarine submitted to the Confederate Patent Office. No records have been found indicating if, or when, this submersible was ever built. *Courtesy of an anonymous collector*

manually powered submarine diagrams of Williams' Richmond submarines are in existence, the bronze patent model in question could very well be a model of Jas Patton's submarine boat.[88]

◆　◆　◆

While propellers and air purity occupied the attention of some in the Navy Department, a Washington inventor named Pascal Plant was nearing completion of an ingenious rocket-powered torpedo he hoped to sell to the Federal navy. Plant, confident his idea would prove useful to the Union cause, approached President Lincoln several months earlier with his plans for a submarine vessel to be used against the *CSS Virginia.* Lincoln was impressed with the plans (he often met with inventors and even personally tried out advanced weaponry) and submitted them to the Navy Department for consideration.

As strange as it seems today, Navy Secretary Gideon Welles witnessed a test of Plant's "self-propelled torpedo" while visiting the Washington Navy Yard in December of 1862. Two of Plant's torpedoes were sighted on a target anchored in the river and fired from a test platform. The first struck a distant mud bank, while the second veered off course and sank the small schooner *Diana*, anchored some distance from the proposed target. Although the botched test resulted in history's first recorded sinking of a vessel by a self-propelled torpedo, Union naval personnel were unimpressed and wished nothing more than to wash their hands of the whole affair.[89]

Some weeks later another test of a self-propelled torpedo was conducted at the Washington Navy Yard resulting in yet another naval first. Shortly after firing the device at a floating target anchored in the Potomac, the torpedo soared into the air, and stayed airborne for over a hundred yards before splashing down into the muddy river. The Union naval officers who witnessed this demonstration failed to see the potential weapon that could be fashioned from this strange invention, and left in disgust.[90]

The rest of 1862 was spent by both opponents attempting to develop a workable submarine and a place to put it into service with a reasonable likelihood of success. Little could Samuel Eakins have guessed that far to the south, along the docks of Mobile, Alabama, a rival team of Confederate submariners consisting of Horace Hunley, James McClintock, and Baxter Watson, were themselves busily constructing a modified propulsion system for a submarine boat of their own.

CHAPTER 3

1863:
ADVANCES & SETBACKS

"Please expedite transportation of Whitney's submarine boat from Mobile here, it is much needed."

—*Telegram from Gen. P. G. T. Beauregard in Charleston, SC, to railroad agents in Alabama*

By early January 1863, James McClintock, Baxter Watson, Horace Hunley, and their assistant, Lt. William Alexander, had reached the conclusion that the steam engine they had designed to propel their Mobile submarine (christened by some historians as the *Pioneer II*), was inadequate for the job. Exactly when they reached that conclusion is not known, although the modifications allowing the boat to be powered by hand were complete and being tested as early as February 1863. The failure of both the electro-magnetic engine (although they were still tinkering with the idea) and steam engine methods of propulsion forced the inventors to turn to a more practical form of propulsion: muscle power. When all else failed, explained McClintock to Matthew Maury after the war, "I afterwards fitted cranks, to turn the propeller by hand, working four men at a time, but the air being so closed, and the work so hard, that we were unable to get a speed sufficient to make the boat of service against vessels blockading this port [Mobile]."[1]

The slow and cramped five-man *Pioneer II* was launched in late January 1863. With the Union blockade tightening around Mobile, it was decided that an attempt had to be made—despite the submarine's obvious shortcomings—to sink one or more of the Federal warships steaming back and forth beyond the range of Southern coastal guns. While men like McClintock and others spent months experimenting with ways to

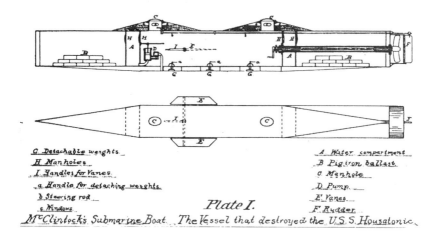

G Detachable weights
H Manholes
I Handles for Vanes
a Handle for detaching weights
b Steering rod
c Windows

A Water compartment
B Pig iron ballast
c Manhole
D Pump
E Vanes
F Rudder

Plate I.

McClintock's Submarine Boat. The Vessel that destroyed the U.S.S. Housatonic.

This diagram, drawn in the presence of James McClintock, was probably the *Pioneer II*, even though it is labeled "The vessel that destroyed the *Housatonic.*" William Alexander wrote a letter to the Navy Department in 1902 stating that the vessel shown in plate I was the submarine built after the loss of the *Pioneer*. *Eustace Williams Collection*

efficiently propel their underwater boats, the Federal blockade was slowly beginning to have an effect on Southern imports. Several major ports had already fallen, and by early 1863 the only harbors of significance that remained open were Mobile, Alabama, Charleston, South Carolina, Galveston, Texas, and Wilmington, North Carolina. Since ships of a more traditional nature, as well as the new breed of Rebel ironclads, were unable to break the blockade, hopes and energies were placed in producing unconventional weapons that at least had a chance of doing so.[2]

On August 26, 1862, Franklin Buchanan was promoted to admiral and given command of the naval forces at Mobile. Buchanan, who had been wounded while in command of the *CSS Virginia* on March 8 in her historic duel with the Federal frigates *Cumberland* and *Congress,* was an old salt whose first assignment as a midshipman dated back to 1815. His resume was impressive by any standard and included a stint as the first superintendent of the U.S. Naval Academy. His age and experience with sailing ships (much like his Federal counterpart Louis Goldsborough) perhaps prejudiced him against inventions he did not fully understand or appreciate. Navy Secretary Stephen Mallory, however, was a driving force in the development of new weapons, and Buchanan kept his superior well apprised of the submarine experiments taking place in Mobile Bay. In response to Mallory's inquiry as to the boat's status, Buchanan acknowledged that Alabama officials were fully cooperating in an attempt to finish the submersible. "Mr. McClintock has received from this state, from General [James] Slaughter commanding her, and myself all the assistance and facilities he requested to complete his boat," he wrote. "Within the last week or ten days," continued the admiral, "we succeeded in getting a man from New Orleans who was to have made the 'magnetic engine' by which it was to have been propelled," an interesting aside indicating that the inventors had not yet fully abandoned the idea of an electric motor. Still, Buchanan was not impressed with the contraption. "I have witnessed the operations of the boat in the water when propelled by hand, the steam engine being a failure and had to be removed. On that occasion its speed was not more than two miles per hour. Since then other trials have been made all proving failures."

The end of Buchanan's letter to Mallory contained news which surely disappointed the beleaguered navy secretary:

> The last trial was made about a week since when the boat was lost off this harbor and was sunk, the men came very near being lost. I never entertained but one opinion as to the result of this boat, that it should prove a failure, and such has been the case. The original intention of going under a vessel and attaching a torpedo to her was abandoned, the torpedo or explosive machine was to have been towed by a rope from the boat and when under the vessel was to have been exploded. I considered the whole affair as impracticable from the commencement.[3]

The story of the *Pioneer II*, however, does not end with Buchanan's scribbled description of its fatal demise. Indeed, a fascinating mystery surrounds its final days before it was lost. McClintock and company had towed the submarine to Fort Morgan, an 1834-era brick fortress named after Revolutionary War hero Daniel Morgan and erected on Mobile

Point. From this new location, it was hoped that the boat would be close enough to the Federal warships to mount an attack with some prospect of success. Evidence that an attack was undertaken comes from a Confederate deserter named James Carr, a 19-year-old New York native who claimed he was conscripted into the Confederate Navy while working on a Mississippi river boat docked near New Orleans. On February 23, after being sent ashore to hunt for oysters, James Carr and two sailors attached to the gunboat *CSS Selma* deserted their vessel and surrendered to the crew of the Federal ship *USS Clifton,* anchored near Horn Island. After supplying a detailed and generally accurate account of Mobile's defenses and the armaments of the *Selma,* Carr stunned his captives with an incredible tale. "On or about the 14th [February]," he said,

> an infernal machine, consisting of a submarine boat, propelled by a screw which is turned by hand, capable of holding 5 persons, and having a torpedo which was to be attached to the bottom of a vessel and exploded by means of clockwork, left Fort Morgan at 8 p.m. in charge of the Frenchman who invented it. The intention was to come up at Sand Island, get the bearing and distance of the nearest vessel, dive under again and operate upon her; but on emerging they found themselves so far outside of the island and in so strong a current (setting out) that they were forced to cut the torpedo adrift and make the best of their way back. The attempt will be renewed as early as possible, and three or four others are being constructed for the purpose.[4]

Setting aside the submarine attack for a moment, Seaman Carr's testimony is detailed, accurate in most respects, and seemingly confidently presented. There is little doubt the New York native was convinced an attack on the blockading fleet had indeed been attempted by an "infernal machine" less than ten days before his desertion. Oddly enough, news of the alleged attack was taken in stride by Commodore Robert B. Hitchcock, the Federal officer who reported the information to Washington in a nonchalant manner.

But did the attack actually take place, and if so, was it conducted by the *Pioneer II?* James McClintock does not mention any attempt with

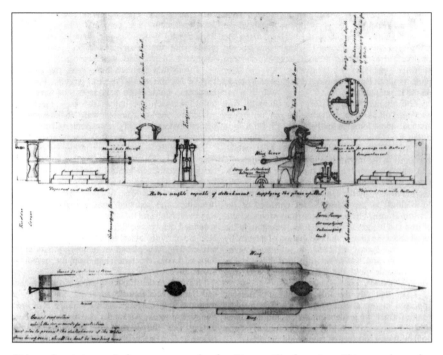

Side and top views of what appears to be the *Pioneer II* submarine. This was drawn by James McClintock in the fall of 1872 while attending secret meetings with British naval officials in Nova Scotia. *British Admiralty, London*

the *Pioneer II* against the Federal ships at Mobile in his postwar accounts on the subject. McClintock's reminiscences, however, are by no means definitive, for they do not even discuss the eventual fate of the Mobile submarine. Lieutenant William Alexander, however, confirmed that the submersible was towed to the masonry fortress and that an attack was planned. "It [the submarine] was towed off Fort Morgan," he explained to a New Orleans newspaper after the war, "intended to man it there and attack the blockading fleet outside, but the weather was rough, and with a heavy sea the boat became unmanageable and finally sank, but no lives were lost." Did it sink while attempting the attack or during additional trials? Unfortunately, Alexander does not elaborate or specify the date on which the submarine was lost. Records on file at the Mobile Bar Pilots Association confirm Alexander's reminiscence with evidence that a Mobile captain named George Cook was to take the *Pioneer II* out. Was it lost with Cook in command?

Since Buchanan mentioned the boat was lost "a week since," in his February 14 letter to Mallory, and Carr contended it took place "on or about the 14th," perhaps the answer is simply that it was not the *Pioneer II* that made the attempt. Carr mentioned in his statement that "three or four others [submarines] are being constructed for the purpose" of attacking the Federal warships off Mobile, and that the mid-February effort was "in charge of the Frenchman who invented it." None of the men associated with the *Pioneer II* were French. Definitive answers, unfortunately, may never be known, for few documents have survived from wartime Mobile that could shed more light on this question.[5]

Shortly after the loss of the *Pioneer II*, Admiral Buchanan received a short inquiry concerning the submarine from the Confederate Navy Department. One of the three partners, Baxter Watson, had already written to Navy Secretary Mallory to inform him of the loss and request government assistance in its salvage. Mallory apparently sought additional information from Buchanan as to whether it was worth the time and effort to recover the boat. Not surprisingly, he was not enthusiastic about the idea. "The boat can not be of any possible use in Mobile Bay in consequence of its shallow water," Buchanan concluded, not altogether accurately. "I don't think it could be made effective against the enemy off the harbor as the blockading vessels are anchored in water too shallow to permit the boat to pass under." Without Buchanan's blessing the *Pioneer II's* owners had to abandon any hopes of salvage. As a result, the small submarine's exact location was soon forgotten. She rests today where she sank on that February morning so long ago.[6]

The real loser from the *Pioneer II's* untimely demise was Horace Hunley, the sole financier of the group's second ill-fated submarine. Since the early days of the war Hunley had remained closely involved in several operations relating to the breaking of the Federal blockade. His submarine activities appear to have comprised but one segment of his overall efforts toward obtaining this goal. It is not known how much Hunley invested in the *Pioneer II* since no records on that subject have come to light. The loss of the second submarine, however, must have discouraged the Louisiana inventors, for without government assistance construction of yet a third vessel seemed doubtful.[7]

◆   ◆   ◆

While the *Pioneer II* was being put through her trials in Mobile Bay (and perhaps making an unsuccessful attack on the Union fleet off Fort Morgan), the *Alligator* at the Washington Navy Yard was still being tested in the muddy waters of the Potomac River. The modified propulsion system for the Federal submarine had been completed, and she was almost ready to return to active service. Gustavus Fox, in a telegram to Samuel Eakins, informed him on February 10 that he would "be at the Yard with Professor Trosford at half past two tomorrow afternoon to witness trial of the *Alligator*." No record of the result of this trial has been discovered.[8]

The Navy Department had recently decided that a commission of specialists was necessary to evaluate inventions like the *Alligator*, and on February 11—the same day Fox and others were witnessing the submarine's new trials—a board called the Permanent Commission was appointed by the Secretary of the Navy to "handle all plans and inventions submitted to the Navy Department," with the authority "to call in other experts whenever needed." Rear Admiral Charles H. Davis was chosen to head up the commission. Davis was perfectly suited for the task. Although he had seen action during the expeditions at Cape Hatteras, Port Royal, and with the Mississippi flotilla under David Farragut, Gideon Welles considered the Harvard-educated officer to be "more of a scholar than a sailor." Davis' three advisors on the commission included the Superintendent of U. S. Coastal Survey, A. D. Bache; Secretary of the Smithsonian Institution, Joseph Henry; and Assistant Superintendent of Weights and Measures, Joseph Saxton.

It is interesting to note that in early February 1940, the American Military Institute formally requested information as to whether a similar commission had been formed in the South to consider submarine inventions submitted to the Confederate Navy Department. "No record is found in this office relative to any boards or committees formed to consider submarines for the C. S. Navy," responded a member of the United States Naval Archives.[9]

Although the United States Naval Archives was unable to discover any information regarding official commissions in the South, evidence exists indicating that such a group of evaluators was in fact formed to assess inventions. A Prussian aristocrat named Victor Ernest Rudolph von Sheliha, formerly chief engineer for Dabney H. Maury in Mobile, published a book following the war on coastal defenses in which he discussed "examining committees" overseeing new inventions of several varieties. "The War Department and the Chief Engineers of the several departments were worse than importuned by the applications of inventors," he remembered,

> every one of whom demanded an examination of his plan or model. Such requests having to be granted for fear of possibly overlooking a perhaps useful invention, the attention of examining committees would, naturally enough, often be called to the most absurd schemes. There were torpedo twin boats, propelled by rockets; diving apparatus by means of which torpedoes might be attached to the bottom of the enemy's ships; balloons that were to ascend, and, when arrived just above the vessel, were to drop some kind of torpedo on the deck of the ship; rotation torpedo rockets to be fired underwater; submarine boats with torpedoes attached to their spar; in fine, any variety of plans, and yet but few, very practicable ones.[10]

The Prussian seems to have had as much faith in underwater boats as Admiral Buchanan or, for that matter, Flag Officer Louis Goldsborough.

While it is likely the *Alligator's* sea trial of February 11 was undertaken, its success or failure remains in doubt. So, apparently, was Samuel Eakins' relationship with the Navy Department. On February 12, a telegram to the Washington Navy Yard summoned "Mister Eakins," as opposed to Acting Lieutenant Eakins, as had been his title on a telegram sent by Assistant Secretary Fox just forty-eight hours earlier, "to report in person to the Department at half past nine tomorrow morning." Why Eakins was directed in so terse a fashion to repair to Washington is not known. The diminished paper trail regarding the *Alligator's* (and her crew's) status after the aborted James River expedition at least suggests a conscious effort to shroud the entire affair in secrecy. What is known is that Eakins' affiliation with the *Alligator* was quickly coming to an end. Entries in the payroll books kept at the Washington Navy Yard demonstrate he remained on duty until March 9, 1863, when

Acting Master Samuel Eakins commanded the Federal submarine boat *Alligator* through much of 1862 and 1863. *U.S. Naval Historical Center*

he was discharged by the Secretary of the Navy, "His services no longer being needed."[11]

For most of February and early March, no records exist as to the condition or status of the submarine boat. In all probability the *Alligator* spent this time in a refitting and testing mode. All that is known with certainty is that on March 10, the day following Eakins' discharge, the *Alligator* was ordered towed to Hampton Roads, Virginia, where it was to be delivered to Admiral Samuel P. Lee, Goldsborough's successor. Exactly who was in charge of the boat at this time or how large the crew was is unknown. After his apparent dismissal by the Navy Department, Eakins had returned to Philadelphia. While there, he received on March 16 a rather cryptic telegram from Assistant Secretary Fox: "Would like to see you in Washington ready to go south with the *Alligator*." If there had been a falling out between Eakins and the Navy Department—as suggested by the Washington Navy Yard's record books—Fox's telegram indicates a resolution had been reached. In any event, by March 20, Eakins was back at the Washington Navy Yard.[12]

The imbroglio, if there was one, may have been over rank (perhaps related to his abandonment of the *Alligator* during the Seven Days Battles). On the day Eakins returned to Washington, however, Secretary Welles sent him a telegram addressed to "Acting Master Samuel Eakins." Eakins was officially promoted on March 24, 1863, when Welles conferred the rank on him, with these words: "Sir: I hereby have the honor to accept the appointment of Acting-Master in the Navy of the United States for temporary service in the command of the submarine boat *Alligator.*" For whatever reason and whatever the circumstances related to these strange goings-on, Samuel Eakins was once again affiliated with the *USS Alligator.*[13]

Attempts to get the *Alligator* into action continued at a brisk pace. On March 25, Andrew Harwood, the Commandant of the Washington Navy Yard, telegraphed Assistant Secretary Fox "acknowledging the receipt of your letter of today directing me to deliver to Acting Master Samuel Eakins an electro magnetic [Magneto Electric Machine] wire and cartridges." Whatever this strange electrical device was, it was not self-explanatory. "Acting Master Henry Rogers will give Mr. Eakins the necessary instruction in regard to the use of the apparatus as directed by the Department," concluded Harwood. Assignment orders were sent the next day to the *Alligator's* skipper from the Secretary of the Navy, acknowledging his earlier March 10 directive to tow the boat to Hampton Roads. Welles' orders also confirm for the first time that Virginia was intended as but a brief stopping point before moving further south, and that the boat was about to receive a new executive officer. "You will proceed to Hampton Roads in the steamer *Philadelphia* this evening, taking with you Acting Masters Mate Moser, and all the freight for the *Alligator,*" instructed Welles. "On your arrival at Hampton Roads, report to Acting Rear Admiral S. P. Lee, commanding the North Atlantic Blockading Squadron, who will afford you the earliest opportunity to reach Port Royal with the *Alligator* and freight, where you will report to Rear Admiral Du Pont for such duty as he may assign you."[14]

The submarine's new destination was Port Royal, South Carolina. The town and its deep-water sound were captured on November 7, 1861, by the Federal Navy. Since that time, it had been utilized as a supply depot and relay station for both the blockading fleets stationed off Charleston, South Carolina, and Savannah, Georgia. The *Alligator* was at last about to be used for the purpose for which she had been designed: to operate against underwater obstructions and the hulls of enemy vessels anchored in a deep harbor. Charleston, a major blockade-running port for the Confederacy, was the home of Fort Sumter and witnessed the opening shots of the war. To many in both the North and South, Charleston was considered the very embodiment of secession, the "Cradle of the Confederacy"; as long as Charleston held out against the Federals, the South would follow suit. This public perception of the city, together with its important logistical significance to the Confederacy, drove the Lincoln Administration to regard the capture of the city as a top priority.[15]

At the time of the *USS Alligator's* deployment to Port Royal, Admiral Du Pont, the Commander of the South Atlantic Blockading Squadron, was planning a bold attack on Charleston. In addition to his wooden steamers were the monitors *Montauk, Weehawken, Patapsco, Catskill, Nantucket, Nahant, Passiac,* and the double-turreted *Keokuk.* His plan was to send his iron fleet into Charleston Harbor and bombard Fort Sumter "beyond precedent." The only problem with this daring idea was what to do about the numerous underwater contact mines and obstructions thought to be just below the surface at the harbor's entrance. Although evidence is sketchy, Admiral Du Pont may have remembered the submarine boat that had been built in Philadelphia while he was Commandant of the Philadelphia Navy Yard in 1861, and requested it be sent to Port Royal to destroy the underwater obstructions at the mouth of Charleston Harbor prior to sending in his ironclads. If he did not request its use, then perhaps Welles or Fox determined it may be of use to the admiral in his forthcoming assault on Charleston. Either way, on March 30, one week before the planned attack on Fort Sumter, Acting Master J. F. Winchester of the *USS Sumpter* was ordered to "Choose favorable weather and proceed [to] Port Royal, agreeably to your orders from the Navy Department. You will take in tow the submarine boat *Alligator,*" instructed Admiral Lee, "and deliver her to Rear Admiral Du Pont on your arrival."[16]

Throughout the morning of March 31, Samuel Eakins and the sailors on the steamer *Philadelphia* transferred the *Alligator's* unique

Civil War sketch of a submarine boat believed by many to be based on the *USS Alligator*. *Author's Collection*

"freight," whatever it might have been, to the cargo hold of the waiting *Sumpter*. As sailors hoisted the numerous large lead ingots that would be used for the *Alligator's* ballast onto the deck of the *Sumpter*, Acting Masters Mate Moser numbered the containers and cases that held the submarine's mysterious machinery. From a letter sent to the Secretary of the Navy several weeks later, we now know that some of the articles taken aboard the steamer included cases containing "submarine cable" and a "Beardslees magnetic machine with coils of covered wire," along with a large "doubled barrel air pump with hose." On the morning of April 1, the *Alligator's* Acting Master Samuel Eakins and his First Officer, Masters Mate Moser, walked up the *Sumpter's* gangplank for what was expected to be an uneventful towing of the *Alligator* to Port Royal. Ten months earlier, Eakins had taken a similar cruise down the Chesapeake from the Philadelphia Navy Yard with an inadequately tested and underpowered submarine. Now he was on his way to Port Royal with an extensively modified boat that was going to be deployed in a theater of operations for which she had been designed.[17]

As the little submarine rocked from side to side at the end of her long tow line, Eakins and Moser stood at the stern of the *Sumpter* watching the ropes strain under the weight of their partially submerged iron monster. With the harbor of Newport News steadily disappearing over the horizon behind them, the United States Navy's only pair of submarine officers talked between themselves about the hazardous mission that lay before them far to the south. Throughout the afternoon that followed, Eakins and Moser probably walked the decks of the little steamer answering the many questions put to them by the curious crew of the *Sumpter*. As the sun slowly disappeared over the calm horizon that first evening, two sailors hung oil lanterns at the stern masthead so as to keep a watchful eye on the strange contraption that all hoped would soon punch a hole in the underwater defenses of Charleston Harbor.

The first day of towing proved uneventful with clear weather and a smooth sea. On the following day, however, a heavy storm was encountered. "In my experience of over 25 years at sea," reported Acting Master Winchester of the gale, "I have never before seen equaled." According to Winchester's official report,

At half past 9 p.m. (the first day) made Cape Hatteras light. At 1:30 a.m. second Cape Hatteras light bore northwest distant in my judgement about 15 miles. At 3 a.m. found the temperature of the water had risen to 68. The wind increased from west south west, and making little headway. At 8 a.m. set fore and aft sails. At noon got an observation and found Latitude 34.43 Longitude 75.20 water still at 68 degrees.

The wind by this time had increased to a very heavy gale from the south and west, and a very heavy sea causing the ship to labor very heavily but the *Alligator* towing very well astern. From 2 to 4 p.m. the wind rapidly increased in force, the sea running higher causing the ship to plunge heavily and labor hard. At 3:30 the ship was plunging under to the foremast, the weight of water she shipped broke the windlass, and hatches forward and flooded the Berth deck and hold with water.

At 5 p.m. the wind still increasing and the *Alligator* towing hard parted the Port hawser, hauled it in and payed out full to starboard hawser. At 5:30 the wind had increased to a furious gale from the Southwest. The *Alligator* was steering wildly and threatening to snap the hawser, and it being evident that we would soon lose her I called a council of all the officers including Acting Master Eakins, her commander, where it was unanimously concluded that to keep her longer would greatly endanger the ship.

I was compelled reluctantly to give the order to cut her adrift, all expressed a desire to save her if possible but the danger to the vessel

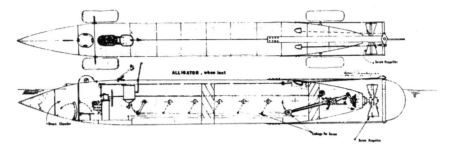

Sketch of the *USS Alligator* as she is thought to have looked at the time of her disappearance. *U. S. Naval Historical Center*

being so imminent, having then over two feet of water in the hold, and the ship straining badly. I gave the order to cut at 6 p.m. and the ship instantly surged ahead and cleared a very high and heavy sea that partly broke over her stern. The engine needed some repairing at this time but it was impossible to stop.[18]

According to Acting Master Winchester, the storm battered his vessel for days and washed overboard two sailors, Ensign R. Bentson and Seaman O. Lea. With the *Alligator* lost, it was decided to head for New York Harbor for much needed repairs. Once there, Acting Master Samuel Eakins wrote the Secretary of the Navy with the news, confirming in all respects Winchester's account of the *Alligator's* tragic loss. "I concurred in the opinion of the other officers of the ship and the order was given to cut the hawser, which was accordingly done," wrote Eakins with cool scientific detachment. The submarine's demise also meant the end of Eakins' commission, and Welles confirmed as much when he endorsed the letter, "This appointment and that of the acting Masters Mate with him to be revoked, their services being no longer required."[19]

The loss of the boat incensed its designer, Frenchman Brutus de Villeroi. After the war, the *Alligator's* inventor dripped both vitriol and inaccuracies from his pen: "The boat was sent to Washington and Fortress Monroe, and from there to the coast of Charleston, where it was abandoned to the Rebels." For several years following the end of the war, de Villeroi barraged the Navy Department with requests for payment of outstanding bills related to his ill-fated submarine from which so much had been expected. There is no record of payment.[20]

On the morning of April 7, 1863, just five days after the loss of the Union Navy's secret weapon off the coast of Cape Hatteras, Du Pont launched his attack on Fort Sumter and Charleston Harbor. With the submarine no longer at Du Pont's disposal, a large wooden raft was constructed and floated in front of the leading ironclad in order to snag or detonate the underwater mines. Everything went very wrong from the beginning of the operation. After the lead monitor spotted a line of harmless floating barrels, it veered off course and disrupted the alignment of the entire attack. Du Pont's vaunted ironclad monitors were only able to fire 139 rounds in the battle, and but 55 of these struck Sumter. Seventy-seven guns from Forts Sumter and Moultrie and elsewhere expended a total of 2,200 shots, 400 of which slammed into the monitors. Although only one Union sailor was killed in the action, all the ironclads sustained substantial damage, especially the riddled *Keokuk*, which sank that night. The botched attempt to take the defiant city cost Admiral Du Pont his command, and the Federals gave up on the idea of taking Charleston by direct sea attack.[21]

On the morning of April 27, 1863, some three weeks after Du Pont's attempt to take the city had failed, the *Charleston Mercury* printed a story detailing the loss of the *Alligator*, prior to Du Pont's attack, that was undoubtedly of great interest to the citizens of the defiant city. Unfortunately the Northern newspaper from where this startling information was derived was never revealed. "The Yankee Torpedo Battery Which Was Lost." It was announced just before the attack on Charleston that a submarine battery—the *Alligator*—had been lost at sea while being towed to that city to aid in the assault, by discovering and exploding the torpedoes in the harbor. The Northern papers furnished a description of the lost battery, which is interesting. It had been at Washington on exhibition. The account says: The machine was about thirty feet long and six or eight feet in diameter, and with conical ends. It was made of iron, with the upper part pierced for small circular plates of glass, for light, and in it were several water tight compartments.

When it arrived at Washington there were sixteen paddles protruding through the sides; but this plan was subsequently changed, and the paddles were removed and a propeller substituted, which worked by a crank.

By letting water in the compartments the machine was submerged, and, by first calculating the bearings of the torpedo or ship on which it was intended to work, the operator could approach sufficiently near to it (the machine being steered from the inside) to answer the purpose required.

The experiments were at first unsatisfactory, the machine on one occasion springing a leak and sinking beside the wharf; but after the propeller was attached to it the experiments were successful, a speed of about seven miles per hour being attained, and the machine showing a capacity of moving underwater, at the option of those controlling it. The *Alligator* was to be manned by sixteen men, besides one in submarine armor, who was the explorer, and a captain, who was to steer the craft. An air pump in the center of the machine, to which were attached two air tubes, attached to floats, was to furnish air to the occupants, the machine being of course air tight. The entrance to it was through a man-hole at one end, which was covered with an iron plate and leather packing. Ironically, within a matter of weeks after undergoing extensive modifications to their respective propulsion systems, both the Union *Alligator* and the Confederate *Pioneer II* met their ends in a stormy sea while being towed to their appointed theaters of operations. Neither have ever been found, and so to this day the exact location of their rusting hulls remains a mystery. It is impossible to know whether the *Alligator* would have reached Admiral Du Pont's fleet in time to have played a significant role in his attack, or whether it could have accomplished much when it got there. The sea floor is carpeted with the hulls of dead submarines whose last encounter was the accidental bumping of a mine—and Charleston Harbor was loaded with them. But the effort was never made, so the impact the *Alligator* may have had there will never be known. The loss of the *Alligator* falls into the category of another one of military history's "what ifs."[22]

Although both sides had recently lost their most advanced submarines, underwater submersible experimentation and construction continued on both sides of the Mason-Dixon Line.

◆　　◆　　◆

It was about this time that Horace Hunley, James McClintock, and Baxter Watson joined a recently formed organization of engineers at Mobile, Alabama. Under guidelines set forth by the Confederate government, this group would be entitled to 50 percent of the value of any vessel of war and any other Federal property destroyed as a result of their inventions, "with the necessary ammunition and materials for manufacturing their devices, as well as free transportation for both men and machines." The group's founder was a 37-year-old burly Texan named Edgar C. Singer. A self-styled mechanical engineer from Port Lavaca, Singer, along with a small group of ex-Texas artillerists, was manufacturing the most widely used underwater contact mine in the Confederacy. In the early weeks of April this group consisting of: J. D. Breaman, R. W. Dunn, B. A. (Gus) Whitney, D. Bradbury, James Jones, and several others had entered into a contract with the military defenders of Mobile to mine Mobile Bay with Singer Torpedoes. Within weeks after the signing of this contract, Horace Hunley, James McClintock, and Baxter Watson were asked to join the unique organization.[23]

The three inventors from New Orleans added both encouragement and experience to the group. After all, they had already built two underwater vehicles. As a result, the Singer Submarine Corps (also known as the Singer Secret Service Corps), as the men would later style their organization, decided to invest in an underwater torpedo boat submitted for consideration by McClintock, Hunley, and Watson. Four men stepped forward from within the ranks of this unique group to buy shares in the proposed venture. E. C. Singer, the group's founder and chief explosives designer, purchased one-third of the vessel at a cost of $5,000. Horace Hunley retained another one-third and sold the remaining shares to R. W. Dunn, B. A. Whitney, and J. D. Breaman. The total cost of the proposed submarine boat was $15,000, a considerable sum in 1863.[24]

Situated on a solid financial foundation, construction of the Louisiana inventors' third and final submarine boat began at the Park and Lyons machine shop under the direction of Lieutenant Alexander and James McClintock. "We decided to build another boat," remembered Lieutenant Alexander after the war in a detailed description of how the craft was designed and constructed that deserves reprinting in full:

> . . . and for this purpose took a cylinder boiler which we had on hand, 48 inches in diameter and twenty-five feet long. We cut this boiler in two, longitudinally, and inserted two 12-inch boiler iron strips in her

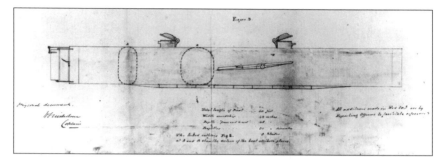

A sketch of the *Hunley* drawn by designer James McClintock during the fall of 1872. McClintock attended secret meetings in Nova Scotia with officials of the British Navy who were interested in building a submarine vessel of their own. *British Admiralty, London*

sides; lengthened her by one tapering course fore and aft, to which were attached bow and stern castings, making the boat about 30 feet long, 4 feet wide and 5 feet deep. A longitudinal strip 12 inches wide was riveted the full length on top. At each end a bulkhead was riveted across to form water-ballast tanks they were used in raising and sinking the boat. In addition to these water tanks the boat was ballasted by flat castings, made to fit the outside bottom of the shell and fastened thereto by 'Tee' headed bolts passing through stuffing boxes inside the boat, the inside end of the bolt squared to fit a wrench, that the bolts might be turned and the ballast dropped, should the necessity arise.

In connection with each of the water tanks, there was a sea-cock open to the sea to supply the tank for sinking; also a force pump to eject the water from the tanks into the sea for raising the boat to the surface. There was also a bilge connection to the pump. A mercury gauge, open to the sea, was attached to the shell near the forward tank, to indicate the depth of the boat below the surface. A one and a quarter shaft passed through stuffing boxes on each side of the boat, just forward of the end of the propeller shaft. On each side of this shaft, outside of the boat, castings, or lateral fins, five feet long and eight inches wide, were secured. This shaft was operated by a lever amidship, and by raising or lowering the ends of these fins, operated as the fins of a fish, changing the depth of the boat below the surface at will, without disturbing the water level in the ballast tanks.

The rudder was operated by a wheel, and levers connected to rods passing through stuffing boxes in the stern castings, and operated by the captain or pilot forward. An adjusted compass was placed in front of the forward tank. The boat was operated by manual power, with an ordinary propeller. On the propelling shaft there were formed eight cranks at different angles; the shaft was supported by brackets on the starboard side, the men sitting on the port side turning on the cranks. The propeller shaft and cranks took up so much room that it was very difficult to pass fore and aft, and when the men were in their places this was next to impossible.

In operation, one half of the crew had to pass through the fore hatch; the other through the after hatchway. The propeller revolved in a wrought iron ring or band, to guard against a line being thrown in to foul it. There were two hatchways—one fore and one aft—16 inches by 12, with a combing 8 inches high. These hatches had hinged covers with rubber gaskets, and were bolted from the inside. In the sides and ends of these combings glasses were inserted to sight from. There was an opening made in the top of the boat for an air box, a casting with a close top 12 by 18 by 4 inches, made to carry a hollow shaft. This shaft passed through stuffing boxes. On each end was an elbow with a 4 foot length of 1 1/2 inch pipe, and keyed to the hollow shaft; on the inside was a lever with a stop-cock to admit air.[25]

At some point during the boat's construction, Lt. George E. Dixon, a fellow officer in William Alexander's 21st Alabama Regiment, joined the team of builders and designers. A Kentucky native and mechanical engineer by trade, Dixon entered Confederate service as a private in the spring of 1861 after he left his post as an engineer aboard a riverboat to enlist in the regiment. Although he managed to rise steadily in rank, he suffered a severe leg wound at Shiloh on April 6, 1862, his first engagement of the war. Unfit thereafter for field service, Dixon was convalescing in Mobile when he apparently crossed paths with the group of underwater adventurers. He may have been on detached duty with Lieutenant Alexander at the Park and Lyons machine shop, although his compiled service record is unclear on this point.[26]

At about the same time that the Singer Submarine Corps was drawing up plans for its new submarine boat, a similar company was being

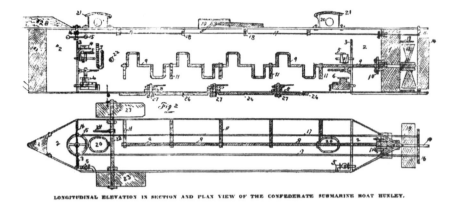

LONGITUDINAL ELEVATION IN SECTION AND PLAN VIEW OF THE CONFEDERATE SUBMARINE BOAT HUNLEY.

CSS H. L. Hunley (1863–1864). This duel view was drawn by William A. Alexander, who directed her construction. *U.S. Naval Historical Center*

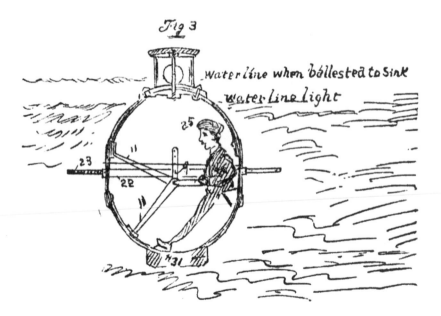

This cutaway of the *Hunley* is from a sketch by William A. Alexander, who directed her construction. *U. S. Naval Historical Center*

formed 1,200 miles away in the Confederate capital at Richmond. A letter sent to the Confederate War Department by Virginia Senator A. J. Marshall held that he and three others were planning to invest in a submarine venture from which they "Desire to secure all the rewards promised such enterprises by the Act of Congress." The enterprise, explained Senator Marshall, was called the Triton Company, and its actions would "require the utmost secrecy." The venture would be financed through private funds, Marshall went on, and the company investors or "planners should be considered in the service of the Confederate States so that if captured they will be regarded as prisoners of war."[27]

The five faded pages outlining Marshall's plan to the Confederate Secretary of War revealed that the other three investors in the enterprise were: C. Williams of St. Louis, Missouri; Jeremiah Morton of Virginia; and E. Allen of Texas. In addition to asking for special passes to travel to Charleston, South Carolina, explained the senator, "I request the aid of Thomas M. Smith, an engineer and machinist now in the employment of the government at Selma, Alabama . . ." Smith, continued Marshall, "besides having great mechanical skill and ingenuity has a familiarity with the subject. I therefore ask that T. M. Smith be specially detailed to go with me to Charleston." Just where Smith had obtained his "familiarity with the subject" of submarine boats is not known, although there is some evidence that he may have been the brother of Reverend Franklin Smith, the underwater visionary whose letter advocating "Submarine Warfare" appeared throughout the Confederacy in June of 1861.[28]

Senator Marshall was deadly serious about his intent to construct and launch a workable submarine. Rufus Rhodes, the Confederate Commissioner of Patents, confirmed as much on August 13, 1863, when he issued a secret patent for the submarine vessel soon after Marshall and his associates formed their unique organization. In a letter to "Mr. C. Williams"—one of the four founding members listed in Senator Marshall's letter—Rhodes wrote: "Your papers relating to a caveat (patent) for a submarine boat and enclosed eleven dollars have been received, and the caveat has been filed in the *Secret Archives* [emphasis added] of this office as directed."[29]

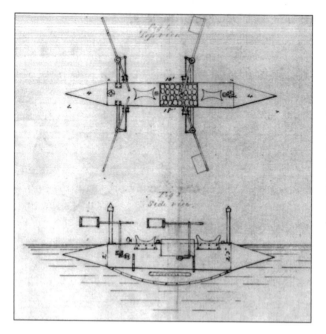

The Richmond-based Triton Company submitted designs of this oar-powered submarine to the Confederate Patent Office during the spring of 1863. *National Archives*

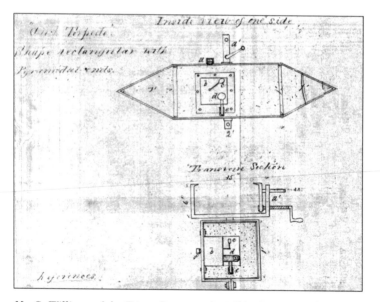

Mr. C. Williams of the Triton Company drew this diagram of the "Clock Torpedo" (an attachable mine) that was to be used with that group's submarine boat. *National Archives*

While Marshall and the other founders of the Triton Company tried to secure the services of engineer-machinist Thomas Smith, E. C. Singer and his group of Mobile engineers, including Hunley, McClintock, and Watson, may have been taking notice of a strange contraption being tested in Mobile Bay. Extant descriptions show the invention was similar in design to the weapon tested by Pascal Plant in the Potomac River the year before. The new device was called a "rocket-powered torpedo." Like most other secret weapons tested during the Civil War, documentation on this invention is incomplete and confusing. This variety of rocket torpedo was born in the imagination of Col. E. H. Angamar, a Louisiana engineer engaged in planting underwater mines in Mobile Bay. Colonel Angamar's "Submarine Rocket Project" first appears in Confederate records in early November 1862, and according to the Confederate Engineering Bureau, he was assigned "to make satisfactory experimental tests of an invention designed to destroy the ships of our enemy."[30]

It is not known whether Colonel Angamar and his men had any ties to Singer's group of engineers, then hard at work building their submarine boat in the Park and Lyons machine shop. It appears as though the two groups of men had radically different ideas regarding marine warfare, for Colonel Angamar was not only trying to develop a rocket-powered torpedo, he was also attempting to build a rocket-powered torpedo boat from which to deploy his weapon. Whether the colonel was a good engineer is unknown, but he certainly had a knack for financing a far-sighted project: according to records kept by "The Committee of Safety" at Mobile, Colonel Angamar received some $20,000 to finance his scheme.[31]

In late April of 1863, Angamar's "rocket boat and the twin boats from between which the rocket boat is to be started" had been completed. Confederate records indicate the "rocket propellant" for the project was shipped from the Confederate powder works at Augusta, Georgia, on April 15, and that "Angamar expected in a short time to attack one of the enemy's ships." According to Mobile's chief engineer, Confederate Brig. Gen. Danville Leadbetter, Colonel Angamar was sent to Richmond on May 22 to report on his rocket-powered torpedo experiments. By June 4, Angamar and his staff had completed their rocket-powered boat, "drawing 18 feet of water, and a twin boat for rowing and aiming it." "A flat boat with cranes for hoisting the torpedo boat," had also been built. According to Angamar, his experiments with the novel craft had been a success, although General Leadbetter let Richmond know that he had "no confidence" in the project.[32]

By July 1, as Robert E. Lee was feeding troops into the spreading conflagration at Gettysburg, Colonel Angamar and his staff of nineteenth-century rocket engineers were apparently ready to unleash their secret weapon on the Union fleet anchored at the mouth of Mobile Harbor. Angamar requested from the Mobile Engineering Department charts of Mobile Bay and tracing paper from which he planned to plot his course of attack. Unfortunately, this is the last bit of information concerning either the colonel or his rocket-powered torpedo boat. No records regarding his alleged attack are known to exist, and the name of E. H. Angamar disappears from the surviving Mobile war records. Whether he was killed in his attempt or whether in fact such an attack ever took place remains a mystery. The lack of information regarding the fate of Colonel Angamar and his $20,000 rocket-powered torpedo boat is a good example of how vague and incomplete surviving Civil War records are—especially in the area of experimental weaponry.[33]

◆   ◆   ◆

While the mysterious Colonel Angamar and his staff of Mobile engineers were putting the finishing touches on their rocket boat, members of the Permanent Commission, which had been established as an oversight committee by the Navy Department in Washington, D.C., some months earlier, were examining diagrams of a new submarine that was in many ways decades ahead of its time.

The design of the boat was submitted by a "Professor Horstford" from Cambridge, Massachusetts. At first glance, Professor Horstford's diagrams appear to be almost modern in concept, and it's difficult to imagine they were drawn during the mid-nineteenth century. One of its most striking features, and one that sets the vessel apart from other submarine concepts of the day, is the employment of a periscope. "A telescope with reflectors

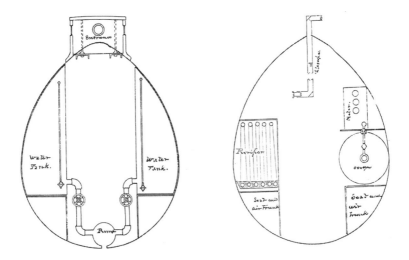

(Top left) The forward conning tower and side mounted ballast tanks in Professor Horstford's original 1863 blueprints. (Top Right) Cutaway view of Horsford's submarine showing the periscope, air purifier, and tank of compressed oxygen. *National Archives*

will be passed through a stuffing box in the top to any required height," explained the professor, "by which the relative positions of objects may be ascertained without exposure of the vessel." Although crude periscopes were occasionally used on some Union ironclads, Horstford appears to have been the first to propose their use aboard a submarine.[34]

In addition to a periscope, Horstford also proposed utilizing a forward lockout chamber that could be pressurized from a large tank of compressed air carried within the hull. When this compartment's internal air pressure matched the water pressure outside, two men outfitted with "submarine armor" could exit the vessel by way of the chamber's bottom hatch. This method of dispatching divers outside was first used aboard the ill-fated *Alligator*, and these diagrams depicting how the forward lockout chamber functioned may be quite similar to the one utilized aboard de Villeroi's invention.[35]

The boat itself was a large one—55' in length—and was intended to carry a crew of twenty-six. In order for light to enter his vessel from the

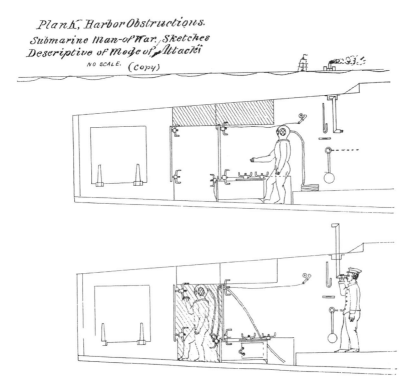

Plank, Harbor Obstructions.
Submarine Man-of War, Sketches
Descriptive of Mode of Attack.
NO SCALE. (copy)

These 1863 diagrams (above and right facing page) were submitted to the Navy Department by Professor Horstford illustrating how a diver could exit his submarine by way of a forward lockout chamber, attach a mine to the rudder assembly of a Confederate ironclad or ship, and reenter. *Hortsford File, Submarine Force Library and Museum, Groton, Connecticut*

outside, Horstford proposed placing view ports in the sides and bottom of the submarine, or "in convenient places for looking out into the water." Air aboard the submarine would stay pure through an ingenious air purifying system. This device was described in detail in a postwar article written by Commander G. W. Baird, the same officer who examined James McClintock's *Pioneer* with his superiors after the fall of New Orleans in 1862. "A tank of oxygen gas, compressed to one-fifteenth its volume was used," explained Baird. "[Horstford] employed a great surface of woolen cloth, which passed over pulleys and was dipped in lime water. A blower

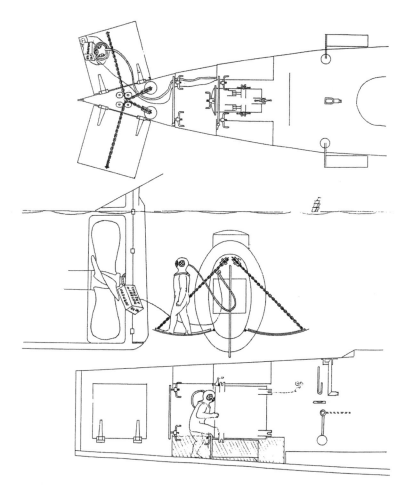

kept the air moving over the wet surface. The lime water absorbed the carbonic acid gas. As this gas is absorbed and a small amount of oxygen liberated, the air may be kept nearly at normal purity."[36]

Professor Horstford's submersible would be propelled manually by twenty-four men who sat on either side of a long crankshaft attached to a stern propeller. It would not be a surprise if we someday learn that the professor possessed detailed information on Brutus de Villeroi's invention. Horstford's means and method of propulsion may have been the same configuration adopted by the *Alligator* while undergoing

Top view of Professor Horstford's 1863 submarine diagram. *National Archives*

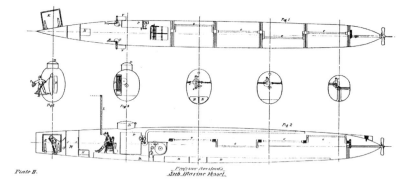

Professor Horstford's submarine as pictured in a 1902 Naval Institute publication

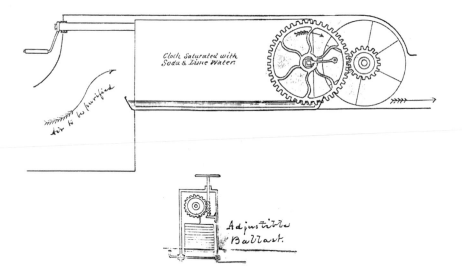

Professor Horstford removed the carbonic gas (CO_2) from within the hull of his submarine by forcing it through a saturated cloth of soda and lime water. *National Archives*

modifications at the Washington Navy Yard in the winter of 1862. The appearance of the vessel, as set forth in Horstford's diagram, is an upgraded version of de Villeroi's *Alligator*, and may in fact be based on the *Alligator's* original blueprints.[37]

◆   ◆   ◆

As the war dragged on, the once sieve-like blockade of the Confederate coastline grew more effective. The twin defeats at Gettysburg and Vicksburg, together with their long casualty lists, dampened morale across the South. It was becoming increasingly obvious that if the Confederacy was going to realize its independence, the Federal blockade, which was slowly choking life from the Confederate war effort, would have to be broken. A handful of inventors were determined to achieve that goal.

In July 1863, shortly after the devastating news of the surrender at Vicksburg, Mississippi, reached Mobile, a new submarine slid down wooden ramps into the harbor at the Theater Street Dock. The boat would become one of the most famous submarines in maritime history and was christened on behalf of her largest contributor: *H. L. Hunley.*[38]

The *Hunley* was not a rebuilt *Pioneer*. The Louisiana inventors had learned much from the two previous vessels they had constructed in 1861 and 1862, and with this experience they appreciated what worked and what did not. For example, prior experience taught them that a submerged submarine tilted dangerously whenever a crew member shifted his body weight only a foot or so. To arrest this problem, an assigned spot at the propeller shaft was given to each of the eight men who propelled their newest vessel. The skipper, or ninth man in the crew, stood at the forward hatch peering through small glass view ports located at the front and sides of a narrow conning tower. In one hand was the lever that controlled the port and starboard diving planes, and in the other was the wheel that manipulated the rudder. Whenever the boat ran beneath the surface, the commander knelt next to a flickering candle and monitored the dimly lit depth gauge and compass in order to keep the vessel on course while approaching an enemy ship.

No one knows who was the first commander of the *Hunley*. In all likelihood it was either Lt. George E. Dixon or chief designer James McClintock. Both men later commanded the small submarine in action against the Union fleet, so it seems safe to say that one of them was at the diving planes during her July 1863 harbor trials. Regardless of who piloted the novel craft that day, all who witnessed the tests agreed that this third submarine was a success, and would be a formidable adversary to any blockading fleet.

Satisfied with the performance of their latest effort, representatives of the Singer Submarine Corps arranged a demonstration of the *Hunley's* attack capabilities for Mobile's naval commander, Admiral Franklin Buchanan. Some months earlier Buchanan had witnessed trials of the *Hunley's* predecessor, *Pioneer II,* and had come away less than impressed. However, Buchanan was farsighted enough to realize that any vessel that could possible sink an enemy ship—or help break up the Federal blockade—should be given serious attention, regardless of how outlandish. The *Hunley* would soon have an opportunity to prove her worth.[39]

◆　◆　◆

While members of the Singer Submarine Corps were arranging for their submarine demonstration before Mobile's naval commander, the Permanent Commission (the Northern oversight committee) heartily endorsed the construction of Professor Horstford's submarine boat. On July 27, committee chairman Rear Admiral Charles Davis wrote to Horstford to advise him of their decision. "I have the pleasure to inform you that several conferences on the subject have resulted in a determination on the part of the commission to recommend to the department the construction of a submarine boat upon your plan, the cost of construction to be borne partly by yourself, and partly by the department."[40]

Another new Federal submarine, one more advanced then anything that had come before, was about to be constructed.

◆　◆　◆

Within seventy-two hours after the Permanent Commission informed Professor Horstford of its favorable decision regarding the construction of his submarine vessel, an old coal-hauling flatboat in far-off Alabama was towed to the middle of the Mobile River and anchored. On shore were several high-ranking Confederate officers who had assembled to witness the destructive capabilities of a unique underwater diving machine that had recently been completed in the Park and Lyons machine shop by engineers attached to E. C. Singers Submarine Corps.[41]

While Admiral Buchanan and his staff of naval officers restlessly mingled on the muddy banks of the Mobile River, several hundred yards upriver the submarine's commander squeezed through the forward hatch and took his place at the forward diving planes. With all hands at their stations, he ordered the hatches sealed and the man at the rear station opened the sea valve to let water into the ballast tanks. As water splashed into both the forward and rear tanks, the commander's view of the event through the small glass view ports in the conning tower was limited. When the water had risen 3 inches above the black iron hull, he ordered the sea valves closed and the long propeller shaft began to turn.

Once the boat was underway, the commander steered for the flatboat anchored in the river, peering through the forward view port that remained a few inches above the water. In the submarine's wake trailed a long tow rope which held a powder-filled cylinder bristling with contact detonators rigged to explode at the slightest touch. As the submarine approached the old coal-hauling flatboat, a candle was lit next to the compass and depth gauge. The commander depressed the diving planes and the little submarine slowly descended beneath the muddy surface and disappeared before the eyes of the assembled crowd.

Once the mercury depth gauge displayed 20 feet, the diving planes were leveled out. Two or three minutes passed, and the only sound was the creaking of the long iron propeller shaft turning in the hands of the submarine's anxious crew. Whether the commander had a way of judging when he was under the flatboat is unknown. Without warning to the crew, a huge concussion was heard and its shock waves enveloped the narrow iron hull, causing it to shutter and list to one side. Once the powerful wave had passed and the small submarine was again stable, its commander ordered the fore and aft ballast tanks pumped out. Within a few minutes the boat reappeared on the surface of the muddy river. In all probability, the first sound the crew heard when the boat's heavy iron hatch covers were pushed open was that of a cheering crowd. The little

Hunley's efforts were indeed impressive. Her "victory," however, was against an unarmed stationary derelict in a small river under ideal conditions. Whether she was ready to travel out to sea and attempt the same thing against a blockading Federal warship anchored at the harbor's mouth was another thing altogether.

Several eyewitness accounts of these underwater experiments have been located. Brigadier General James Edward Slaughter, who for a time in 1863 commanded the Mobile defenses, was one of these witnesses. "In company with Admiral Buchanan and many officers of the C. S. Navy and Army," Slaughter remembered in a postwar letter, "I witnessed her operations in the river and harbor of Mobile. I saw her pass under a large raft of lumber towing a torpedo behind her which destroyed the raft. She appeared three or four hundred yards beyond the raft and so far as I could judge she behaved as well under water as above it. I will add that I witnessed her experiments more than a dozen times with equal satisfaction," he concluded, thereby confirming the *Hunley* had conducted numerous and successful trials. Captain Peter U. Murphy (Murphey) of the *CSS Selma*—the ship James Carr abandoned in late February before testifying to Federal authorities about an alleged submarine attack on the blockading fleet off Fort Morgan—also saw the *Hunley's* experiments. "Whilst lying at Mobile in company with my officers and others of the C.S. Navy," he remembered, "I witnessed the experiments of the Submarine Boat which appeared to be a perfect success."[42]

With the efficacy of the small submarine no longer in question, military commanders in Mobile unanimously decided to put the *Hunley* into action as soon as possible. Her home port, however, posed several vexing problems made visible once the submarine's limitations had been exposed. In addition to Mobile's relatively shallow water, the Federal ships were often far out to sea—perhaps too far for the *Hunley* to safely reach and return to port. Turning her propeller was exhausting, back-breaking labor, and operating the boat several miles out and back in search of a suitable target appeared to be a risky proposition. After the loss of two boats, the inventors were leery about casually thrusting the *Hunley* into action. After some debate they agreed: Mobile was not conducive to submarine operations. Charleston, South Carolina, seemed better suited to underwater operations. The blockaders often operated

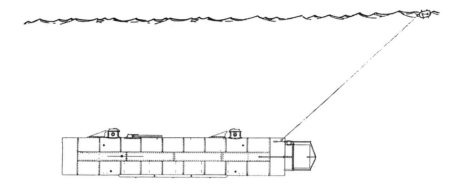

A sketch of the *Hunley* showing how her torpedo was to be delivered. *Caldwell Whistler*

within reach of the *Hunley's* propeller power, and the area was rich with potential targets. For over a month the city's fortifications had been subjected to a daily bombardment from the Federal fleet. If Charleston fell, only Wilmington, North Carolina, would remain open on the Atlantic coastline. Charleston, then, would be the *Hunley's* port of operations.[43]

From Mobile, General Slaughter penned a letter of introduction on July 31, 1863, to Charleston's commander, Gen. P. G. T. Beauregard. The letter was handed to Beauregard personally by inventor Baxter Watson and investor and member of the Singer Submarine Corps, B. A. (Gus) Whitney. These men, explained Slaughter to Beauregard, invented a submarine which they "desire to submit to you for examination, and if it meets your approval to test its usefulness in Charleston Harbor. So far as I am able to judge I can see no reason why it should not answer all our sanguine expectations. Nothing appears to me wanting but cool and determined men to manage it, but you will see and judge for yourself.[44]

On the following day Admiral Buchanan sent a similar communication to Charleston's naval commander, John Tucker. Although Buchanan had been unimpressed with the *Hunley's* predecessor *Pioneer II*, the *Hunley's* apparent abilities won him over. "I yesterday witnessed the destruction of a lighter or coal flat in the Mobile River by a torpedo which was placed under it by a submarine iron boat, the invention of Messrs. Whitney and McClintock," explained Buchanan by way of introducing Tucker to the subject. "Messrs. Watson and Whitney visit Charleston for the purpose of consulting General Beauregard and yourself to ascertain whether you will try it." The men "will explain all its advantages, and if it can operate in smooth water where the current is not strong as was the case yesterday, I can recommend it to your favorable consideration." The engineers had been able to radically increase their third boat's speed: "It can be propelled about four knots per hour, to judge from the experiment of yesterday. I am fully satisfied," concluded the admiral, "it can be used successfully in blowing-up one or more of the enemy's ironclads in your harbor. Do me the favor to show this to General Beauregard with my regards."[45]

Shortly after Flag Officer Tucker received Buchanan's letter, Baxter Watson and Gus Whitney arrived at the busy Charleston Railroad Station. The submarine builders sought and obtained an audience with Charleston's military commander, Pierre Gustave Toutant Beauregard. The French Creole general had experienced a prominent, if uneven, Civil War career. It was Beauregard who ordered Southern guns to open on Fort Sumter on April 12, 1861. Riding high in the popularity polls, he went on to greater heights after leading a Confederate army to victory at First Manassas (Bull Run). Problems with President Davis, however, coupled with a checkered record in the Western Theater cost Beauregard his command. Transferred to command Charleston, he viewed the assignment as the demotion it was and seethed at the embarrassment. For several months, however, Beauregard had ably defended the important city and had done a credible job improving its defenses. With a flair for unconventional and out-of-the-ordinary schemes, Beauregard examined the diagrams presented to him by his enthusiastic visitors from Mobile. The general loved the idea of having a submarine boat. "Please expedite transportation of Whitney's submarine boat from Mobile here," he wired railroad agents on August 7, "it is much needed."[46]

In Mobile, the Singer Submarine Corps received General Beauregard's telegram with great enthusiasm. At last their invention would be used against the enemy's fleet. Now they had to figure out how to transport the heavy submarine without damaging it. The boat would have to be carefully removed from the harbor, transferred to the Mobile railroad station, hoisted aboard two flat cars, strapped down, and sent on its way to South Carolina. It was a daunting task. News that the submarine was heading for the Atlantic coast traveled quickly. Stationed in Mobile was Lt. James Williams, of the 21st Alabama Regiment, a friend of Lt. George Dixon's, the detached engineer working in the Park and Lyons machine shop. On the same day General Beauregard ordered the *Hunley* sent to South Carolina, Lieutenant Williams notified his wife of its transfer. "I have heard that the submarine is off for Charleston, I suppose that Dixon went with it," he wrote. "With favorable circumstances it will succeed, and I hope to hear a report of its success before this month is out; still there are so many things that may ruin the enterprise that I am not so sanguine of its triumph as Dixon." Williams was in error on one point: his friend Lieutenant Dixon did not accompany the boat as part of its first crew in Charleston. His involvement with the little submarine, however, was far from over.[47]

The job of lifting the *Hunley* out of the water at Mobile and transporting it to the railroad station was given to Lt. George Washington Gift, a ubiquitous naval officer of talent. Gift, who had served on the *CSS Arkansas* during her bloody duels on the Yazoo and Mississippi Rivers in 1862 and was now serving on the *CSS Gaines*, left a remarkable description of the *Hunley* in a letter home:

My Dear Ellen,

I have been employed during the past day or two in hoisting out of the water and sending away toward Charleston a very curious machine for destroying vessels, and which I certainly regard as the most important invention to us that could have been made. It is a submarine boat which is propelled with ease and rapidity underwater. But inasmuch as it will become in a very short time one of the great celebrities in the art of defense and attack on floating objects I will run the risk of inflicting a short description.

In the first place imagine a high pressure steam boiler, not quite round, say 4 feet in diameter in one way and 3 1/2 feet the other—draw each end of the boiler down to a sharp wedge shaped point. On the bottom of the boat is riveted an iron keel weighing 4000 pounds. On top and opposite the keel is placed two man hole plates or hatches with heavy tops. They are just large enough for a man to go in and out.

At one end is fitted a very neat little propeller 3 1/2 feet in diameter worked by men sitting in the boat and turning the shaft by hand cranks. She also has a rudder and steering apparatus.

Embarked and under ordinary circumstances with men and ballast she floats about half way out of the water and resembles a whale. But when it is necessary to go underwater there are compartments into which the water is allowed to flow, which causes the boat to sink to any required depth, the same being accurately indicated by a column of mercury.

Behind the boat at a distance of 100 to 150 feet is towed a plank and under that plank is attached a torpedo with say 100 pounds of powder. I saw them explode a vessel as an experiment. They approached to within about fifty yards from her keeping the man holes just above water. At that distance the submarine sank down and in a few minutes made her appearance on the other side of the vessel.

I consider it a perfect success! and in the hands of a bold man would be equal to the task of destroying every ironclad the enemy has off Morris Island [an island at the mouth of Charleston harbor] in a single night. It is perfectly safe and perfectly sure. She will be ready for service in Charleston by the 18th or 20th of this month.[48]

The intelligent and enthusiastic naval officer could not have been more wrong about both the boat's safety and its certainty of success.

◆   ◆   ◆

While the crew of the *Hunley* road the rails with their iron machine across the Deep South en route to their new base of operations in South Carolina, Union Admiral John A. Dahlgren, the new commander of the South Atlantic Blockading Squadron, was considering a unique strategy for destroying Charleston's underwater obstructions. It was not entirely his own, and in fact something similar had first been proposed by Admiral Samuel F. Du Pont some months earlier.

During the early summer of 1862, Admiral Dahlgren had been Commandant of the Washington Navy Yard. In July of that year, the submarine boat *Alligator* had been sent to his yard from Hampton Roads following her unsuccessful mission up the James River. Therefore he was intimately

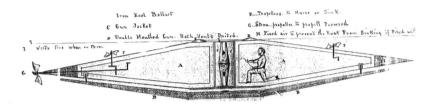

This 1863 submarine diagram was submitted to the Navy Department for consideration by engineer Alfred Luther. The vessel was never built. *National Archives*

familiar with the development of early war submarines and the idea of underwater "infernal machines." The resourceful Dahlgren envisioned something similar to the *Alligator*, although smaller, being dispatched into Charleston Harbor to destroy underwater obstructions. From his flagship *Dinsmore*, he wrote Navy Secretary Gideon Welles on August 11:

> I think the opportunity may occur where explosions may be made useful under water; wherefore, I would like to have a vessel constructed of corrugated iron, fashioned like a boat, but closed perfectly on the top, so that it could be submerged very quickly. There might be air vessels at each end, which, when exhausted, would float the top of the magazine even with the water, when air is allowed to enter, would cause the vessel to sink.
>
> With such a contrivance a quantity of powder could be brought to bear upon obstructions, which would dislocate any nice arrangements. It may be that Francis could fit three or four of his metallic boats in this way and send them to me speedily.[49]

The race for developing an underwater machine of war for use off Charleston was underway.

◆　　◆　　◆

Within hours of Admiral Dahlgren's request for three or four small submarine boats from the Washington Navy Department, Beauregard dispatched an anxious telegram to Mobile inquiring as to the status of the *Hunley.* "General Maury," asked Beauregard, "has the submarine boat been sent from Mobile? If so when did it leave for Charleston?" Perhaps even before he heard back from Maury, Beauregard's answer arrived. The next morning, the train hauling the submarine and her crew slowly lumbered into the busy Charleston Railroad Station. For over four days the submarine had made her way across the South, turning the heads of curious citizens as it wound its way to the city that had witnessed the first shots fired in the war.[50]

Although the mere presence of the unique diving machine was raising morale within the besieged city, Beauregard was anxious to get the submarine into action as soon as possible. On the day of its arrival he ordered his chief quartermaster to "furnish Mr. B. A. Whitney on his requisition with such articles as he may need for placing his submarine vessel in condition for service. His requisitions will be approved subsequently at this office." Beauregard was giving Whitney and his fellow inventors carte blanche to proceed however they deemed fit.[51]

An area known as "the cove," located behind Fort Moultrie at the end of Sullivan's Island, was probably the *Hunley's* first base of operations. By hugging the shore at the tip of the island, it would have been easy to avoid the numerous contact mines in the channel and still gain access to the outer harbor and open sea. Although information is sketchy on this point, the *Hunley's* chief designer, James McClintock, was probably in command of the submarine, with part owner Gus Whitney acting as his first officer manning the ballast tank pumps at the rear of the vessel. The two 21st Alabama engineers, George E. Dixon and William Alexander, were left behind in Mobile to continue their detached duty at the Park and Lyons machine shop.[52]

While patriotism seemed to drive the *Hunley's* inventors, a large cash incentive was also dangled before them soon after their arrival in South Carolina. While the submariners were preparing their machine for service, Thomas Jordan, Beauregard's chief of staff, sent them a dispatch that garnered their attention:

I am authorized to say that John Fraser & Co. will pay over to any parties who shall destroy the U.S. steam iron-clad *Ironsides* the sum of

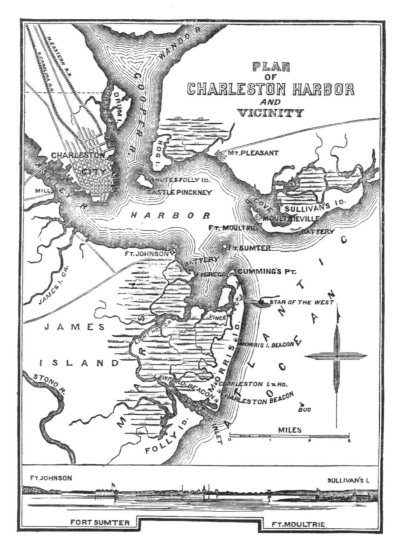

Map of Charleston Harbor

$100,000, a similar sum for the destruction of the wooden frigate *Wabash*, and the sum of $50,000 for every monitor sunk.

I have reason to believe that other men of wealth will unite and give with equal munificence toward the same end.

At the same time, steps are being taken to secure a large sum to be settled for the support of the families of parties, who, making any attempt against the fleet now attacking our outer works, shall fail in the enterprise, and fall or be captured in the attempt.[53]

Matters continued moving forward and Beauregard's cooperation was more than the men could have hoped for. On the day after the generous Fraser & Co. offer had been relayed to the Singer Submarine Corps from Charleston headquarters, Beauregard, via his chief of staff, wired the commander of the city's arsenal to cooperate fully with the submariners. "Render every assistance of material and labor to Messrs. Whitney and Watson, in the construction of torpedoes to be used with their submarine vessel which he regards as the most formidable engine of war for the defense of Charleston now at his disposition."[54]

With the small submarine finally in a position to strike out at the Federal fleet, the underwater raiders wasted no time putting their ambitious plan into motion. During the third week of August, the *Hunley* made at least three nocturnal excursions against the enemy's fleet anchored at the harbor's mouth. None of them were successful, although the crew gained significant experience handling the boat and learned important information regarding the harbor's currents and water conditions. During this period, as remarkable as it might seem, the *Hunley* was almost completely accessible to inquisitive citizens. The submarine was somehow brought to the attention of two curious steam engineers engaged in running the blockade from Nassau, who easily gained access to the boat. Someone acquainted with them named S. G. Haynes sent a letter to Union Secretary of the Navy Gideon Welles to warn him of the impending threat to his ships:

I am informed by two engineers engaged in running the blockade to Charleston, that there is a party of engineers in Charleston who have completed a submarine boat made of boiler-iron in the shape of a Spanish cigar and some forty feet in length, and by means of an air pump capable of remaining under water one hour with this machine. They plan to attach and blow up with torpedoes the iron clads, and men on the blockading squadron that come within reach.

My informants inform me that they have examined the machine in all its parts, and have no doubt of its capability of accomplishing all the purpose. This infernal machine is all ready, and my only fear is that this mail will not reach you in time to put the squadron on their guard.[55]

Haynes had some justification for feeling concerned, for the *Hunley* was already prowling the nighttime waters off Charleston looking for a victim.

◆   ◆   ◆

The letter Haynes had sent Gideon Welles was duplicated and sent to a skeptical Admiral Dahlgren, who was himself waiting for a response to his submarine request of August 11. Plans for building an underwater boat similar to the vessel requested by Dahlgren were under consideration by the Permanent Commission. Diagrams of this craft describe a small one-man submersible that its designer, Ensign Andrew Hartshorn (USN), hoped to use against harbor defenses and river obstructions throughout the Confederacy. Hartshorn claimed that "The small size of the machine renders it perfectly easy to handle, while by the use of the sea cock and force pump, it can rise and sink at will." Ensign Hartshorn apparently tested the craft and was pleased with the results, claiming he could "cut away the hawsers and chains which are stretched across some of the rivers and harbors on the coast, and in short remove in a few days all the obstructions in any one of the harbors."[56]

One of Ensign Hartshorn's most ambitious plans called for blowing up an enemy vessel or ironclad "by fixing a small torpedo between the stern post and hull and explode it by means of a wire connecting with any electric battery." The characteristics of his invention, similar to most of the others built thus far, were as follows: "The draft shows a longitudinal section of the inside of the machine, which is an air tight chamber made of sheets of boiler iron riveted together. The door by which the machine is entered shuts down upon a flange which is covered with rubber packing." The submarine was also to incorporate "Flint glass port-lights or windows, force pumps for forcing the water

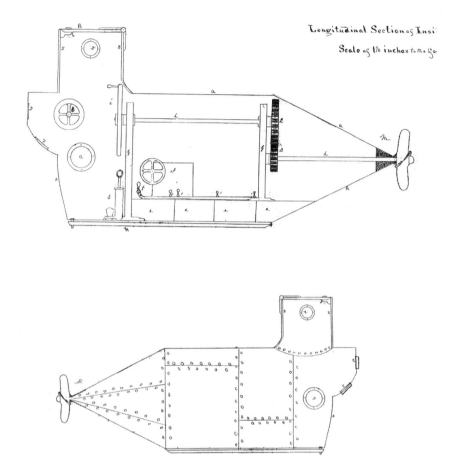

This 1863 diagram of a one-man submarine was submitted to the Navy Department for consideration by Ensign Andrew Hartshorn, USN. *National Archives*

out of the water tanks, and an air pump connecting with a hose upon the outside of the machine and carried to the surface by a buoy."[57]

Whether Ensign Hartshorn's theories regarding mini-submarines could be put to practical use remained to be determined.

◆   ◆   ◆

While Dahlgren waited and Hartshorn schemed, Horace Hunley worried. What would happen to the crew of his submarine if they were captured trying to destroy an enemy ship? Many in the Victorian Age considered inventions such as submarine boats and underwater mines to be "infernal machines," inhuman in their method of attack. If they were treated as war criminals or on the order of spies, they could be hung for their service. In an attempt to legitimize their endeavor—at least in the eyes of the Federals—Hunley placed an order with Charleston's quartermaster on August 21 for "nine grey jackets, three to be trimmed in gold braid." Feeling the need to justify his request, he added that "the men for whom they are ordered are on special secret service and that it is necessary that they be clothed in the Confederate Army uniform."[58]

Less than twenty-four hours after Hunley placed his request for uniforms, the war-weary citizens of Charleston awoke to the sound of a terrific explosion. From Morris Island over four miles away, the Union army had mounted a 200-lb. Parrott Rifle, nicknamed the "Swamp Angel." This siege gun was not aimed at Forts Sumter or Moultrie but at the very heart of the sleeping city. At 1:30 in the morning on August 22, the first shot was fired into the "Cradle of the Confederacy." Fifteen additional rounds followed, and after a break, twenty more shells were arched into the city. Luckily for its citizens, the last shot disabled the large 200-lb. Parrott Rifle and the gun crew withdrew.[59]

The incoming rounds brought with them a new sense of urgency. With the city now under the very guns of the Union Army, something had to be done to drive the invaders away. The city's forts and batteries, while plentiful and powerful, were necessarily restricted to defensive action. Charleston's small flotilla of ironclads and warships was not the answer either, for they were unable to effectively take the offensive against the Federal warships steaming outside the bar. The situation facing Charleston was growing increasingly more desperate, and Battery Wagner on Morris Island was under daily threat of collapse. Thus the hopes of many now rested on the submarine *Hunley*. When day after day passed without results, however, military leaders in the besieged city grew increasingly impatient with their cautious guests from Mobile.

In the early morning hours of August 23, a situation developed that may have contributed to the military's decision to seize the small submarine from her owners. At 3:00 a.m., a group of Federal monitors steamed up to the harbor's entrance and began shelling Fort Sumter. Both Sumter and Moultrie returned fire as a thick fog rolled in, rendering the targets invisible. When the fog lifted, it was discovered that one of the enemy's ironclads had run aground. As the cannons from both forts started to site in on the helpless warship, fog rolled in again and obscured the target. In his report on the event, a disgusted Thomas Clingman, the commander of Sullivan's Island, concluded that the enemy ironclad would have been destroyed if only it had been in sight for another thirty minutes.[60]

With the opportunity of destroying one of the enemy's most powerful iron ships foiled by a fluke of nature, General Clingman was in no mood to hear excuses from the ineffective *Hunley* crew. Shortly after writing his report on the matter, Clingman learned that the *Hunley's* attempt at another nocturnal patrol had been scrubbed. "The torpedo boat started at sunset but returned as they state because of an accident," he lamented to his aide, Capt. W. F. Nance. "Whitney says that though McClintock is timid, yet it shall go tonight unless the weather is bad." Clingman's hopes were dashed again a few hours later when he discovered that the boat remained moored in place. "The torpedo boat has not gone out. I do not think it will render any service under its present management."[61]

Clingman's last communication sealed the fate of the small boat and her crew. Within twenty-four hours the *Hunley* was seized by military authorities and turned over to officers of the Confederate Navy.

◆   ◆   ◆

On the same day that the *Hunley* was seized from her owners, a letter was sent from the Washington Navy Department to Admiral Dahlgren outlining the current situation in regard to his submarine request of August 11. "The Department has written to Rear-Admiral Paulding to enquire if such submarine boats as you refer to in your No. 76 can be made by the parties named," explained Gideon Welles, "and if so, to have them prepared."[62]

◆　　◆　　◆

The circumstances surrounding the *Hunley's* sudden seizure are unclear. Theodore Honour, a soldier stationed at Fort Johnson, wrote his wife Beckie about the affair less than a week after it took place. "You doubtless remember, and perhaps you saw while in the city the iron torpedo boat which certain parties brought from Mobile to blow up the *Ironside*. They have been out three times without accomplishing anything," he continued, "and the government suspecting something wrong, proposed to them to allow a Naval officer to go with them on their next trial, which they refused. The boat was therefore seized and yesterday some men from one of the gun boats was placed in her to learn how to work her, and go out and see what they could do."

The military could get a chance soon. By August 26 the underwater machine was under the full control of the Confederate Navy. The military bureaucracy had moved quickly, and a volunteer crew was now seated along the propeller shaft and a naval officer manned the helm. With the *Hunley* now in the possession of the Confederate government, a board of advisors was established to determine the value of the novel craft. The group of naval experts established the price of the unique diving boat at $27,500. Whether this sum was ever paid to the Singer group has not been established. All that is known for sure is that shortly after the submarine's confiscation, E. C. Singer and his assistant, J. D. Breaman, traveled to Richmond to meet with Navy Department officials concerning the continued deployment of underwater contact mines. Gus Whitney and Horace Hunley appear to have remained in Charleston, while McClintock and the rest of the submarine's crew returned to Mobile to continue planting and maintaining underwater obstructions in the harbor. Whether they left in anger or with a sense of relief is not known.[63]

Some of the members of the Singer group who had accompanied the submarine from Mobile remained behind in South Carolina in an advisory capacity. One of them penned a note recommending to General Beauregard on August 26 that "the bearer, C. L. Spraige, has come recommended as one ingenious in matters relating to submarine torpedoes and is directed to report to you to be attached to the submarine vessel of Whitney and company." Spraige, the note continued, "may be of service to the Naval officer who has volunteered to take that vessel in hand, and it were well to place them in communication as also with Mr. Whitney." Whitney's involvement with the submarine after its seizure is unclear. The aforementioned note at least implies that he remained behind in some position of authority or involvement with the *Hunley*. Sadly, he would not live long enough to witness the boat's climatic triumph—or suffer the consequences of its fate. A short time after the above order was issued, Gus Whitney, chief spokesman and part owner of the *Hunley*, died of pneumonia. Perhaps he contracted the illness as a result of his nocturnal activities aboard the damp submarine. The unfortunate Whitney can thus perhaps be considered the first casualty associated with the *Hunley*, which many would come to describe as a "peripatetic coffin."[64]

The new volunteer commander of the small submarine was Lt. John A. Payne, a distinguished veteran of the Confederate Navy recently assigned to the Charleston-based ironclad *CSS Chicora*. Payne's crewmen also were drawn from the ironclad and included Charles Hasker, an English immigrant who had served as a boatswain aboard the *CSS Virginia* during her duel with the *Monitor*. Recently promoted to lieutenant, Hasker was good friends with Payne and shared his interest in the submarine torpedo boat from Mobile. Payne was also experienced in combat. A little more than a year before he had served aboard one of the *Virginia's* support vessels during her short but spectacular career in Hampton Roads. With the fall of Norfolk and the scuttling of the ironclad, Payne had been reassigned to the naval force operating in Charleston Harbor. He had taken a keen interest in the *Hunley* ever since her arrival in the city, and eagerly volunteered to take command of her once the navy had taken control of the craft. The new commander was soon able to pilot the small submarine with some ability, and could be seen diving the boat under numerous ships at anchor around the harbor shortly after taking command. A daring officer with little regard for caution, he wasted no time preparing his raw crew of sailors for action against the ever-growing enemy fleet.[65]

James McClintock did not seem to think much of placing a raw crew on board the submarine, and he implied as much to Matthew Maury after the war. "The boat and machinery was so very simple, that many persons at first inspection believed that they could work the boat without practice, or experience," McClintock remembered, "and although I endeavored to prevent inexperienced persons from going underwater in the boat, I was not always successful in preventing them." McClintock was undoubtedly referring to the eager Lieutenant Payne and his crew of neophyte submariners.[66]

It was shortly after the seamen from the *Chicora* volunteered for duty on the *Hunley* that disaster struck. After diving and surfacing the submarine several times around the harbor during the afternoon of August 29, Payne ordered his crew to head for the docks at Fort Johnson. Either while the submarine was approaching the busy mooring site or shortly after she had tied up, something occurred that caused the small craft to submerge without warning and while the hatches were still open. There are several conflicting accounts relating to the cause of the accident. Probably the most likely description of what went so terribly wrong that day was based on an account told to historian Simon Lake in 1898 by Charles Hasker, who had paid a visit to Lake's New Jersey home to examine the inventor's recently completed submarine boat *Argonaut*. "When experimenting with the *Argonaut*," recalled Lake, "I received a visit from Charles H. Hasker, of Richmond, Virginia. He had volunteered as one of the party to try the *Hunley*." According to Hasker, the *Hunley* . . .

> parted away from the dock in tow of the gunboat *Ettawan* [*Ettiwan*] by a line thrown over the hatch combing. She had been trimmed down so that she had very little freeboard, and as she gained headway she started to 'sheer' due to her peculiar flatiron-shaped bow.
>
> Lieutenant Payne who was in command, attempted to throw the tow line off the hatch combing, but got caught in the bight of the line. On his struggle to free himself he knocked a prop from under the tiller of the horizontal diving rudder, which had been set to hold the bow up. As soon as the prop was knocked out the tiller dropped down and inclined the horizontal rudder to dive, and the vessel dove with her hatches open.
>
> Lieutenant Payne freed himself, and Charles Hasker managed to get partly out of one of the hatches before the vessel sank, but the inrushing force of the water closed the hatch door, which caught him by

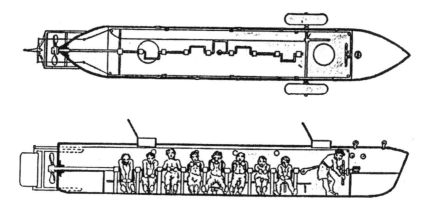

This sketch of the *Hunley* appeared in the January 1899 edition of *McClure's Magazine*. It was drawn by *Hunley* survivor Charles Hasker while visiting New Jersey submarine designer Simon Lake in 1897.

the calf of his leg, and he was carried with the vessel to the bottom in forty-two feet of water. However he maintained his presence of mind, and when the vessel became full it balanced the pressure so he could release himself from the hatch cover. He was a good swimmer and escaped to the surface. Two men escaped from the other hatch. The other five members of the crew were drowned in the vessel.[67]

Although the *Hunley* was known thereafter (and today as well) as a dangerous craft, one of her builders and probably her first commander, James McClintock, disagreed. "Although she proved fatal to a number of persons," he explained, " it was from no fault of the boat, or machinery, but want of sufficient knowledge of those in charge of the boat." Theodore Honour, the soldier stationed at Fort Johnson where the tragedy took place, confirmed McClintock's assessment that the deaths were the result of accident and not a design defect with the boat. "Just as they were leaving the wharf at Fort Johnson, where I was myself a few minutes before," he explained to his wife in a letter home on August 30, "an accident happened which caused the boat to go under the water before they were prepared for such a thing, and five out of the nine went down in her and were drowned. The other four made their escape. They had not up to last night recovered either the boat or the bodies. Poor fellows, they were five in one coffin."[68]

The *Charleston Post and Courier* reported the unhappy event to the citizens of the city on the front page of the next morning's edition. "Unfortunate Accident," shouted the headline. "On Saturday last while Lieutenants Payne and Hasker, of the Confederate Navy, were about experimenting with a boat in the harbor, she parted from her moorings and became suddenly submerged, carrying down with her five seamen who were drowned. The boat and bodies had not been recovered up to a late hour on Sunday. Four of men belonged to the gunboat *Chicora,* and were named Frank Doyle, John Kelly, Michael Cane and Nicholas Davis. The fifth man, whose name we did not learn, was attached to the *Palmetto State.*" A sailor on board the *Palmetto State* was struck by the sudden and horrible death suffered by his comrade. "We had quite a sad accident yesterday," he wrote in a letter home. "A 'machine' we had here and which carried eight or ten men, by some mismanagement filled with water and sank, drowning five men, one belonging to our vessel, and the others to the *Chicora.* They were all volunteers for the expedition and fine men too, the best we had. It has cast quite a gloom over us. Strange, isn't it, that while we hear with indifference of men being killed all around us, the drowning of one should effect us so."[69]

Although some of the crew were dead, the boat was still intact and salvageable. On September 1, three days after the *Hunley* disappeared off the end of the Fort Johnson wharf, General Beauregard utilized rather cryptic language to instruct Brig. Gen. Roswell Ripley, the commander of the First Military District on the far side of Charleston Harbor, to "Fish Torpedo still at bottom of bay, no one working on it. Adopt immediate measures to have it raised at once. Put proper person in charge of the work. Inform Lieutenant Payne of my orders." The monumental task of raising the heavy iron machine was given to two civilian divers named Angus Smith and David Broadfoot. These two Scottish immigrants held a virtual diving monopoly around Charleston Harbor and had been employed by the government on several occasions.[70]

The two underwater adventurers gathered up their own crew and set course with Lieutenant Payne for the unlucky wharf at Fort Johnson. It

did not take long after Smith and Broadfoot arrived at their site of operations for them to realize that they would be conducting their salvage
efforts almost under the guns of the enemy. Fort Sumter, only a few hundred yards away, was under a slow continuous bombardment, and the
sounds of explosions shattering her walls and splitting the warm summer air were heard by everyone at Fort Johnson.

For well over a week both Angus Smith and David Broadfoot groped
around the cold dark bottom of Charleston Harbor in their heavy lead
diving boots, attaching ropes and chains to the hull of the dormant submarine. The work was tedious and difficult. Finally, on or about September 13, the two exhausted divers were finally able to free the unlucky
Hunley from the black mud at the bottom of Charleston Harbor and
hoist her slowly to the surface. Once there, a pump was installed to remove the seawater, and within a short time the boat regained positive
buoyancy and once again floated at the Fort Johnson wharf. Once the
water was removed, the grisly task of removing the bodies of the unfortunate seamen was undertaken.[71]

By the time the *Hunley* was pried loose from the depths, Morris Island was under Federal control. On the night of September 6, with all
hope of holding out against the Federal onslaught gone, the soldiers
holding Battery Wagner drove iron spikes into the touch holes of their
artillery pieces and abandoned the position. Fort Sumter was now within
point blank range of the Federal guns.

◆　◆　◆

As General Beauregard pondered what to do, if anything, about the
Hunley's fatal plunge, Gideon Welles sent Admiral Dahlgren on September 11 a discouraging dispatch. In reference to your application "to
have submarine boats forwarded to you," explained the Navy Secretary,
"I have enclosed herewith a copy of a letter from Captain Drayton, assistant inspector of ordnance at New York, in which he states that nothing can be done towards their construction without further details and
more definite instructions." Although Welles was dropping the ball back
into Dahlgren's lap, work was apparently still progressing on the admiral's underwater idea. By early October, Dahlgren may have accepted
the secret delivery of at least two small submarines.[72]

◆   ◆   ◆

On the afternoon of September 19, the answer as to what to do with the submarine boat arrived at General Beauregard's headquarters in the form of a letter. It had been written earlier that same day by Horace Hunley, who wanted to take charge and recrew the unlucky boat himself. "I am part owner of the torpedo boat the *Hunley*," he began, and "have been interested in building this description of boat since the beginning of the war, and furnished the means entirely of building the predecessor of this boat, which was lost in an attempt to blow up a Federal vessel off Fort Morgan in Mobile Harbor. I feel therefore a deep interest in its success." Having established his credentials and patriotism to the general, Hunley jumped to the real reason for his letter. "I propose if you will place the boat in my hands to furnish a crew (in whole or in part) from Mobile who are well acquainted with its management and make the attempt to destroy a vessel of the enemy as early as practicable."[73]

Beauregard mulled the offer over for three days before finally reaching a decision. Writing through his chief of staff Jordan, the general informed the city's arsenal commander, Maj. J. T. Trezevant, that the boat was now in the hands of Capt. H. L. Hunley. Beauregard appreciated that swift cooperation from Trezevant was needed in order to get the submarine ready for action. "With a view to prompt repairs . . ." directed aide Jordan, "I am instructed to request you to have all work done for Capt. Hunley that he may require with the utmost celerity and to supply such material as he will requisition as the mechanics under his control can apply. His requisitions will be approved at these Head Quarters." According to Beauregard's postwar recollections, "After the recovery of the sunken boat, Mr. Hunley came from Mobile, bringing with him Lieutenant Dixon, of the 21st Alabama Volunteers, who had successfully experimented with the boat in the Harbor of Mobile, and under him another crew volunteered to work it." To Beauregard, Hunley probably seemed to be the logical successor to command the boat. However, whether Hunley had any practical training with the submarine up to this time is not altogether clear. Beauregard's statement is awkwardly written, and he could have been referring to either man—Hunley or Dixon—in reference to the successful experimentation of the machine in Mobile. It seems logical to assume Hunley had some experience inside the craft, but whether or not he had actually been at the forward diving planes will probably never be known.[74]

While an anxious Hunley monitored the repairs to his namesake boat, a new crew to man the resurrected submarine was being selected from those who had built and tested her in far away Alabama. It is possible that some of these men had been part of James McClintock's crew, recently returned from Charleston after the military authorities seized the boat. If so, they appreciated the perils that awaited them outside that besieged harbor. In 1902, forty years after the events in questions, William Alexander remembered the exciting time and activities at the Park and Lyons Mobile shop:

> General Beauregard . . . turned the craft over to a volunteer crew from Mobile known as the 'Hunley and Parks crew,' Captain Hunley and Thomas Parks, a member of the firm in whose shop the boat had been built, were in charge, with Brockband, Patterson, McHugh, Marshall, White, Beard and another (Lt. Dixon) as the crew. Until the day this crew left Mobile, it was understood that I was to be one of them, but at the last moment Mr. Parks prevailed on me to let him take my place. Nearly all of the men had some experience in the boat before leaving Mobile, and were well qualified to operate her.[75]

Whether this new crew would have any better luck with the boat remained to be seen.

◆　　◆　　◆

At about the same time the "Hunley and Parks crew" was being selected in Mobile, far to the north at New York's Brooklyn Navy Yard, a Union officer was about to test a small submarine the navy hoped would soon be at work removing obstructions from beneath the surface of a blockaded Rebel harbor. During the spring of 1862, Capt. Edward B. Hunt of the Army Corps of Engineers had been selected to take part in a special—and perhaps secret—submarine project the Navy Department was staging off Long Island, New York. Hunt was promoted to major on March 3, 1863, and by the early fall of that year had developed a small

Horace Hunley's September 19, 1863, letter to General Beauregard in which he requested command of the submarine boat that bore his name. *National Archives*

one-man submarine boat that may have been similar in appearance to the vessel designed by Ensign Hartshorn several months earlier.[76]

Unfortunately neither diagrams nor a history of this vessel have yet turned up, and it may be that the project was eventually abandoned following submerged tests conducted at the Brooklyn Navy Yard. The underwater tests were not successful and cost the life of Major Hunt, who died a horrible (and lingering) death of asphyxiation after his submarine was trapped on the bottom. According to naval doctor Thomas L. Smith of the U.S. Naval Hospital in Brooklyn, New York, Hunt "departed this life, at the U.S. Navy Hospital . . . at one o'clock P.M. October 2, 1863." The unfortunate officer "died of the effects of the respiration of the Mephitic air [carbon dioxide or air exhausted of oxygen and containing chiefly nitrogen] evolved in the hold of the vessel, where he was making experiments with his 'Submarine Battery.'" How, exactly, Hunt was recovered from his submarine still alive is not known, but he was "received into this Hospital on the afternoon of September 30th, the day of the accident, in a comatose condition, in which he continued until one o'clock P.M. October 2nd when he died."[77]

An article the next day in the *New York Times* confirms both Hunt's death and the existence of the submarine, which the paper claimed was "well known." The death of Major E. B. Hunt, "which occurred at the Brooklyn Navy Yard," recounted the article,

> will cause profound regrets among a large and devoted circle of friends, both in the army and private life. Major Hunt had, it is well known, been engaged for many months in the construction of a new submarine battery of his own invention, which promised to give the most important results.
>
> For many months subsequent to the opening of the war he was engaged in the construction of the fortifications of Key West, Florida. Sometime after his return North he commenced devoting himself to the modeling of his submarine, from which he was up to the time of his death, sanguine of obtaining the most gratifying and valuable results.
>
> He died, although not on the battle-field, yet in harness, devoted, with all his powers of soul, mind and heart to the service of his country. His sad death takes from our midst one of the noblest and purest of spirits.[78]

Two months after Major Hunt's tragic accident, a government pension of $25 a month was allotted to his widow and eight-year-old son. Of more historical significance is the fact that Major Hunt's death was the first Union submarine fatality of the Civil War. Like his Confederate counterpart, the late Charles G. Wilkinson of Savannah, Georgia, Hunt died as a result of operations in a submarine vessel of his own design.[79]

◆   ◆   ◆

About the same time that Hunt was lying comatose in the Brooklyn Navy Yard Hospital, the second crew of Mobile, Alabama, submariners was en route to South Carolina to take over the submarine that had already cost the lives of five of their fellow countrymen. From the sparse information that exists relating to that first week of renewed operations, it appears that Lieutenant Dixon was in actual command of the submarine. His first officer was Thomas Park, the son of the owner of Park and Lyons. It was Park's duty to man the aft ballast pumps and sea valves.

With the little *Hunley* once again in the hands of a crew practiced in the operations of the machine, she was once more seen moving and diving about the harbor by soldiers and sailors who only a few weeks earlier referred to her as a "peripatetic coffin." While newly mounted Federal batteries on Morris Island continued their slow bombardment of Charleston, the crew of the *Hunley* continued training by staging mock attacks against the *CSS Indian Chief* anchored in the Cooper River.[80]

◆   ◆   ◆

While the Mobile-based *Hunley* crew continued training in preparation for a real attack against a Federal warship, an interesting observation was made by Confederate sentries stationed on Sullivan's Island. "There is no material change in the fleet off the harbor this morning . . . ," recorded a watch officer on October 4 in the Charleston Harbor Journal of Operations. "Several large vessels arrived today from the north. It is not believed they brought any troops. Probably loaded with ordnance and other stores. A small submarine affair was observed today with the fleet and was towed over the bar and was brought inside by one of the blockading vessels."

A Federal submarine operating with the fleet off Charleston? The entry is the first solid evidence that Admiral Dahlgren may have taken delivery of at least one of the small submarines he had requested two months earlier. If so, the affair must have been a closely guarded secret, for no mention of a submarine vessel appears in any official South Atlantic

Blockading Squadron document, dispatch, or communication circulated during this period, or in any of Dahlgren's official papers. The following day, October 5, another entry was scribbled in the Charleston Harbor Journal of Operations substantiating and building on the previous day's observations: "There are inside the bar this morning the *Ironsides,* four Monitors, two mortar and seven gunboats plus 20 supply vessels, also a small craft having the appearance of a submarine boat."[81]

The sighting by the Confederates of a submarine boat operating before Charleston with the blockading fleet was the subject of some concern and speculation. Three days later on October 8, the movements of the boat—or perhaps boats—was again noted and recorded in the Journal of Operations: "The two nondescript affairs previously reported inside the bar are now thought to be constructed to remove torpedoes," wrote one officer, substantiating that there were a pair of submarines with the blockading fleet. His observation also is in line with what Dahlgren had proposed they be used for, i.e., removing obstructions. "As seen from Sullivan's Island," continued the recorded observation, "they are described as elliptical in shape, low in the water and flush deck." Since Union documents pertaining to these two mysterious vessels have not come to light, how they were used and what their ultimate fate was is subject to speculation. They were never seen again by the Confederate sentries on Sullivan's Island, and thus the October 8, 1863, entry in the Charleston Harbor Journal of Operations is the last mention of them.[82]

While Beauregard and his staff no doubt discussed the sudden appearance of small submarines off their city, a crew of Charleston-based naval personnel—not the crew of the *Hunley*—were planning an attack on the blockading fleet with a secret semi-submersible war vessel of their own. The attack craft was a cigar-shaped wooden boat about 50' long and steam-driven. Operated by a crew of three, it made about seven knots. The Federals referred to this style of torpedo boat as a "David," and although several were built, none were christened with formal names. Although not a true submersible, the method of attack was similar to the *Hunley* and other submarines, and her success is worthy of noting.

On the night of October 5, 1863, the day after Admiral Dahlgren's assumed submarine boat was first detected, the "David" made a nocturnal attack on the most powerful ship in the blockading fleet, the USS *New Ironsides*. With an explosive device attached to the end of a long spar, and her narrow hull all but hidden beneath the dark surface, the sleek wooden cigar had been able to approach the massive vessel undetected. When the contact torpedo slammed into the warships's thick iron hull at 9:15 p.m., a huge geyser of water and fragments was thrown high into the air, sending some of the water into the "David's" tiny smokestack. The seawater extinguished the torpedo boat's fires and the vessel was swamping badly. Lt. William T. Glassel, the torpedo boat's commander, ordered his men to abandon ship. Within minutes after jumping overboard, Glassel and his fireman were both captured and taken aboard the wounded ship. The *New Ironsides'* commanding officer, Capt. Stephen C. Rowan, filed an official report of the incident the following day:

> About a minute before the explosion, a small object was seen by the sentinels and hailed by them as a boat, and also by Mr. Howard, Officer of the Deck, from the gangway, receiving no answer, he gave the order 'fire into her,' the sentinels delivered their fire, and immediately the ship received a very severe explosion, throwing a column of water upon the Spar deck, and into the engine room. The object fired at proved to be, (as I subsequently learned from one of the prisoners), a Torpedo Steamer, shaped like a cigar, fifty feet long by five feet in diameter, and of great speed, and so submerged, that the only portion of her visible was the combings of her hatch, which were only two feet above the waters edge, and about ten feet in length.
>
> The Torpedo boat was commanded by Lt. Commander Glassel, formally a Lieutenant in our navy, and now our prisoner. He states that the explosion threw a column of water over the little craft, which put out the fires and left it without motive power, and it drifted past the ship.
>
> Nothing could be seen from the gun deck and to fire at random would endanger the fleet of transport and other vessels near us. The Marine guard and musketeers on the Spar deck saw a small object at which a very severe fire was kept up, until it drifted out of sight. Two of our cutters were dispatched in search of it, but returned without success.
>
> I hope our fire destroyed the Torpedo steamer. Lt. Commander Glassel acknowledges that he and Engineer Tombs, and the Pilot, who

constituted the crew at the time of the explosion, were compelled to abandon the vessel, and being provided with life preservers swam for their lives. Glassel hailed one of our coal schooners as he drifted past, and was rescued from a grave he designed for the crew of this ship.[83]

Unbeknownst to Captain Rowan, as the little "David" slowly drifted away from the New Ironsides, Assistant Engineer Tomb had swum back to the crippled vessel and found the pilot, who could not swim, clinging to the rudder of the lifeless craft. The two men climbed aboard the vessel, relit the fire, and limped back into Charleston Harbor. Upon inspecting the craft the following day, her hull was found to contain no less than thirteen bullet holes, undeniable proof of the two men's narrow escape. The Federals were doubly fortunate. Not only did the New Ironsides not sink (although she was damaged worse than believed), but Commander Glassel and his fireman were both found to have detailed diagrams of the David in the pockets of their uniforms. Within hours, the entire blockading fleet had drawings of the vessel, along with a full description of her capabilities. "Among the many inventions with which I have been familiar," wrote Admiral Dahlgren, "I have seen none which have acted so perfectly at first trial. The secrecy, rapidity of movement, control of direction, and precise explosion indicate, I think the introduction of the torpedo element as a means of certain warfare. It can be ignored no longer."[84]

While Dahlgren was duly impressed with the invention, he put on quite a show for the general public over the attack. Both prisoners, he maintained, should be taken to New York Harbor, tried, and hanged "for using an engine of war not recognized by civilized nations." Privately, Dahlgren was so taken with the design of the "David" that early the following year he requested that "Torpedo Boats be made and sent here with dispatch; Length about forty feet—Diameter amidship five to six feet, and tapering to a point at each end—Small engine and propeller—an opening about fifteen feet above [smokestack], with a hatch combing to float not more than eighteen inches above water, somewhat as this sketch. I have already submitted a requisition on the Bureau of Construction for some craft of this kind which with the great mechanical facilities of the North, should be very quickly supplied."[85]

In the days following the attack on the *New Ironsides,* divers were dispatched to inspect the damage inflicted by the torpedo. The ship's external hull had only been slightly dented, and it was initially believed that the *New Ironsides* could remain on station with the rest of the blockading fleet. For several weeks she remained in position, but as the mounds of coal in her hull diminished, signs of interior damage were found. The ship's carpenter made an immediate inspection and recommended that repairs be made at once. On November 28, Captain Rowan sent a communication to Admiral Dahlgren stating that the *New Ironsides* was "very seriously injured, and ought to be sent home for repairs." The ship was dispatched to the Philadelphia Navy Yard but was unable to return to active service before the end of the war. The Federal navy kept the *New Ironsides'* damage a closely guarded secret, and Beauregard and his men never learned how effective the attack actually was until after the war was over.[86]

◆   ◆   ◆

As Admiral Dahlgren pondered the potential effectiveness of the newly discovered Confederate threat, the crew of another menace was honing its skills in the Cooper River. General Beauregard's confidence in the *Hunley* was probably restored as he and his men watched it surface, maneuver, and dive at will without incident. "Raining again this morning, and too hazy to get report on the fleet," recorded an officer in the Charleston Harbor Journal of Operations on October 15. The dreary overcast morning did not prevent the *Hunley's* men from continuing their training, and the confident submariners squeezed through the submarine's narrow hatches and took their places at the long propeller shaft. Lieutenant Dixon was absent, and Horace Hunley decided to take the boat out in his stead. He took his position standing in the forward hatch, a post that was, according to William Alexander, familiar to him. It was 9:25 a.m.[87]

The exact sequence of events that transpired within the submarine's cramped hull forever remains a mystery. No one standing on the Cooper River docks or crewed aboard the *Indian Chief* recorded that anything was awry with the boat that morning. The submarine was preparing to make a typical dive under the *Indian Chief,* and she approached the vessel in normal fashion. When the *Hunley* was about 200 feet off the starboard side of the ship, her diving planes were depressed and she disappeared beneath the surface at 9:35 a.m. Large gulps of bubbles were seen breaking the surface . . . and then nothing. For a second time the ill-fated submarine had taken her occupants on a fatal dive; this time, none would return.

"An unfortunate accident occurred this morning with the submarine boat, by which Captain H. L. Hunley and seven men lost their lives in an attempt to run under the navy receiving ship," is how the Charleston Harbor journal reads. "The boat left the wharf at 9:25 a.m. and disappeared at 9:35. As soon as she sunk air bubbles were seen to rise to the surface of the water, and from this fact it is supposed the hole in the top of the boat by which the men entered was not properly closed. It was impossible at the time to make any effort to rescue the unfortunate men, as the water was some 9 fathoms deep." The loss must have crushed General Beauregard's hopes for an effective Charleston-based submarine. "Lieutenant Dixon made repeated descents in the harbor of Charleston, diving under the navy receiving ship which lay at anchor there," he reported. "But one day when he was absent from the city, Mr. Hunley, unfortunately, wishing to handle the boat himself, made the attempt. It was readily submerged, but did not rise again to the surface, and all on board perished from asphyxiation." The iron boat had now cost the lives of two crews.[88]

Why had she sunk? Lieutenant Dixon had not encountered any serious problems with the boat, so perhaps the answer was human error. If the submarine could be found and raised, maybe what went wrong could be discovered and corrected. A search and salvage operation to locate and raise the missing *Hunley* was put into motion the following day. Once again Angus Smith and David Broadfoot donned their crude diving gear and returned to the black and muddy bottom of Charleston Harbor in search of the *Hunley.* On the same day the two divers began work, Brig. Gen. Roswell Ripley, who was engaged in defensive operations around Charleston, authorized Lieutenant Dixon and a companion to travel to Mobile and back. The determined Alabamian—the only surviving crew member—had not yet given up on the unlucky *Hunley.* Intent on making her a success, he intended to travel to Mobile to enlist the services of his friend and fellow engineering officer William Alexander, who was on detached duty in the Park and Lyons machine shop.[89]

◆   ◆   ◆

On the day the *Hunley* was declared lost, Maj. Gen. Jeremy F. Gilmer, the commander of the Engineering Office, Department of South Carolina, Georgia, and Florida, sat down at his desk and took his pen in hand. Gilmer, a career soldier who had been wounded at Shiloh, now had enough evidence to satisfy him that submarines were both a waste of money and lives. His letter was directed to Secretary of War James Seddon, and it outlined numerous design flaws in the submarine boat that the Triton Company (Senator A. J. Marshall's group) was proposing to build in Charleston. Gilmer viewed the submarine with such disfavor he recommended that neither government funding nor facilities be granted to the Virginia senator and his partners. "I examined carefully the plan of a boat intended for a submarine approach as proposed by Mr. A. J. Marshall of Richmond," began Gilmer, "and was forced to the conclusion that it must fail in practice, and for the following reasons:

1. The propelling power will prove insufficient for the management of the boat in a tide way.

2. The sacks for receiving air from the interior of the boat—thus giving greater buoyancy—are badly adjusted and in my opinion not reliable for the purpose intended should the boat sink to a depth greater than the length of the tubes projecting upwards from the deck. Water compartments that can be filled and emptied at will by force pumps are better and safer than air sacks.

3. The leverage of the air tubes will be too great for the stabilizing of a boat having only a five foot beam—and again it will not be possible for the 'lookout' to raise and lower himself in a tidal current with the facility described by Mr. Marshall.

4. The air pump is liable to get out of order, and should this occur when the boat is submerged, it causes the loss of boat and crew.

5. The arrangement for attaching the boat to a ship for adjusting a torpedo to the side or bottom are not explained.

6. The materials required for making the boat and marine armor (diving gear) can not be had in the Confederacy—It is proposed to build the boat of thick boiler plate iron—the armor of india rubber.

I can not recommend that the Government should furnish any materials for constructing boats after Mr. Marshall's plan, or even offer facilities for doing the work in the public shops.[90]

General Gilmer's death sentence for the Triton Company boat is not the end of the story for Senator Marshall's submarine. Six weeks later, a copy of the Triton Company's submarine plans were accidentally captured when two Mississippi mail couriers were surprised by a Union foraging party and taken prisoner. The plans which Gilmer reviewed with such disfavor in Charleston were considered so important by Maj. Gen. Nathaniel P. Banks, the Union Commander of the Department of the Gulf, that the diagrams were immediately forwarded to the Secretary of War in Washington. "A rebel mail was captured a few days since while its bearers were attempting to cross the Mississippi River near Tunica Bend," reported Banks through his chief of staff Charles P. Stone. "The capture was made by the Lieutenant-Colonel of the Sixth Regiment Michigan Volunteers, who was there with a foraging party." Although the letters were "mostly of an unimportant character," he continued,

one, which seems to be from the principal contractor for building torpedo vessels, gives instructions for the building of some west of the Mississippi River and for Texas. This letter, a copy of which is enclosed herewith, encloses the plan of construction of these torpedo vessels, which is also enclosed.

I would most respectfully recommend that a careful examination of this project be made by competent machinists, as it appears to me to be a feasible and dangerous one. The letter throws considerable light on the details of construction and use.

The War Department immediately turned Banks' diagrams and letters over to engineering officers, who in turn suggested that "the papers be submitted to the proper Navy Department for review."[91]

The captured plans were drawn up by C. Williams, one of the four founding partners of the Richmond-based Triton Company. Unfortu-

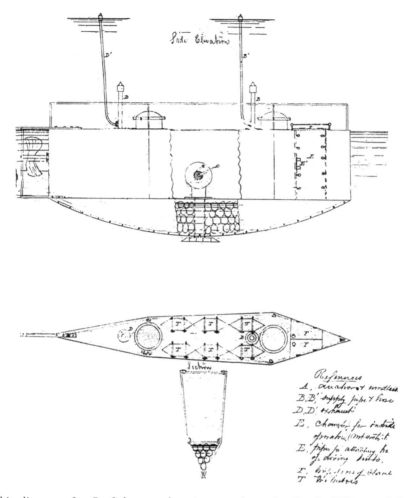

This diagram of a Confederate submarine was drawn by Mr. C. Williams of the Richmond-based Triton Company. This plan, together with other secret information, was captured by the Federals. *National Archives*

nately the letter that once accompanied these fascinating diagrams has either been misplaced or lost. This is indeed unfortunate, for it would have shed more light on the clandestine activities of the Triton Company, which was in all probability "the principal contractor for building torpedo vessels" referred to by Banks. The plans were a copy of the same diagrams inspected by Charleston's Major General Gilmer, and most of the boat's unique features are mentioned in Gilmer's summary to James Seddon. Although Gilmer may have had an unfavorable opinion of these diagrams, several feasible and ingenious devices were incorporated in the vessel.[92]

The dimensions and features of this undersea craft suggest it was an upgraded version of the submarine vessel seen and reported on by Union spy "Mrs. Baker" in 1861. Of all the submarines known to have been built in the Confederacy, only those constructed in Richmond at the Tredegar Iron Works incorporated the use of a diver housed in a "false bow." Mrs. Baker, Allan Pinkerton's operative, reported to her boss that the vessel she witnessed in the James River had men "provided with submarine diving armor, which enabled them to work under the water and attach the magazine to the ship intended to blow up." These diagrams, drawn two years later by Mr. Williams, also incorporate the use of a diver. There were other similarities as well. "The only visible sign of its existence was a large float that rested on the surface of the water," reported Baker, "and which was connected with the vessel below, designed to supply the men who operated it with air." The submarine described in the Triton Company's diagram also calls for the use of a floating snorkel assembly attached to air pumps within the vessel. The Triton Company, it will be recalled, was a Richmond-based business. Thus some or all of its members may have been associated with or knew of William Cheeney's early war submarine experiments in the James River. If so, they may have taken the knowledge gained during those experiments to design the vessel portrayed in the captured diagrams. The connection admittedly is but a theory, although a logical one given the similarities involved.

The Williams (Triton Company) boat was built to operate at a relatively shallow depth. This drawback was pointed out by Major General Gilmer when he reported, "should the boat sink to a depth greater than the length of the tubes projecting upward from the deck," the result would be a loss of the boat and crew. A detailed set of instructions as to how the diver was to be supplied with air were once enclosed with the diagrams but are no longer available. Their absence makes it difficult to interpret exactly how the vessel was to be handled. The little submarine was to be manned by a crew of three men: one to turn the propeller shaft, one to steer the vessel, and one stationed on the outside in "submarine armor" to fasten the torpedo to the hull of the intended victim. The hoses attached to floats on the surface—marked "B.B. supply pipe and hose" and "D. D. exhaust pipe and hose"—supplied air to the men inside as well as the diver in the forward chamber outside. The two attachments pictured within the "Chamber for outside operations," according to the diagrams, are "Pipes for attaching hose of diving suits." Since two pipes are pictured, it is assumed that one was designed to introduce air into the diver's helmet, while the other pipe served as an exhaust system which flowed from the diver back to the interior of the submarine. If this was indeed the arrangement intended, it would have eliminated bubbles that could have been seen by enemy sentries. The "anchor and Windlass" seem to be the only mechanism by which the vessel was to be sunk and raised, for no ballast compartments appear on either the interior or exterior of the vessel. No records exist indicating whether or not this Triton Company boat was ever built. Judging from the description of the letter that once accompanied this diagram, it seems possible that others had already been fabricated by the Triton Company, for General Stone, in his communication to the War Department, claimed that the diagram "seems to be from the principal contractor for building torpedo vessels." Stone's statement at least implies that he believed other such vessels had already been built, or he had evidence to that effect.[93]

One final piece of this submarine puzzle was written fifty-five years later. Isaac Ball, who had close personal ties to the Smith family of Columbia, Tennessee—the same Smith family of which Reverend Franklin Smith was a member—penned a letter in 1918 to a family friend discussing Reverend Smith's Civil War submarine diagrams and early-war proposals. "Unknown to Rev. Smith at the time," wrote Ball, "his brother was also engaged in submarine design and construction in Charleston, South Carolina." It will be recalled that Virginia Senator A. J. Marshall and Triton Company founder had requested that engineer and machinist Thomas M. Smith—who according to Senator Marshall had "a familiarity with the subject" of submarine vessels—be detailed to the Triton Company. Was a submarine built (or in the process of being built when the war ended) in Charleston by Reverend Smith's brother and the Richmond-based Triton Company in spite of General Gilmer's lack of confidence in the project? The secrecy surrounding this subject accounts for the paucity of surviving records, so we probably will never know if the *Hunley* had direct competition in Charleston.[94]

◆ ◆ ◆

If another boat was indeed being built in Charleston by the Triton Company, General Beauregard probably had as little faith in its efficacy as he did in the *Hunley*. The Singer Submarine Corps' most promising boat was stuck firmly in the muddy bottom of the city's harbor, a mass coffin holding the corpses of eight men, including Horace Hunley. Divers Smith and Broadfoot were once again groping about in the darkness in search of the ill-fated boat. On October 18, three days after the *Hunley* disappeared beneath the hull of the *Indian Chief,* an officer recorded that "Mr. Smith provided with submarine armor, found the sunken submarine boat today in 9 fathoms of water. The engineering department was instructed to furnish Mr. Smith all facilities in the way of ropes, chains, etc., that an attempt might be made to recover the boat."[95]

The unlucky submarine was not found resting on the bottom, as had been the case at Fort Johnson. Instead, her bow was buried deep in the mud with her iron hull protruding from the bottom at about a 30-degree angle. Further investigation by the pair of divers determined that the hatches remained bolted shut from the inside, with the emergency drop weights still attached to the bottom of the keel. Since there were no visible holes found in the vessel, it appeared that the cabin had not flooded. It was obvious that the mystery to this tragic sinking would not be solved until the submarine was once again hoisted to the surface and her narrow hatches forced open. The task of raising the boat was a difficult one, and she did not break the surface of the harbor until November 7, just over three weeks after the *Hunley* had taken down her second crew.[96]

A crowd, some certainly drawn to the event out of morbid curiosity, gathered about the dock as authorities prepared to open the *Hunley's* hatches. Years after the war, General Beauregard still could not shake his reaction to the scene that met his eyes when the hatches were swung wide. "When the boat was discovered, raised and opened the spectacle was indescribably ghastly," remembered Charleston's commander. "The unfortunate men were contorted into all kinds of horrible attitudes, some clutching candles, evidently endeavoring to force open the manholes; others lying in the bottom, tightly grappled together, and the blackened faces of all presented the expression of their despair and agony."[97]

Were it not for postwar writings on the subject by William Alexander, the cause of the unfortunate accident would have remained a mystery. In an article he penned for the *New Orleans Picayune* on June 29, 1902, Alexander described exactly what happened on the tragic morning thirty-nine years earlier:

The position in which the boat was found on the bottom of the river, the condition of the apparatus discovered after it was raised and pumped out, and the position of the bodies in the boat, furnished a full explanation for her loss. The boat, when found, was lying on the bottom at an angle of about 35 degrees, the bow deep in the mud. The bolting-down bolts of each cover had been removed. When the hatch covers were lifted considerable air and gas escaped. Captain Hunley's body was forward, with his head in the forward hatchway, his right hand on top of his head. In his left hand was a candle that had never been lighted, the sea-cock on the forward end, or *Hunley's* ballast tank, was wide open, the cock-wrench not on the plug, but lying on the bottom of the boat. Mr. Park's body was found with his head in the after hatchway, his right hand above his head. He also had been trying to raise the hatch cover, but the pressure was too great. The sea-cock to his tank was properly closed, and the tank was nearly empty. The other bodies were floating in the water. Hunley and Parks were undoubtedly asphyxiated, the others drowned. The bolts that had held the iron keel ballast had been partly turned, but not sufficient to release it.

In the light of these conditions, we can easily depict before our minds, and almost readily explain, what took place in the boat during the moments immediately following its submergence. Captain Hunley's practice with the boat had made him quite familiar and expert in handling her, and this familiarity produced at this time forgetfulness. It was found in practice to be easier on the crew to come to the surface by giving the pumps a few strokes and ejecting some of the water ballast, than by the momentum of the boat operating on the elevated fins. At this time the boat was under way, lighted through the dead-lights in the hatchways. He partly turned the fins to go down, but thought, no doubt, that he needed more ballast and opened his sea-cock. Immediately the boat was in total darkness. He then undertook to light the candle. While trying to do this the tank quietly flooded, and under great pressure the boat sank very fast and soon overflowed [into the cabin proper], and the first intimation they would have of anything being wrong was the water rising fast, but noiselessly, about their feet in the bottom of the boat. They tried to release the iron keel ballast, but did not turn the keys quite far enough, therefore failed. The water soon forced the air to the top of the boat and into the hatchways, where Captains Hunley and Parks were found. Parks had pumped his ballast tank dry, and no doubt Captain Hunley had exhausted himself on his pump, but he had forgotten that he had not closed his sea-cock.[98]

The day before the divers made their final adjustments to the numerous chains that would hoist the silent submarine back into the world of the living, orders issued from Beauregard's Charleston headquarters authorizing that "Captain Hunley [be] buried with the military honors due to an officer of his rank." Two days later, Hunley's remains, together with those of his crew of Mobile adventurers, were laid to rest in Magnolia Cemetery on the banks of the Cooper River. The *Charleston Mercury* covered the solemn ceremony and wrote about it on November 9. "Last Honors to a Devoted Patriot," read the headline:

> The remains of Captain Horace L. Hunley were yesterday interred in Magnolia Cemetery. His body was followed to the grave by a military escort, and a large number of citizens.
>
> The deceased was a native of Tennessee, but for many years past has been a resident of New Orleans. Possessed of an ample fortune, in the prime of manhood—for he was only thirty-six at the time of his

death—with everything before him to make life attractive, he came to Charleston, and voluntarily joined in a patriotic enterprise which promised success, but which was attended with great peril. Though feeling, as appears from the last letter which he wrote to his friends, a presentiment that he would perish in the adventure, he gave his whole heart, undeterred by the foreboding, to the undertaking, declaring that he would gladly sacrifice his life in the cause. That presentiment has been mournfully fulfilled. Yet who shall call that fate a sad one, which associates the name of its victim with those of his country's most unselfish martyrs?"[99]

◆ ◆ ◆

On October 18, 1863, while Smith and Broadfoot were beginning their search for the lost *Hunley*, Lt. George Dixon and Henry Dillingham walked through the doorway of the busy Park and Lyons machine shop in Mobile. It was probably only then that the machine shop's workers learned of the submarine's most recent fatal mishap that had taken the life of Horace Hunley and so many of their friends—including Mr. Park's son. One of the engineers there was another member from the 21st Alabama, William Alexander, who was also intimately familiar with the boat. The *Hunley*, Dixon informed his friend, needed another crew.[100]

◆ ◆ ◆

As the cold winter winds were blowing across the harbor city of Newark, New Jersey, on November 2, 1863, an underwater enthusiast named Scovel Merriam entered into a contract with Augusta Price and Cornelius Bushnell for one iron submarine boat of Merriam's design. According to the guidelines of the agreement, Bushnell and Price would fund the venture up to an estimated cost of $15,000. Within a year, the union formed by the partnership would be incorporated into an enterprise known as the American Submarine Company, and the boat fabricated by the partners became the property of the United States Navy. Unfortunately for the Union war effort, cost overruns and construction

The *Intelligent Whale* (photo taken at the New York Navy Yard on July 27, 1915) was an experimental submarine built in 1863–1864 but not completed until 1866. A number of sailors died in her during sea trials. *U. S. Naval Historical Center*

delays kept the submarine in dry dock until April of 1866, exactly one year following the end of the war.[101]

◆ ◆ ◆

While Merriam, Price, and Bushnell hammered out the details of their joint submarine venture in faraway New Jersey, a discouraged General Beauregard was trying to send a telegram to Lt. George Dixon in Mobile. The message, dispatched from Charleston on November 5, was not good news for Dixon and his associates. "I can have nothing more to do with that Submarine boat," concluded Beauregard. "It is more dangerous to those who use it than the enemy." Dixon, however, probably never saw the telegram. He was not assigned to any post in the city, and the message was addressed simply, "Dixon Geo. E. Lieutenant. Mobile, Ala." No response to the message was received in Charleston.[102]

Whether Dixon saw the telegram or not, General Beauregard harbored grave reservations regarding the continued use of the *Hunley*.

Even though Dixon had proven that he could safely operate her, Horace Hunley—a man who had been involved with these machines since the beginning of the war, and who had personally requested that the craft be put under his control—went down with her. Although it is not known exactly when Dixon arrived back in Charleston, he and his comrades were in the city no later than the afternoon of November 12. The *Hunley* had only recently disgorged her gruesome contents, and Dixon hurried to examine the boat shortly after reaching the city. It was presumably this inspection of the salvaged machine, coupled with interviews with those who had removed the bodies, that helped determine the cause of the accident.[103]

Dixon immediately pled his case to an unmoved Beauregard. The Alabama engineer, however, was not easily dissuaded. Dixon, who had begun the war with a serious wound at Shiloh, "was very handsome, fair, nearly six feet tall, and of most attractive presence," remembered his former company commander long after the war. "I never knew a better man; and there never was a braver man in any service of any army." It was probably this air of self-confidence, dedication to duty, and unyielding faith in the capabilities of the *Hunley* that finally convinced the doubtful Beauregard to grant Dixon one last opportunity to command the small submarine in action against the Union blockading fleet. It had been close, for Beauregard changed his mind only after a lengthy discussion with Thomas Jordan, his trusted chief of staff. Dixon's cause was assisted by the presence of fellow engineer William Alexander. The submarine's former crew member had accompanied Dixon back to South Carolina to take over as the *Hunley's* first officer, meaning he would man the rear ballast tank pump and sea valves. Even with Alexander helping Dixon, Beauregard insisted on putting restrictions on the boat's use.[104]

Lieutenant Dixon immediately set out to make his endeavor a success, but the stench and rot clinging to the inside of the boat stopped him cold. In addition to brushes and soap, lime was needed to sanitize the *Hunley*. Dixon and his crew were not about to scrub the interior themselves. "Before I can proceed with my work of cleaning the Sub-Marine boat," he wrote Beauregard's chief of staff, "I shall have to request of you an order on the Quartermaster or Engineer Department for ten Negroes." Additional work on the boat also needed to be done at the city arsenal, and Dixon wanted Beauregard to issue the appropriate order allowing it to be completed. "In order to make all possible haste with this work, I would be pleased to have those orders granted at your earliest convenience," he concluded.[105]

Once the boat was scrubbed clean, Dixon determined to completely overhaul it. The force with which it struck the bottom on October 15 may well have caused some damage to the bow or forward diving planes, but she was in need of general maintenance regardless. The ten men assigned to assist him hoisted the *Hunley* from her slip in the harbor and placed her in dry dock for the repairs. She was positioned atop two wooden pilings on a Mount Pleasant dockside. With the *Hunley* cradled between the two beams, it would have been an easy task to turn the bolts that held the emergency drop weights attached to the bottom of the vessel. With these keel weights removed, the stuffing boxes that prevented the water from entering the vessel through the bolt holes could be repacked, as could the boxes that kept water from entering by way of the propeller shaft, diving planes, and snorkel assembly.

It was during this period of maintenance and repair that Mr. Williams, a member of the Richmond-based Triton Company, sent a letter in late November to the "Proprietors of the submarine torpedo boat at Charleston." Although the letter itself has long since disappeared, an annotation of its contents was recorded: "Mr. Williams requests attention to certain improvements in submarine operations described in enclosed communication . . ." What, exactly, were these "improvements" that the Triton Company was willing to share with the Singer group? Had the two groups been sharing information all along? Just how closely involved were these two clandestine organizations? Unless additional documentation comes to light, we will never have specific answers to these questions, or know whether any of Williams' suggestions were implemented on the *Hunley*.[106]

"We soon had the boat refitted and in good shape," remembered Alexander long after the war. Now that it was ready for additional sea trials, a crew had to be found. Dixon and Alexander already had two unidentified crew members with them in Charleston—perhaps they came with them from Mobile—so five more men were needed to fully man the submarine. Where would they come from? Alexander and Dixon repaired to General Beauregard's headquarters, where they "reported to General Jordan that she was ready for service, and asked for a crew." Although Beauregard had already given Dixon permission to repair and command the vessel, the issue of where the crew would be found generated some heated debate. "After many refusals and much discussion," Alexander wrote, "General Beauregard finally assented to our going aboard the Confederate receiving ship *Indian Chief* and calling for volunteers. He strictly enjoined upon us to give a full and clear explanation of the desperately hazardous nature of the service required."[107]

With the permission they needed to seek out a new crew, Lieutenants Dixon and Alexander walked down to the Cooper River docks, boarded a skiff, and were rowed out to the harborbound *Indian Chief.* After presenting Beauregard's orders to the vessel's captain, the entire ship's company was called to assemble on the quarterdeck. The selection of the *Indian Chief* was probably no accident. Her crew had seen the *Hunley* on numerous occasions propelling around the harbor and launching mock attacks against their ship. The crewmen were also aware of the submarine's tragic past, and that her last accident took place while she was attempting to dive beneath the *Indian Chief*'s hull. Still, whatever Dixon said that day was persuasive enough to cause several sailors to put aside their fears and step forward to crew the diving machine. "We had no difficulty in getting volunteers to man her," recalled Alexander, perhaps with some surprise. "I don't believe a man considered the danger which awaited him. The honor of being the first to engage the enemy in this novel way overshadowed all else."[108]

The rigorous nature demanded by undersea duty likely prompted Dixon and Alexander to select the most physically fit seamen available. The engineers knew well from firsthand experience that the new sailors would labor under grueling, claustrophobic, and cold conditions, using their arms and upper back muscles to turn the cranks that propelled the iron submarine for hours on end, miles out to sea and back. This duty was not for the faint of heart. Whatever criteria was utilized to select who would have the "honor of being the first to engage the enemy in this novel way," the two Alabama engineering officers chose Boatswain's Mate James A. Wicks, Seaman Arnold Becker, Seaman Joseph Ridgeway,

Frank J. Collins, and Seaman C. Simkins. The seven men set out for the Mount Pleasant docks, where repairs to the submarine had essentially been completed. Dixon did not want to waste any time acquainting his new crew with how the boat operated and what was expected of them. Sailors are a superstitious lot, and one wonders how long it took before some of them realized the *Hunley* had taken thirteen souls with her to the bottom.[109]

Since the *Hunley* was still cradled atop the two wooden pilings, Dixon's task of explaining the various components and features of the vessel was greatly simplified. Beauregard had demanded the officers explain fully to each volunteer the "desperately hazardous nature of the service required," and surely Dixon did so, pointing out in turn how each could have been easily avoided. Thereafter, the five volunteers took turns squeezing through the *Hunley's* tiny hatches to get a first glimpse inside the vessel in which they would soon be gambling their lives.

◆   ◆   ◆

By late 1863, Wilmington, North Carolina, was perhaps the most important port city in the Confederacy. Defended by mammoth Fort Fisher and numerous shore batteries, the Cape Fear River city hosted a booming blockade-running business. Although more difficult to blockade than Charleston, the Federal naval grip on Wilmington was beginning to tighten. Perhaps that is the reason why the authorities there were considering building a submarine of their own. Although the design of the proposed vessel has not come to light, one of the *Hunley's* owners, R. W. Dunn, was requested to serve as a consultant on the project—an indication that they may have decided to pattern the boat after the *Hunley*. On November 30, 1863, the Commander of Wilmington, Maj. Gen. William Henry Chase Whiting, wrote the Secretary of War in Richmond requesting plans for what he called "torpedo boats," as well as the services of Robert W. Dunn. The term "torpedo boat" was often used interchangeably with "submarine." Whiting's letter was referred to the Engineering Department, which responded on December 16. "On conference with Captain James, Chief Engineer of your department, I find that the Bureau has no drawings on that subject different from those already in your possession," came the reply. "Mr. Dunn, alluded to in your letter will be informed of your wish that he should proceed to Wilmington to aid in the construction of the torpedo boats. I am authorized by the Secretary of War to inform you that there are already agents in foreign countries qualified to select and purchase materials for the submarine batteries needed for the defense of Wilmington, and that for this reason, he must for the present decline to send Captain Bolton abroad for that purpose."[110]

It seems fairly clear that Whiting was considering a fully submersible boat as opposed to a semi-submersible David-type craft. Why else would he have asked for Robert Dunn? A member of the Singer Submarine Corps, Dunn was considered knowledgeable in the construction of submarines. Since his only known education on the subject was derived from his association with the *Hunley,* his expertise extended only to hand-cranked iron submersibles—not semi-submersible steam-powered Davids.

On the same day that General Whiting was reading his mail from the Richmond Engineering Department, another letter was being sent to Robert W. Dunn, who was attending a meeting in the Southern capital. The communication informed Dunn of Whiting's request for his services and asked that he contact the Engineering Bureau "on the subject." Thereafter, the trail grows cold, and the role Dunn played with the proposed Wilmington boat, if any, is not known.[111]

Although Dunn's role remains a mystery, evidence exists that some of the Wilmington boat's parts were manufactured at the Tredegar Iron Works in Richmond. On December 23, an engineering officer dispatched a letter to the iron works. "The bearer Captain Henry Bolton will submit to you the drawings of a forty two inch (42") propeller screw for a torpedo bearing boat now constructing at Wilmington, N.C. The Honorable Secretary of War has referred papers to me in this connection with favorable endorsement. I therefore respectfully ask that you will cause to be prepared as speedily as may be the necessary patterns and have the castings made." Information available only in Captain Bolton's compiled service record seems to substantiate the Wilmington "torpedo boat" was indeed a submarine. Bolton was "detailed on application from General Whiting to lay submarine mines for the defense of Wilmington," and was "experienced in submarine galvanic batteries."[112]

Like virtually every other submarine project in the South, remaining papers on the subject are scattered and fragmented. The letter regarding the construction of the 42" propeller, for example, is the last written evidence discovered concerning the Wilmington boat. By the middle of February 1864, Robert Dunn was back working in Mobile, Alabama, so if he joined General Whiting in Wilmington to work on a boat of any kind, it was only for a very short period.[113]

◆　◆　◆

The *Hunley* meanwhile, once again ready for water, was hoisted from her makeshift cradle and returned to the dark tides of Charleston Harbor. Although no one wrote about it, the boat's first excursion in late 1863 almost certainly was nothing more than a careful trial in shallow water. The new crewmen had to gain confidence in the machine before Dixon would risk their lives with more dangerous maneuvers. Before long, however, the *Hunley* was again seen by Rebel sailors and civilians prowling here and there and diving around the harbor and beneath friendly ships. Even though the trials were being successfully conducted, it would not be long before the boat would acquire a new nickname: "the Murdering Machine."[114]

The boat was ready for the real thing on December 14, 1863, when Special Orders No. 271 were issued by Beauregard legitimizing Dixon's command and ordering him out to sea. "First Lieut. George E. Dixon, Twenty-first Regiment Alabama Volunteers," read the directive, "will take command and direction of the Submarine Torpedo-Boat *H. L. Hunley,* and proceed tonight to the mouth of the harbor, or as far as capacity of the vessel will allow, and will sink and destroy any vessel of the enemy with which he can come in conflict." Knowing that Dixon may require assistance in the way of special ordnance or other items of supply, Beauregard added, "All officers of the Confederate army in this department are commanded, and all naval officers are requested, to give such assistance to Lieutenant Dixon in the discharge of his duties as may be practicable, should he apply therefore." Dixon and his new crew of underwater raiders were at last ready to be unleashed on the unsuspecting Union fleet. Tension must have run high that afternoon as the *Hunley's* crew readied the diving machine for her first nocturnal excursion outside the harbor. No one knew what to expect. They could not direct the boat against a specific ironclad since these warships wisely changed position each night. They all knew, though, that once the *Hunley* passed beyond the relatively safe waters of the harbor, she was completely on her own.[115]

With Morris Island dominated by the Union Army, the cove behind Fort Moultrie—the presumed mooring used by the McClintock crew in late August—was considered too close to the Union positions for the submarine's activities to go unobserved. Mount Pleasant, although further from the harbor's entrance, was a better choice and appears to have remained the *Hunley's* base of operations into 1864. This first nocturnal patrol from Mount Pleasant was probably an awkward experience plagued with minor mistakes and stressful uncertainty. According to William Alexander, the strong currents at the harbor's entrance wreaked havoc with the submarine and its towed cargo. "The torpedo was a copper cylinder holding a charge of ninety pounds of explosive, with percussion and primer mechanism, set off by triggers," explained the boat's First Officer. "It was originally intended to float the torpedo on the surface of the water, towed by the boat, which was to dive under the vessel to be attacked. In experiments made with some old flat boats in smooth water, this plan operated successfully, but in a seaway the torpedo was continually coming too near our craft." Being blown up by their own torpedo was not what the sailors from the *Indian Chief* had volunteered for, and the men immediately began pondering another method for delivering the charge. Since they were limited in their choices, the obvious alteration was a spar apparatus mounted on the front of the submarine.

Another problem presented itself when the outbound journey from Mount Pleasant to the harbor proved longer and more arduous than expected. The several hours of prolonged cranking produced nothing but unnecessary fatigue. This problem was solved when Dixon decided to have the *Hunley* towed to the mouth of the harbor whenever possible by another vessel. Whatever the problems encountered by the *Hunley* on her first night out, they were surmountable, and the boat made it back safely early the next morning.[116]

Shortly after Dixon decided to have a steam vessel tow his submarine, Beauregard's headquarters directed his request to Chief Engineer

James Tombs, the skipper of the small steam-powered torpedo boat "David." There is a high probability that Dixon and Tombs knew one another prior to their meeting to discuss the nightly towing of the *Hunley*. Both men commanded similar vessels, and each would have been interested in the other's operations. According to the David's commander, "There was a submarine torpedo boat, not under the orders of the Navy, and I was ordered to tow her down the harbor three or four times by Flag-officer Tucker, who also gave me orders to report as to her efficiency as well as safety." While we do not know what Dixon thought of the cigar-shaped David, we know Tombs held the *Hunley* in low regard. "Lieutenant Dixon was a very brave and cool headed man, and had every confidence in his boat, but had great trouble when under the water from lack of air and light. She was very slow in turning, but would sink at a moment's notice and at times without it."[117]

Before long, Engineer Tombs voiced concerns over the way in which the small submarine was to attack her victims. His intent was to strike from beneath the surface of the sea. "In my report to him [Flag Officer William Tucker]," explained Tombs in January 1865, "I stated that the only way to use a torpedo was on the same plan as the 'David'—that is, a spar torpedo—and to strike with his boat on the surface, the torpedo being lowered to 8 feet. Should she attempt to use a torpedo as Lieutenant Dixon intended, by submerging the boat and striking from below, the level of the torpedo would be above his own boat, and as she had little buoyancy and no power, the chances were the suction caused by the water passing into the sinking ship would prevent her from rising to the surface."[118]

Dixon's standing December 14 order to "proceed to the mouth of the harbor and sink any vessel of the enemy which comes in conflict" granted him a license to act whenever the weather permitted, and he took every opportunity to do so. The *Hunley* was towed to the mouth of the harbor several times during late December 1863, but none of her nocturnal expeditions sent a Federal warship to the bottom. They did prove conclusively that the boat, if well handled, was not the death trap so many believed her to be. On one of these missions it was determined that the Union Navy had deployed an elaborate system of chain booms around its ironclads, designed to defend their hulls against an attack from a David-style contact torpedo. Much to Dixon's dismay, this same system also proved to be a very effective defense against the type of attack the *Hunley* was capable of making.

In spite of this disturbing discovery, Engineer Tombs continued to tow the *Hunley* past Fort Sumter whenever weather conditions allowed. This arrangement continued until one unlucky night in early January 1864, when near disaster forced an end to the operation. During one of the hauling operations, the "David" slowed down or stopped for a reason that is not readily apparent. The torpedo line that towed the explosive device behind the *Hunley* drifted alongside Tombs' little torpedo boat and became entangled in her rudder assembly. While both crews held their collective breaths, a brave and as of yet unnamed hero dove into the freezing water and somehow managed to clear the tow line from the rudder and push the deadly device back to where it belonged. Dixon's "torpedo got foul of us and came near blowing up both boats before we got it clear of the bottom, where it had drifted," reported Tombs. "I let him go after passing Fort Sumter, and on my making report of this, Flag-Officer Tucker refused to have the David tow him again."[119]

◆   ◆   ◆

While Dixon and Alexander were successfully propelling their iron boat outside Charleston Harbor in search of a victim, Confederate Engineering officers in Richmond were examining yet another set of submarine diagrams submitted to their department on December 28, 1863. The thin written record demonstrates that the diagrams were for one submarine vessel and prepared by the Triton Company's ubiquitous C. Williams. Nine days later, confirmation of the submission was mailed to Williams. "Your letter of the 28th accompanied by drawings and descriptions of your submarine apparatus for operating with torpedoes etc. has been received," wrote Lt. Col. A. L. Rives, "and your plans will be subjected to consideration at the earliest opportunity."[120]

Perhaps Williams and the Triton Company finally decided it was time to share their submarine plans with Confederate engineers. Whether Williams was submitting these diagrams on behalf of himself or the Triton Company may never be known. In fact, it is not known whether the Triton Company was still in existence by late December 1863. Little could Williams have guessed that Union naval officers in Washington, D. C., already had access to his unique diagrams, for they were in all likelihood merely copies of the same plans that had been captured from a Mississippi mail courier several weeks earlier.

CHAPTER 4

1864:
CONSUMMATION & PATHOS

"The destruction of the Sloop-of-War *Housatonic,* off of Charleston harbor, demonstrates very conclusively that the rebels have anticipated us in the practical application of engines of submarine warfare."

—*March 19, 1864 editorial in the* Army & Navy Journal

The odds of winning the Civil War had swung decidedly against the Confederacy by January 1, 1864. During 1863, each of its principal armies had been roundly beaten in the field.

After a spectacular but costly victory at Chancellorsville in May, Lee's Army of Northern Virginia marched north and was tactically and strategically defeated in the Gettysburg Campaign. Out west, the much-maligned Gen. Braxton Bragg stumbled into the Army of Tennessee's only major victory of the war at Chickamauga in September. Like Lee, Bragg followed his success with a catastrophic defeat on the hills above Chattanooga two months later. Lt. Gen. John C. Pemberton's luck was even worse. Promoted above his abilities, Pemberton allowed his army in Mississippi to become bottled up in the defenses of Vicksburg, where it met its dénouement against a resourceful and dogged U. S. Grant on the 4th of July. Pemberton's defeat—followed quickly by the loss of Port Hudson, Louisiana— was significant, for it guaranteed Federal dominance of the entire Mississippi River from St. Louis to New Orleans. The Trans-Mississippi was effectively cut off from logistical and political centers east of the river.

Desertions plagued both armies, but Southern soldiers, many of whom had families living behind enemy lines, were especially hard hit. While Confederate armies were giving up large chunks of territory, the

Federal blockade was growing more effective by the month. In addition, inflation was rocking Confederate currency, and the hope for foreign intervention had vanished.

It was perhaps a feeling of hopelessness that drove two sailors attached to the Charleston-based *Indian Chief* to steal a skiff and desert to the Union fleet. On the night of January 5, 1864, Seamen Shipp and Belton surrendered themselves to the Federal Navy. When questioned about Charleston Harbor defenses and the current location of the "David," Union naval officers were told a tale that sent shock waves through the blockading fleet. Lengthy reports from the deserters were obtained with detailed descriptions of harbor defenses, shore batteries, ironclads, life in the city, and military morale. But what interested Federal authorities the most had nothing to do with those matters. The Confederacy, they were informed, not only possessed a steam-powered torpedo boat that could be submerged up to her smokestack, but also had an iron submarine capable of delivering a death blow to any ship afloat without ever coming to the surface.[1]

This enemy submarine, learned the stunned Federal officers who took it all down in a long report,

is about 35 feet long, height about the same as the David [5' 6"]. Has a propeller at the end, she is not driven by steam, but her propeller is turned by hand. Has two man heads on the upper side about 12 or 14 feet apart. The entrance into her is through these man heads, the heads being turned back, they are all used to look out of.

She has had bad accidents but was owing to those in her not understanding her. She can be worked perfectly safe by persons who understand her. Can be driven 5 knots an hour without exertion to the men working her. When she went down the last time, was on the bottom 2 weeks before she was raised. Saw her when she was raised the last time. They then hoisted her out of the harbor, refitted her and got another crew. Saw her after that submerged, saw her go under the *Indian Chief,* and then saw her go back under again. She made about 1/2 mile in the dives.

Saw her go under the *Charleston*—went under about 250 feet from her and come up about 300 feet beyond her, was about 20 minutes under the water. Believe she is at Mount Pleasant. One of her crew who belongs to his vessel came back for his clothes and said she was going down there as a station.[2]

Two days later, on January 7, Admiral Dahlgren issued Order No. 2 to his fleet with specific details on how to combat against this type of warfare. "I have reliable information that the Rebels have two torpedo boats ready for service, which may be expected on the first night when the weather is suitable for their movement. One of these is the David which attacked the *Ironsides* in October, the other is similar to it." There was also one "of another kind," wrote the admiral,

> which is nearly submerged, and can be entirely so; it is intended to go under the bottoms of vessels and there operate. This is believed by my informant to be sure of well working, though from bad management it has hereto met with accidents, and was lying off Mount Pleasant two nights since. There being every reason to expect a visit from some or all of these torpedoes, the greatest vigilance will be needed to guard against them. The ironclads must have their fenders rigged out, and their own boats in motion about them. A netting must also be dropped overboard from the ends of the fenders, kept down with shot, and extended along the whole length of the sides; howitzers loaded with canister on the decks and a calcium (search light) for each monitor. The tugs and picket boats must be incessantly upon the lookout, when the water is not rough, whether the weather is clear or rainy. I observe the ironclads are not anchored so as to be entirely clear of each other's fire if opened suddenly in the dark. This must be corrected, and Captain Rowan will assign the monitors suitable positions for this purpose, particularly with reference to his own vessel.

"It is also advisable not to anchor in the deepest part of the channel," concluded Dahlgren, "for by not leaving much space between the bottom of the vessel and the bottom of the channel, it will be impossible for the diving torpedo to operate except on the sides, and there will be less difficulty in raising a vessel if sunk."[3]

With information as to the *Hunley's* whereabouts in hand, the admiral issued his precautionary orders. Unbeknownst to him, however,

A 1902 photograph of the *CSS Hunley's* First Officer, William Alexander. *Mobile Museum*

plans were being made by Lieutenants Dixon and Alexander to relocate the submarine away from Mount Pleasant so they could focus on the wooden vessels anchored further out to sea. With the "David's" towing services abruptly canceled by Flag Officer Tucker, the two Alabama engineering officers had to find another mooring from which to strike out at the enemy fleet. "On account of chain booms having been put around the ironsides and the monitors in Charleston harbor to keep us off these vessels," later recalled Alexander, "we had to turn our attention to the fleet outside. We were ordered to moor the boat off Battery Marshall, on Sullivan's Island. The nearest vessel which we understood to be the United States Frigate *Wabash*, was about twelve miles off, and she was our objective point from this time on." The submarine's new base off Battery Marshall was Breach Inlet, a small and rather treacherous passage between Sullivan's Island and the Island of Palms.[4]

It is unknown when, exactly, Dixon and Alexander fitted their boat with its distinctive spar apparatus, but it was around the time the *Hun-*

ley was moved to Breach Inlet. The harpoon-like contraption allowed the submarine to deliver her explosive device ahead of her instead of towing the deadly cargo at the end of a long tow line, miles out to sea in unpredictable currents. An article from the *Charleston Daily Republican* on October 8, 1870, "The remarkable career of a remarkable craft," claimed that P. G. T. Beauregard was the originator of the boat's new paraphernalia. "General Beauregard changed the arrangement of the torpedo by fastening it to the bow," wrote a reporter. "Its front was terminated by a sharp and barbed lance-head so that when the boat was driven end on against a ship's sides, the lance head would be forced deep into the timbers below the water line, and would fasten the torpedo firmly against the ship. Then the torpedo boat would back off and explode it by a lanyard."[5]

While contemporary writings suggest that this new form of torpedo delivery was introduced at about the same time the *Hunley* was being relocated to Sullivan's Island, this type of torpedo configuration may have been regarded as a secondary means of attack since the boat's earliest days in Mobile. With the waters of Mobile Bay so shallow, a spar torpedo probably was considered as a method of attack long before the submarine ever prowled Charleston Harbor. If so, once the submarine was brought to Charleston that method of attack would have been abandoned, since a lance-headed torpedo could not be used against the hulls of ironclads.

A very interesting piece of evidence supporting this theory comes from a sketch drawn by artist Conrad Wise Chapman on December 2, 1863. Conrad's drawing clearly shows a reel spindle behind the forward conning tower, cocked off to the side so that the line running from it would not interfere with the forward diving planes. Whether or not this torpedo design was first introduced by Engineers Dixon and Alexander while still in Mobile may never be known. However, there is little doubt that this new method of attack was utilized exclusively after the *Hunley* moved to her new mooring at Battery Marshall off Sullivan's Island.[6]

A collection of Charleston torpedo diagrams, including a detailed blueprint of the Singer Torpedo used aboard the *Hunley,* was seized by Federal troops at the end of the war. They were then copied by Union torpedo engineer Capt. Adalfus Luettwitz, 54th New York Volunteers, and it is his drawings that exist today. The angle of the shaft extending from the torpedo makes it clear that the explosive device carried at the end of the spar was able to be lowered several feet beneath the surface of the water prior to detonation. This torpedo configuration was standard on the "David" class torpedo boats, and now evidence exists that the designers of the "David's" torpedo had a hand in helping redesign the *Hunley's* revised spar apparatus. A letter to Capt. Francis Lee, the designer of the "David's" spar-mounted torpedo system, from the Confederate Engineering Department in early March of 1864, praised the captain for his contribution toward designing the delivery system on the submarine boat.[7]

Further evidence pointing to the fact that the *Hunley* adopted a David-style torpedo configuration is found in a diagram of the boat drawn for Simon Lake by Englishman and former crew member Charles Hasker, during his visit with Lake in the summer of 1897. Hasker's drawing depicts the submarine's diving planes in an upright position—to keep the forward view port above the surface while trimmed at neutral buoyancy—with the spar of the *Hunley* angled down beneath the bow. Since the powder-filled explosive device had a positive buoyancy (and would therefore have to be forcibly lowered beneath the surface), no secondary means other than the sleeve shown in the captured diagrams, would have been necessary for securing the torpedo to the spar.[8]

According to First Officer William Alexander, even after the small submarine had been relocated to Breach Inlet, the crew of the *Hunley* remained quartered several miles away at Mount Pleasant. This inconvenient arrangement continued until the end of January 1864, when quarters for Dixon's men were finally provided on Sullivan's Island. During this period (about January 14–20), the crew of the *Hunley* practiced the new method of attack in an area described by Alexander as the bay behind Battery Marshall. "Our daily routine," recalled the Alabamian, "whenever possible, was about as follows: Leave Mount Pleasant about 1 P.M., walk seven miles to Battery Marshall on the beach (this exposed us to fire, but it was the best walking), take the boat out and practice the crew for two hours in the Back Bay."[9]

The boat's practice consisted of mock attacks with their new torpedo system against the hull of an old flatboat anchored behind Battery Marshall, practice dives, navigation, and other similar actions. Delivering a charge with the new spar required the crew of the *Hunley* to literally ram an enemy vessel with the harpoon mounted on the bow of the submarine. Once the torpedo's barbed lance head was driven deep into the vessel's wooden hull, the crew would reverse the propeller and back away, leaving the harpoon head and explosive device attached to the ship. When the line or lanyard carried in a reel outside the hull (as sketched by Chapman) reached the end of its 150-foot tether, the explosive was detonated.

After practicing with the crew in the Back Bay for a couple of hours in the late afternoon, remembered Alexander,

> Dixon and myself would then stretch out on the beach with the compass between us and get the bearings of the nearest vessel as she took her position for the night; ship up the torpedo on the boom, and when dark, go out, steering for that vessel, proceed until the condition of the men, sea, tide, wind, moon and daylight compelled our return to the dock; un-ship the torpedo, put it under guard at Battery Marshall, walk back to quarters at Mount Pleasant and cook breakfast.[10]

While Admiral Dahlgren and the crews of the various ironclads prepared their vessels for a nocturnal visit from the *Hunley,* Lieutenants Dixon and Alexander—unaware that the existence of their small submarine had been compromised just days earlier—finalized plans for an attack out of Breach Inlet two and one-half miles up the coast. As rumors of this new underwater menace spread throughout the Union fleet, Dixon continued to sharpen his crew's skills in the brackish but calm bay behind Battery Marshall. The plan at this time, remembered William Alexander in 1902, "was to take the bearings of the ships as they took position for the night, steer for one of them, keeping about six feet under water, coming occasionally to the surface for air and observation, and when nearing the vessel, come to the surface for final observation before striking her, which was to be done under the counter, if possible."[11]

As preparations for an attack intensified, Seaman Belton, one of the deserters from the *Indian Chief,* had been busy constructing a detailed model of the little submarine for Admiral Dahlgren. After carefully examining Belton's model, Admiral Dahlgren sent it to Gideon Welles, the Secretary of the Navy, on January 22, 1864. "I transmit by the *Massachusetts,* a model of the 'Diver' which is said to have been built at Mobile by the rebels, and brought to this place for use against the vessels in this Squadron," reported Dahlgren. "The Department will find a brief description of her in my communication of the 13th [see Chapter 3]. The model was made by E. C. Belton who is a mechanic, and ran an engine on the Montgomery and Mobile Railroad for some time. He worked in a building near where it was built—and claims to understand fully its construction," continued the admiral, who was fully convinced the ordinary seaman knew what he was talking about. "It has been very unlucky in the trials made with it, and is stated to have drowned at different times three crews of seventeen men."[12]

While Dahlgren was keeping Washington abreast of naval matters off Charleston, Dixon and Alexander were preparing to lead their crew on their first nocturnal excursion against the wooden fleet from their new mooring at Breach Inlet. As the flickering light of campfires appeared behind the sand and log walls of Battery Marshall, the *Hunley's* crew could be seen preparing the little submarine for the long and dangerous night that lay ahead. She presented quite an appearance. Her once freshly painted black hull was but a memory, for months of immersion in saltwater had encrusted her iron skin with small crustaceans. Streaks of rust ran down the exposed surfaces of the hull. The submarine's interior was even worse. The cramped compartment reeked of musty candle smoke and mildew, while mold had grown around the rivet heads that held the hull together. If not routinely cleaned, the ceiling around the forward hatch would have been thick with soot from the dozens of candles that had been burned immediately beneath by the commander.

While the crew sat at the propeller shaft preparing themselves for their perilous journey, Commander Dixon would have lit one of the candles he had brought on board. Condensation or a dusting of frost would have been wiped from the submarine's view ports, and the boat's mercury gauge would have been checked out. First Officer Alexander squeezed through the small rear conning tower and took his place at the rear ballast tank pump. Soon the order to move out was given. As the long cold propeller shaft started turning in the capable hands of Dixon's crew, the young engineering officer stood with his head above the hatch

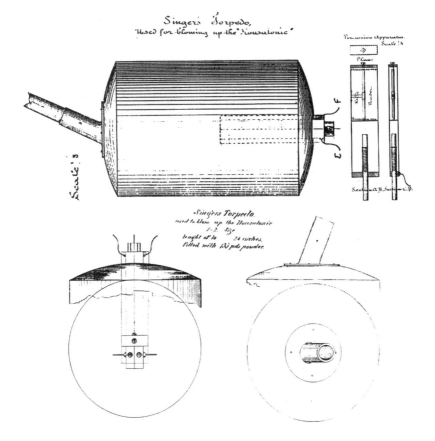

Singer Torpedo and fuse diagrams captured in 1865 show how the *Hunley's* explosive device was secured and detonated. *National Archives*

rim, steering his small submarine toward the open sea and the faint bobbing lights of the Union fleet that lay at anchor several miles off shore.

The routine would be repeated many times during the nights that followed.[13]

◆   ◆   ◆

It was during these early days of frenetic activity at Breach Inlet that another submarine venture was being proposed to authorities in Richmond. Whether a January 11, 1864, congressional report on "Torpedo

Boats" had anything to do with the formation of this project may never be known, for the earliest information regarding this venture is little more than a recommendation from the Secretary of the Navy Stephen Mallory.

On January 26, the President of the Confederate States of America, Jefferson Davis, granted to John P. Halligan an exemption from military service for the purpose of "constructing a submarine torpedo boat." Just where the 31-year-old Irish immigrant gained his knowledge of submarine vessels is unknown. The earliest mention of him comes from April of 1862, when he was employed by C. Richmond & Company in Memphis, Tennessee, to construct underwater mines for use in the Mississippi River. Although little is known of Halligan's early war activities, it was obvious to President Davis that he had a thorough knowledge of submarines. In fact, Halligan would eventually come to build one of the most advanced undersea vehicles constructed during the Civil War.[14]

◆　◆　◆

Harper's Weekly probably put a healthy dose of fear into some of its readers when on January 30, 1864, it reported one of the most sensational stories to date. The article first appeared in a French paper some weeks earlier, and *Harper's Weekly* picked it up for domestic consumption."REBEL SUBMARINE BATTERY," proclaimed the headline, which was followed by quite a story:

> A. M. Olivier de Jalin sends to the French *Le Monde Illustr'e* drawings of a submarine vessel which we reproduce on this page, abridging his description.
>
> There has just been finished, he says, at Mobile a very curious little vessel, designed by Mr. Anstilt, which seems capable of destroying any ship in the world. It is of iron 23 yards long. The interior is divided longitudinally by a partition into two portions: in the upper is the machinery, armaments, rudders, and reservoirs of compressed air: in the lower are chambers to hold air or water, as the case may demand, coal bunkers, provision lockers, and the like.
>
> On the deck, which is hermetically closed are pipes for discharging air and steam, a smoke-stack, and a look-out, the upper part of

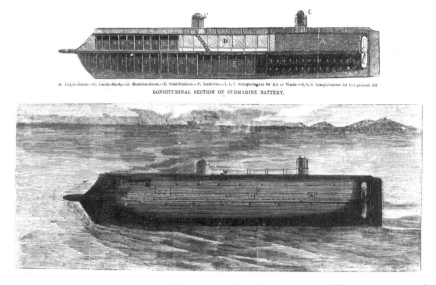

A. Engine-Room.—C. Smoke-Stack.—D. Munition-Room.—E. Coal-Bunkers.—F. Look-Out.—I, I, I. Compartments for Air or Water.—0, 0, 0. Compartments for Compressed Air

LONGITUDINAL SECTION OF SUBMARINE BATTERY.

Confederate "Submarine Battery." Cutaway and underway views of this steam-powered vessel. *Harper's Weekly*

which is of thick glass. The motive-power is a screw, worked either by steam or electricity. At the stern is an ordinary rudder; at the bow another rudder, working on a horizontal axis, the object of which is to raise or lower the vessel.

Now when no enemy is in sight the air-chambers are filled, and the vessel is managed like any other steamer. But when an enemy is in view the air-chambers are filled with water; down goes the vessel, and nobody is the wiser for its presence. Her perpendicular course is determined by the bow rudder, just as her horizontal course is regulated by her stern rudder. Turn it one way and up she goes; turn it the other, and down she sinks. The pressure-gauge shows just the depth to which she has at any moment sunk.

The man in the glass look-out governs the movement of the vessel. If it is sunk three feet below the surface it is invisible. On each side of the deck are placed iron cases filled with powder, joined two-and-two by chains of proper length. If a vessel lying at anchor is to be attacked, the submarine boat dives down, lets slip one of these twin torpedoes directly under the enemy; these rise by their specific gravity, and hug the enemy, one on each side, but kept from escape by the chain which, passing under the keel, unites them.

The submarine, having accomplished her work, backs off to a safe distance, explodes these torpedoes by means of a galvanic battery, and up goes the enemy, in more pieces than one can well count. If a vessel under sail or steam is to be assaulted, the submarine dives down and lies hidden right under the track of her foe; then at the exact moment loosens a torpedo furnished with a percussion apparatus; the enemy strikes this, explodes it, and up she goes past all hope of redemption. The submarine in the mean time, has dived down into the water so deep as to be quite safe from the shock which she has occasioned.

'I can't stop to describe to you,' concluded M. Olivier de Jalin, 'the systems of pumps to drive out the foul air, the air and water-pipes by means of which, with the aid of the compressed air, the air tanks may be in a few moments be filled with water or emptied. We believe M. Olivier has sold our French friend, and think that if our fleet has nothing to contend with more formidable than the invention of Mr. Anstilt it will not suffer much danger.'[15]

There is some evidence that the boat either did exist at one time or plans of it did. Although no records regarding this supposed Mobile-based submarine have come to light on this side of the Atlantic, early French submariners must have had some documentation as to her existence, for detailed diagrams and descriptions far superior to the sketches found in *Harper's Weekly* are found in several respected European texts. Also compelling is the story told by James Carr, the 19-year-old New York native and deserter from the Confederate gunboat *Selma*. Carr, it will be remembered, had abandoned his station in February 1863, and reported on a submarine attack against the Federal blockading ships outside Mobile. "The attempt will be renewed as early as possible," he warned, "and three or four others [submarine boats] are being constructed for the purpose." What happened to these "three or four other" Mobile submarines? Was one of them the monster boat described by *Harper's Weekly?* Perhaps the Anstilt submarine boat was a semi-successful private venture which carried on largely unnoticed in Mobile, but was reported on elsewhere by blockade-running crews who regularly entered French ports. The absence of tangible documentation means the boat's existence may forever remain a subject of speculation.[16]

◆　◆　◆

While Northern families sat around mid-nineteenth-century breakfast tables and marveled at the story presented in *Harper's Weekly,* Dixon and his crew continued to put to sea in their submarine boat whenever weather conditions allowed. The physical strain on the crew of the *Hunley* during this period must have been exhaustive. After hiking seven miles from their quarters at Mount Pleasant to Breach Inlet, the seamen took the submarine into the Back Bay and practiced for a couple of hours, keeping their skills sharp for their night attack. Several hours later they pumped the cranks through miles of seawater on their long, cold, and lonely search for prey. The level of tension inside the boat must have been palpable. Knowing the submarine's history, every sudden bump or dip must have triggered a sudden start and nervous sweat. Each time they surfaced for air—and they did this numerous times each night—could spell the doom of their submarine if a Yankee picket boat spotted them as they opened their hatch. From the time the men took their places at the long propeller shaft until the following dawn, the flickering candle light revealed almost nothing but the shadows of their fellow crew members and the dripping condensation running down the interior of the *Hunley's* gloomy iron walls. It was their own voluntary form of Hell. And still they went out.

Long after the war, Lieutenant Alexander expounded on the issue of the dangers faced by the *Hunley's* crew. "It was Winter, therefore necessary that we go out with the ebb and come in with the flood tide, a fair wind and a dark moon," the First Officer recalled. "This latter was essential to success, as our experience had fully demonstrated the necessity of occasionally coming to the surface, slightly lifting the after hatch-cover and letting in a little air. On several occasions we came to the surface for air, opened the cover and heard the men in the Federal picket boats talking and singing." Surprising to many, the small submarine "went out on an average of four nights a week, but on account of the weather, and considering the physical condition of the men to propel the boat back again, often, after going out six or seven miles, we would have to return. This we always found a task, and many times it taxed our utmost exertions to keep from drifting out to sea, daylight often breaking while we were yet in range."[17]

Their numerous near-fatal encounters with enemy picket boats and the unavoidable dilemma of the sunrise finding the boat in enemy waters convinced Dixon and Alexander that a test should be conducted to determine just how long the *Hunley* could remain submerged without exhausting the air supply. Alexander brought up another reason for conducting the test: It was "also our desire to know," he wrote, "in case we struck a vessel (circumstances required our keeping below the surface), suggested that while in safe water we make the experiment to find out how long it was possible to stay under water without coming to the surface for air and not injure the crew." The test was simple yet dangerous, and Alexander told the story well:

It was agreed to by all hands to sink and let the boat rest on the bottom, in the Back bay, off Battery Marshall, each man to make equal physical exertion in turning the propeller. It was also agreed that if anyone in the boat felt that if he must come to the surface for air, and he gave the word 'up,' we would at once bring the boat to the surface. It was usual, when practicing in the bay, that the banks would be lined with soldiers. One evening, after alternately diving and rising many times, Dixon and myself and several of the crew compared watches, noted the time and sank for the test. In twenty-five minutes after I had closed the after manhead and excluded the outer air the candle would not burn. Dixon forward and myself aft, turning on the propeller cranks as hard as we could. In comparing our individual experience afterwards, the experience of one was found to have been the experience of all. Each man had determined that he would not be the first to say 'up!' Not a word was said, except the occasional, 'How is it,' between Dixon and myself, until it was as the voice of one man, the word 'up' came from all nine. We started the pumps. Dixon's worked all right, but I soon realized that my pump was not throwing. From experience I guessed the cause of the failure, took off the cap of the pump, lifted the valve, and drew out some seaweed that had choked it.

During the time it took to do this the boat was considerably by the stern. Thick darkness prevailed. All hands had already endured what they thought was the utmost limit. Some of the crew almost lost control of themselves. It was a terrible few minutes, 'better imagined than described.' We soon had the boat to the surface and the manhead opened. Fresh air! What an experience! Well, the sun was shining when we went down, the beach lined with soldiers. It was now quite dark, with one solitary soldier gazing on the spot where he had seen the boat before going down the last time. He did not see the boat until he saw me standing on the hatch combing, calling to him to stand by to take the line. A light was struck and the time taken. We had been on the bottom two hours and thirty-five minutes. The candle ceased to burn in twenty-five minutes after we went down, showing that we had remained under water two hours and ten minutes after the candle went out.

The lone (and no doubt surprised) sentry promptly informed Dixon, Alexander, and their men that they had been "given up for lost," and "that a message had been sent to General Beauregard at Charleston that the torpedo boat had been lost that evening off Battery Marshall with all hands." According to a relieved Alexander,

We got back to our quarters at Mount Pleasant that night, went over early next morning to the city (Charleston), and reported to General Beauregard the facts of the affair. They were all glad to see us.

After making a full report of our experience, General [Gabriel] Rains, of General Beauregard's staff, who was present, expressed some doubt of our having stayed under water two hours and ten minutes after the candle went out. Not that any of us wanted to go through the same experience again, but we did our best to get him to come over to Sullivan's Island and witness a demonstration of the fact, but without avail.[18]

While Dixon was sharpening his crewmen for their dangerous occupation, his superior officer in the 21st Alabama Regiment—the unit from which both Dixon and Alexander had been detached for special duty—was lobbying to get him back in the ranks and away from Charleston. In 1900 an article was published in Montgomery, Alabama, claiming that Capt. John Cothran was requesting Dixon to return to his post at Mobile. "While contemplating this hazardous enterprise, Lieutenant Dixon received from his old officer, Captain Cothran of Mobile, a letter entreating him to give up the frightful venture saying that he needed Dixon in his command. This gentleman is still living in Mobile . . ." Dixon, claimed the article, made a "heroic reply, refusing to retreat from the post of danger he had sought."[19]

This "heroic reply" was published in, the *Mobile Register* a short time later under the heading, "Lieutenant Dixon's last letter." Given its poignant contents and Dixon's major role in developing early submarines, the letter is worthy of reprinting in its entirety:

February 5th, 1864.
Captain John F. Cothran.
Commanding Ceder Point, Company "A"
Twenty-first Alabama Regiment,
Mobile, Alabama.

Friend John:
     Your letter of the 29th came to hand today and contents duly noted. I am glad McCullough has gotten to be a Lieutenant, he has served long enough for it. You stated my presence was very much needed on your little island. I have no doubt it is, but when I will get there is far more than I am able to tell at present, for beyond a doubt I am fastened to Charleston and its approaches until I am able to blow up some of their Yankee ships. If I wanted to leave here I could not do it, and I doubt very much if an order from General Maury would have any effect to wards bringing me back.
     I have been here over three months, have worked very hard, in fact I am working all the time. My headquarters are on Sullivan's Island, and a more uncomfortable place could not be found in the Confederacy. You spoke of being on the front and holding the post of honor. Now, John, make one trip to the besieged city of Charleston and your post of honor and all danger that threatens Mobile will fade away. For

the last six weeks I have not been out of the range of the shells and often I am forced to go within very close proximity of the Yankee battery. I do not want you and all the company to think that because I am absent from them that mine is any pleasant duty or that I am absent from them because I believe there is any post of honor or fame where there is any danger, I think it must be at Charleston, for if you wish to see war every day and night, this is the place to see it.

Charleston and its defenders will occupy the most conspicuous place in the history of the war, and it shall be as much glory as I shall wish if I can inscribe myself as one of its defenders. My duty here is more arduous than that of any officer of the 21st. Alabama. Simply because I am not present to fulfill the duties of a Lieutenant there are many that have formed the opinion that I am doing nothing; But I say that I have done more already than any of the 21st. Alabama and I stand ready to prove my assertion by the best and highest military authority. What more I will do time alone will tell. My kindest regards to Charley and all enquiring friends. Hoping to hear from you soon,

I remain your friend.

George E. Dixon.[20]

Clearly Dixon was not about to leave Charleston. But William Alexander did exactly that. On the same day Dixon was writing his letter to Captain Cothran, orders arrived transferring Alexander to Mobile. The directive devastated the entire crew, and perhaps Alexander the most. The boat was preparing to go out again, remembered the distraught lieutenant, "when I received an order which at the time was a blow to all my hopes, although only by obeying it did I live to write this narrative." Alexander was to report to General Thomas Jordan, Beauregard's chief of staff, who would see that he received "transportation and orders to report at Mobile, to build a breech-loading, repeating gun (cannon)." The instruction hit the young Alabamian like a cold wave. "This was a terrible blow, both to Dixon and myself, after we had gone through so much together. General Jordan told Dixon he would get two men to take my place from the German artillery, but that I was wanted in

Mobile." Thinking it best not to tell the crew he had been ordered away, Alexander packed his bags and boarded a train that evening. Alexander would hear from Dixon again on just two occasions, and then he would hear nothing more.[21]

As devastating as was the loss of his First Officer, Dixon had a job to perform. Within a day or so the crew of the *Hunley* was once again operating at full strength following the acquisition of a new volunteer, Cpl. C. F. Carlson, Co. A, South Carolina Light Artillery. Who assumed the reins of First Officer is unknown.[22]

After the first of the year, the Union fleet put into motion a new strategy designed to intercept camouflaged blockade runners as they made their way down the coast and into and out of Charleston. From the sloping walls of Battery Marshall, a swift new Federal sloop-of-war was seen at anchor each evening not three miles past the breakers. The captain of this new vessel, Charles Pickering, was under strict orders to keep up a full head of steam throughout the long night and capture or destroy any blockade runner attempting to reach Charleston. With her twelve large caliber guns loaded and ready for anything, the 207' sloop *Housatonic* gently rocked at anchor within sight of Breach Inlet, unaware that the diving torpedo boat lay in waiting not 50 yards behind its entrance.[23]

Dixon and his men watched the new sloop night after night as the *Housatonic* bobbed at anchor in a heavy sea off Sullivan's Island. To ensure that no Rebel torpedo craft was able to approach the sloop during the night, six well-armed lookouts were posted on deck, one on each cathead, gangway, and quarter. The officer of the deck stood on the bridge; with two other officers posted at the forecastle and quarterdeck, each searching the dark horizon with telescopes hoping to catch a glimpse of a Charleston-bound blockade runner. At the anchor chains, two men stood at the ready to slip the chain and set the ship free at the first sign of trouble. In the hot engine room, soot-covered sailors shoveled coal on the fire throughout the night to keep the pressure within the boiler at a constant twenty-five pounds to ensure that the vessel could steam forward at a moment's notice. On the cold deck above, shivering sailors tried to sleep or played cards around their loaded cannons, ready on a moment's notice to fire on any ship that came within range.

The sight of the new warship anchored there, night after night, must have driven Dixon and his crew to distraction, for the wind and the sea were conspiring against them. Until the former died down and the latter calmed down, Dixon was powerless to act. The weather system, however, refused to cooperate. Instead it continued to hammer the coast with high winds and biting cold. The days passed quickly through the first part of February and soon stretched into the middle of the month. In fact, the winds were so severe during this period that the *Charleston Daily Courier* reported that several Federal ironclads were anchoring at Light House Inlet (on Morris Island) after dark to escape the rough seas offshore. During this time Dixon and his men monitored the weather closely, searching for any sign that it might change long enough for an attack to be made against the wooden sloop blissfully at anchor a mere three miles out to sea.[24]

While Lieutenant Dixon waited for a calm sea, he wrote his old friend William Alexander and informed him of the current status of the crew and situation at Charleston. "I received a note from Lieutenant Dixon, saying that he succeeded in getting two volunteers from the German artillery," explained Alexander, "that for two days the wind had changed to fair, and he intended to try and get out that night." Dixon's brief message was written on the afternoon of February 17, 1864—just hours before the crew of the *Hunley* set out from Breach Inlet and made history.[25]

As the cold afternoon bowed to twilight, Dixon and his sailors prepared their submarine for her dangerous rendezvous with the enemy sloop. Although the weather had finally broken and the sea was relatively smooth, Dixon knew that he would be unable to see the ship from surface level (when they surfaced for air) until quite close to the vessel. The moon that night was almost full, making their task that much more difficult. In spite of the appreciated danger of being spotted by a sentry in the moonlight, Dixon decided that they had waited long enough: the attack would go forward as planned.[26]

While the crew of the *Hunley* patiently waited for the sun to disappear over the marshes behind Sullivan's Island, Capt. Charles Pickering prepared the *Housatonic* for the first calm night at her new station. "The orders to the Executive Officer and the Officer of the Deck were to keep a vigilant lookout, glasses in constant use," remembered Captain Pickering nine days later. "There were three glasses in use by the Officer of the Deck, Officer of the Forecastle and Quarter Master, and six lookouts besides; and the moment he saw anything suspicious to slip the chain, sound the gong, without waiting for orders, and send for me. To keep the engines reversed and ready for going astern, as I had on a previous occasion got my slip rope foul of the propeller by going ahead."

Pickering was not taking any chances. The pivot guns, he reported, were "pivoted in broadside, the 100 pounder on the starboard side, and the eleven inch gun on the Port side; the battery all cast loose and loaded, and a round of cartridges kept in the arm chest so that two broadsides could be fired before the reception of powder from the magazine. Two shells, two canister and two grape were kept by each gun."

Pickering also saw to it that . . .

three rockets were kept in the stands ready for the necessary signal. Two men were stationed at the slip rope, and others at the chain stopper and shackle on the spar deck. The chain was prepared for slipping by reversing the shackle, bow aft instead of forward. The pin which confined the bolt removed and a wooden pin substituted, and the shackle placed upon chain shoes for knocking the bolt out; so that all that was necessary to slip the chain was to strike the bolt with the sledge once, which broke the wooden pin, and drove the bolt across the deck, leaving the forward end of the chain clear of the shackle. I had all the necessary signals at hand, ready for an emergency. The order was to keep up 25 pounds of steam at night always, and have every thing ready for going astern instantly.[27]

At about 7:00 p.m. on February 17, 1864, well over an hour after the sun had disappeared over the winter horizon, Lieutenant Dixon followed his men through the forward hatch of the little *Hunley* and lit the candle next to the tarnished compass. One can easily picture the eery shadows that would have danced across the submarine's damp iron walls as the small flame flickered in the cramped environment. On Dixon's order the men cranked away on their metal bars, turning the heavy iron propeller shaft that in turn moved the iron boat slowly out to sea.

The *Hunley* glided silently out of Breach Inlet and past Battery Marshall, whose commanding officer would wait patiently that night for a signal from the *Hunley*. The signal, which would be in the form of a waving lantern, would alert the shore party to light a beacon fire by which Dixon and his crew could safely return to Breach Inlet.

Unfortunately, the ill-fated *Hunley* would never return to Breach Inlet.

◆   ◆   ◆

While candle wax ran down the bulk head and dripped onto the floor of the submerged *Hunley*, Officer of the Deck John Crosby stood on the bridge of the *Housatonic*, scanning the calm horizon for any sign of a blockade runner. Below deck, Captain Pickering was seated at the desk in his cabin overhauling a book of charts in his collection. Not far from his quarters, Assistant Engineer Holihan stared at the steam gauge in the *Housatonic's* engine room, making sure that the needle never fell below 25 pounds of pressure. Although we will never know what transpired aboard Dixon's *Hunley* on that cold February night, a substantial amount of evidence remains as to what the men of the *Housatonic* experienced.[28]

"I took the deck at 8 P.M. on the night of February 17th," Officer of the Deck John Crosby later testified. "About 8:45 P.M. I saw something on the water, which at first looked to me like a porpoise, coming to the surface to blow. It was about 75 to 100 yards from us on our starboard beam." The disturbance bothered the officer, who called over the quartermaster to take a look through his glasses. "He saw nothing but a tide ripple on the water," remembered Crosby. "Looking again within an instant I saw it was coming towards the ship very fast. I gave orders to beat to quarters slip the chain and back the engine, the orders being executed immediately."[29]

Crosby's testimony confirms that Dixon surfaced the *Hunley* for a final observation just two or three hundred feet from the *Housatonic*. Once he saw how close he was to the vessel's hull, he must have decided to make the final run for the ship. As Dixon steered his little submarine toward its target, Executive Officer Higginson ran to the rail to see what all the commotion was about. "It had the appearance of a plank sharp at both ends," remembered Higginson, "it was entirely on awash with the

The *USS Housatonic* is sunk by the Confederate submarine *H.L. Hunley* in this wartime engraving from *Frank Leslie's Illustrated Newspaper*.

water, and there was a glimmer of light through the top of it, as though through a dead light." At about the same time that Higginson first caught sight of Dixon's candle illuminating the water through the submarine's forward view ports, lookouts on the starboard side started firing their rifles at the mysterious craft that was quickly approaching them.[30]

The musket fire and yelling brought Captain Pickering rushing on deck to find out what was happening and why the ship's company had been called to quarters. "I sprang from the table under the impression that a blockade runner was about," testified the captain, and "on reaching the deck I gave the order to slip, and heard for the first time it was a torpedo, I think from the Officer of the Deck. I repeated the order to slip, and gave the order to go astern, and to open fire. I turned instantly, took my double barrelled gun loaded with buck shot, from Mr. Muzzey, my aid and clerk, and jumped up on the horse block on the starboard quarter which the first Lieutenant had just left having fired a musket at the torpedo."

Pickering left an interesting description of what he saw that night:

I hastily examined the torpedo; it was shaped like a large whale boat, about two feet, more or less, under water; its position was at right angles to the ship, bow on, and the bow within two or three feet of the ship's side, about abreast of the mizzen mast, and I supposed it was then fixing the torpedo on. I saw two projections or knobs about one third of the way from the bows. I fired at these, jumped down from the horse block, and ran to the port side of the Quarter Deck as far as the mizzen mast, singing out 'Go astern Faster.'

At about the same time that three bells were being struck to inform the engine room to go astern, Ensign Charles Craven was rushing on deck. The *Hunley* was bearing down for the starboard hull. Craven's testimony records the sloop's final minutes of life:

I heard the Officer of the Deck give the order 'Call all hands to Quarters.' I went on deck and saw something in the water on the starboard side of the ship, about 30 feet off, and the Captain and the Executive Officer were firing at it. I fired two shots at her with my revolver as she was standing towards the ship as soon as I saw her, and a third shot when she was almost under the counter, having to lean over the port to fire it.

I then went to my division, which is the second, and consists of four broadside 32 pounder guns in the waist, and tried with the Captain of number six gun to train it on this object, as she was backing from the ship, and about 40 of 50 feet off then. I had nearly succeeded, and was almost about to pull the lock string when the explosion took place. I was jarred and thrown back on the topsail sheet bolts, which caused me to pull the lock string, and the hammer fell on the primer but without sufficient force to explode it. I replaced the primer and was trying to catch site of the object in order to train the gun again upon it, when I found the water was ankle deep on deck by the main mast. I then went and assisted in clearing away the second launch.[31]

Craven's detailed testimony suggests that the *Hunley* was much closer to the *Housatonic's* hull when the explosion occurred than Dixon had planned. It's highly unlikely that so much gunpowder (over 130

assignment of a large reward as prize money to crews of boats or vessels who shall capture, or beyond doubt destroy, one of these torpedoes."[37]

Nine days after the fateful night of February 17, Confederate authorities still did not know the identity of the warship resting on the bottom off Breach Inlet. The information finally was obtained in a most unusual manner. On the night of February 26, a Union picket boat accidently strayed too close to Fort Sumter and was captured by a craft belonging to the *Indian Chief*—an irony in and of itself, since several of the crew members on the vanished *Hunley* had once served on the *Indian Chief*. An interrogation of the Federal crew revealed that the name of the warship was the *USS Housatonic*, and that five crewmen had been killed in the attack. The following day, General Beauregard dispatched a telegram to the Inspector General in Richmond. "Prisoners report that it was the U.S. ship of war *Housatonic*, 12 guns, which was sunk on night 17th instant by the submarine torpedo boat, Lieutenant Dixon, of Alabama, commanding," reported Beauregard, who added, "There is little hope of safety of that brave man and his associates, however, as they were not captured."[38]

News of the sinking of the *Housatonic* spread through war-weary Charleston like a brush fire. It was just what the exhausted populace needed: a victory, however slight. "A few nights ago a party of a dozen men went out in a submarine boat, in which they could remain under water for an hour or so, and propel at the rate of four miles per hour," David Barnum, a sailor attached to the *Indian Chief*, wrote excitedly in a short note to a friend in Alabama. "They struck a large vessel with their torpedo and blew all the bottom out of her." The February 29 edition of the *Charleston Mercury* also gloated about the sunken warship. "The news this morning from our immediate vicinity is quite as cheering as that which is echoed along the wires from the far off battlefields of Georgia and the Southwest," began the paper:

> An official dispatch was received from Colonel [Stephen] Elliott at Fort Sumter, on Saturday, conveying the gratifying news that one of our picket boats, commanded by Boatswain Smith, had captured a Yankee picket boat containing one officer and five men. The prisoners have arrived in the city. Their accounts of the success of the pioneer of our fleet of torpedo boats are really exhilarating. They state that the

vessel sunk off the harbor on the night of the 16th, and reported lost in a gale, was the U.S. Steamer *Housatonic,* carrying 12 guns and three hundred men, and that she was blown up by our torpedo boat.

This fine and powerful vessel was sunk in three minutes. The whole stern of the vessel was blown off in the explosion. All the crew of the *Housatonic* are said to have been saved, except five—two officers and three men—who are missing and supposed to be drowned. As a practical and important result of this splendid achievement, the prisoners state that all the wooden vessels of the blockading squadron now go far out to sea every night, being afraid of the risk of riding at anchor in any portion of the outer harbor.

The torpedo boat that has accomplished this glorious exploit was under the command of Lieutenant Dixon. We are glad to be able to assure out readers that the boat and crew are now safe. . . .[39]

Sadly, either the paper had been misinformed or was simply misleading the public, for the gallant little *Hunley* and her brave crew never returned. The Board of Inquiry seated to look into the sinking of the *Housatonic* in mid-February 1864, did not take long to reach conclusions as to how and why the warship was sent to the bottom:

First, That the *U. S. S. Housatonic* was blown up and sunk by a rebel torpedo craft on the night of February 17 last, about 9 o'clock p.m., while lying at an anchor in 27 feet of water off Charleston S.C., bearing E.S.E, and distant from Fort Sumter about 5 1/2 miles. The weather at the time of the occurrence was clear, the night bright and moonlight, wind moderate from the northward and westward, sea smooth and tide half ebb, the ship's head about W. N. W.

Second. That between 8:45 and 9 o'clock p.m. on said night an object in the water was discovered almost simultaneously by the officer of the deck and the lookout stationed at the starboard cathead, on the starboard bow of the ship, about 75 or 100 yards distant, having the appearance of a log. That on further and closer observation it presented a suspicious appearance, moving apparently with a speed of 3 or 4 knots in the direction of the starboard quarter of the ship, exhibiting two protuberances above and making a slight ripple in the water.

Third. That the strange object approached the ship with a rapidity precluding a gun of the battery being brought to bear upon it, and finally came in contact with the ship on her starboard quarter.

Fourth. That about one and a half minutes after the first discovery of the strange object the crew were called to quarters, the cable slipped, and the engine backed.

Fifth. That an explosion occurred about three minutes after the first discovery of the object, which blew up the after part of the ship, causing her to sink immediately after to the bottom, with her spar deck submerged.

Sixth. That several shots from small arms were fired at the object while it was alongside or near the ship before the explosion occurred.

Seventh. That the watch on deck, ship, and ship's battery were in all respects prepared for a sudden offensive or defensive movement; that lookouts were properly stationed and vigilance observed, and that officers and crew promptly assembled at their quarters.

Eighth. That order was preserved on board, and orders promptly obeyed by officers and crew up to the time of the sinking of the ship.

In view of the above facts the court have to express the opinion that no further military proceedings are necessary.[40]

While the Federal Board of Inquiry was absolving Capt. Charles Pickering of any blame for the disaster, Lt. William Alexander remained in Mobile in a state of high anxiety. Word arrived "on February 17th the submarine torpedo boat *Hunley* had sunk the United States sloop-of-war *Housatonic* outside the bar off Charleston, S.C.," remembered the submarine's former first officer. "As I read, I cried out with disappointment that I was not there." Alexander's cries were quickly tempered when he realized something was amiss. "I noted that there was no mention of the whereabouts of the torpedo boat," he lamented. "I wired General Jordan daily for several days, but each time came the answer, 'No news of the torpedo boat.'" Where was the *Hunley?* wondered Alexander. "After much thought, I concluded that Dixon had been unable to work his way back against wind and tide, and been carried out to sea."[41]

Mobile's commanding officer, Dabney Maury, also wanted to know the final fate of Lt. George E. Dixon and the crew of the missing *Hunley*, and he inquired as much to Beauregard's headquarters. Some weeks passed before anything more than a vague answer was provided Maury (which he presumably passed along to Alexander). In reality, absolutely nothing was known as to why the submarine had not returned. Still, Captain Grey of the Charleston Torpedo Service informed the general on April 29 as to what he believed was the fate of the missing boat:

> In answer to a communication of yours, received through headquarters, relative to Lieutenant Dixon and crew, I beg leave to state that I was not informed as to the service in which Lieutenant Dixon was engaged or under what orders he was acting. I am informed that he requested Commodore Tucker to furnish him some men, which he did. Their names are as follows, Viz: Arnold Becker, C. Simkins, James A. Wicks, F. Collins, and—Ridgeway, all of the Navy, and Corporal C. F. Carlson, of Captain Wagner's company of artillery.
>
> The United States sloop of war was attacked and destroyed on the night of the 17th of February. Since that time no information has been received of either the boat or crew. I am of the opinion that, the torpedoes being placed at the bow of the boat, she went into the hole made in the *Housatonic* by explosion of torpedoes and did not have sufficient power to back out, consequently sunk with her.[42]

Captain Grey's ill-conceived theory spawned the popular myth that the submarine perished with her victim.

Although the Federals had closed the book on the *Housatonic* affair, the *Hunley's* saga was only beginning. A one-time friend and executor of the late Horace Hunley's estate, Henry Leovy, heard rumors of the *Housatonic's* destruction. On March 5, he wrote a letter to General Beauregard requesting confirmation of the story and the current status of the submarine, of which he claimed to be part owner. "I am exceedingly anxious to learn whether Lieutenant Dixon accomplished his gallant act with our boat or not, and whether he has escaped," pleaded Leovy. "It will be a source of infinite pride to me to learn this." Five days later, an officer in Beauregard's office responded to Leovy's request for information. "Sir, I am directed by the commanding General to inform you that it was the torpedo boat '*H. L. Hunley*' that destroyed the

Federal man of war '*Housatonic*' and that Lieutenant Dixon commanded the expedition; but I regret to say that nothing has been heard either of Lieutenant Dixon or the torpedo boat, it is therefore feared that gallant officer and his brave companions have perished." [43]

◆   ◆   ◆

As the citizens of Charleston cheered the news of the destruction of a Federal blockader, a pair of letters dispatched to the Navy Department were written by a New York submarine builder named W. L. Barnes. As it turns out, Gideon Welles had already been briefed on the project. In all probability Barnes was a partner of (or associated with) Professor Horstford, the Massachusetts submarine designer who had been favorably contacted by the Permanent Commission regarding the construction of his submarine boat the previous July. Writing from New York on February 29, Barnes opened the letter with a discussion of the loss of the *Housatonic* and "the general subject of submarine operations." Barnes' faith in underwater submarine operations rested in what he believed was a "well planned vessel." I am "confident of substantial success and if the Department will sustain us we will undertake operating in a very short time in Charleston Harbor, and we believe we can destroy their floating batteries and torpedoes without serious difficulty."[44]

Barnes followed up his letter to Welles with another the same day to Welles' immediate subordinate, Gustavus Fox. "I addressed the Secretary of the Navy recently and again today in regard to proposed operations in Charleston Harbor in removing obstructions and blowing up gun boats," began the builder's letter. The vessel, he continued,

is nearly completed—the plan of it you have seen. We are confident of substantial success and will undertake the job if the Department desires it. We would be glad to confer with the Secretary or yourself in regard to it. Our vessel has been quality built and the public knows nothing of it. We can be ready in about two or perhaps three weeks. There is some reason to believe that the machine being operated in Charleston Harbor, and which has finally been successful in destroying one of our vessels, was made in this city.[45]

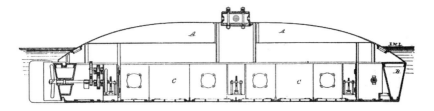

Julius Kroehl's submarine boat *Explorer* was launched during the summer of 1864. *Journal of American Societies of Naval Engineers*

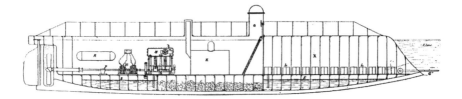

Early-twentieth-century diagram of Anstilt's Mobile-based submarine vessel which appeared in a French book on the history of manned submersibles. *Les Bateaux Sous-Marins*

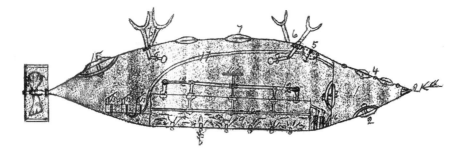

Side view of a submarine boat submitted to the Navy Department in late August of 1864 by an ensign on blockade duty off Mobile, Alabama. The diagram and description speak of a forward lockout chamber and a lime water CO_2 scrubber. *National Archives*

Barnes was under the mistaken impression that the *Hunley* may have been the submarine boat built by New Yorker J. B. Morrell—who had promised the Navy Department in March of 1862 that he could "Blow the Merrimack beyond Davy Jones Locker for three hundred thousand dollars." Since Barnes failed to provide any evidence as to how he reached this conclusion, it will probably remain a mystery as to which New York–based submarine vessel—if not Morrell's—he was referring. The Secretary of the Navy telegraphed Barnes on March 2 that he was interested in the machine. "When your submarine boat is completed the Department will order its examination at your request," wrote Welles.[46]

Thereafter, the historical record between Barnes and Federal naval authorities grows cold, as very little correspondence between them has been found. The next bit of information came about several weeks later when Barnes again wrote to Gideon Welles. The boat was almost finished, implied Barnes on April 23, and he wanted Welles to dispatch an engineering officer to view the submarine and report back to the naval secretary. "In view of the probability that the government, or rather you as secretary may want to control the direction of the vessel after she is completed," explained Barnes, "I would like to have you detail Chief Engineer Stimers to accompany me to Springfield to inspect the vessel and report upon her to you. I will advise with him as to the method of getting the vessel to New York." Welles' terse and unexplained response three days later read simply: "The Department can not comply with your request to detail Chief Engineer Stimers to accompany you to Springfield and examine and report on the submarine boat now building at that place."[47]

Although nothing regarding Barnes' submarine vessel appears in existing naval records for the next several months, work proceeded on the boat. Perhaps Barnes and his partners were not corresponding directly with Washington and instead were in contact with the engineering board finally assigned to evaluate the project. By late July the board had finished its assessment of Barnes' craft. For reasons unknown, it did not find the submarine acceptable. A dismayed Barnes wrote Welles on August 5 pleading for a report on the subject, but Welles refused. "You are informed that the Department does not consider it proper to furnish a copy of the report of the board which examined your submarine boat."

Welles' abrupt termination of the navy's interest in the submarine is the last communication found discussing Barnes' (Horstford's) submarine.[48]

◆   ◆   ◆

"The destruction of the sloop-of-war *Housatonic,* off of Charleston Harbor, demonstrates very conclusively that the Rebels have anticipated us in the practical application of engines of submarine warfare," began a blistering editorial in the *Army & Navy Journal's* March 19, 1864, issue. The loss of the sloop to a submarine attack sent a shockwave through the North—and especially the military establishment. "The fact is a mortifying one," continued the editorial, "but it should invite our inventors to perfect more speedily the appliances which have already been partially developed, especially as other nations seem to be turning their attention to this important subject. By our foreign files we observe that experiments were made a few days ago in the port of Rochelle, to test a submarine vessel of war, the invention of Captain Rochelle, of the French Navy."

The French machine, claimed the magazine,

was so constructed that it might be submerged almost instantly by means of compressed air and a peculiar apparatus with which it was provided. When ready for action, the only part of the craft which remains visible is a small tower whence the commander may observe the position of the vessel to be attacked, and direct the crew which way to steer, in order to strike her hull with the formidable spar which is a chief means of attack of the new contrivance. But the offensive capacity of the craft is not limited to its power as a ram. The spar which discharges this duty is shaped like a tube, and an incendiary shell may be placed in it.

After striking and crushing in the side of a hostile vessel, the PLONGEUR—for that is the name of this naval submarine engine—

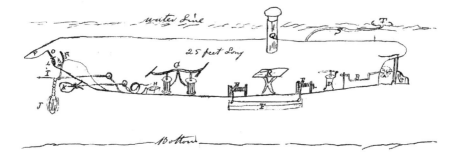

Submarine diagram submitted to the Navy Department on March 12, 1864, by Lt. Hervey of the 11th Connecticut Volunteers. *National Archives*

Just how he came up with this clever system was not revealed in his description of the vessel. His method for sending ships to the bottom of the sea, however, remained primitive. His system was a torpedo attaching device that would drive a short spar fitted with an explosive charge into the victim's hull. To explode the torpedo, the submarine was to back away from the vessel and "electrically detonate by copper wire and galvanic battery."[55]

The Connecticut soldier's ideas were received with some interest by the Permanent Commission. Several weeks of consideration were required before this group of naval experts came to a decision around the middle of July 1864, when a report by Admiral Davis was sent to Secretary Welles. "This invention is not so far advanced in many important particulars as other similar plans before the commission," explained the admiral. "It is especially deficient in the means of providing fresh air, and in the means of regulating the ascent and decent of the boat. Lt. Hervey," cautioned Davis, "has overlooked the fact that the weight worked by a windlass in his plan, would, when resting on the bottom as he proposes, act as an anchor. The Commission, while it appreciates Lt. Hervey's ingenuity and industry, is compelled to say that a trial of his invention would be inexpedient."[56]

While Horace Hervey was no doubt disappointed by the commission's rejection, it may have been prompted in part by the submission of

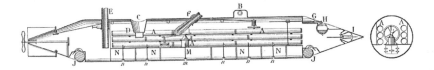

Diagram of Lodner Phillips's 1851 submarine vessel with underwater cannon. *Les Bateaux Sous-Marins.*

another set of diagrams for a similar vessel, a design submitted by perhaps the most knowledgeable submariner in the Union. These plans were advanced by a pair of designers named Lodner Phillips and "Peck." Although Peck's background is unknown, Lodner Phillips' is not. The former shoemaker-turned-submarine-designer had built and tested several small submersibles on Lake Michigan in the decade prior to the Civil War. At least some of Phillips' mid-1850s submarine experiments were geared toward military applications. Why he waited until the summer of 1864 to volunteer his knowledge and assistance with submarines to the Federal government is a mystery.[57]

Perhaps he held grudges. Twelve years earlier, Navy Department officials had demonstrated both a bureaucratic mind-set and spectacular shortsightedness when they snubbed Phillips' offer to sell them a workable submarine. "No authority is known to this Bureau to purchase a submarine boat," croaked the reply. "The boats used by the United States Navy go on and not under the water." The Federal government was a bit more interested in his ideas in 1864—especially with the sloop *Housatonic* resting on the bottom off Charleston. On June 9, 1864, the pair of inventors sent the Navy Department fascinating (and barely believable) information on their early experiments on Lake Michigan. "All the distinctive features were unquestionably demonstrated by the construction of a vessel, forty feet in length, in the year 1850 and by its constant use up to the year 1855," wrote Phillips. His next sentence must have caused even the Navy Department's bureaucrats to sit up and take notice. "The use of shell rockets upon the water line and the discharging of cannon beneath it was coincident with the use of the vessel from 1850 to 1855, hulks having been blown into pieces or sunk on more than one instance." Here, if true, was exactly the type of boat the Federal Navy needed to work its way into Mobile, Wilmington, and Charleston.[58]

On June 28, Admiral Davis recommended to Welles that the navy adopt the submarine boat submitted by Phillips and Peck. Davis' description of the boat is both detailed and fascinating:

> The first vessel described is of a cigar-shape, forty feet in length, and furnished with tubes filled with compressed air sufficient not only to supply breathing air for five men for twenty four hours, but also to be used for the purpose of expelling the water from tanks communicating with the sea, whereby the vessel may be made to rise towards the surface, while it is made to sink by letting the air escape from the tanks into the cabin and readmitting the water, by which the specific gravity of the vessel is increased.
>
> By an ingenious contrivance, and the mere loading of a valve to correspond with the required pressure of the water, a given depth below the surface of the sea may be automatically preserved. This vessel, which is to be propelled by means of man-power, is to be rendered serviceable in attaching torpedoes to the side, or exploding them beneath the bottom of vessels, and to be available in sawing, undermining and otherwise removing obstructions through the agency of compressed air as a motive power. The other vessels proposed are of much larger size, to be propelled by steam, and to be armed with shell rockets to be effective at the surface of the water, and with guns worked on or beneath the surface as occasion may require.
>
> So many conditions are to be fulfilled in order to make successful application of any plan of submarine warfare, that the problem up to this time, within the knowledge of the Commission, has never been successfully solved, or, if so, has not been practically demonstrated. The Commission, however, would not discourage further attempts, and in consideration of the importance of the invention, and the simplicity and apparent feasibility of the plans proposed by Mr. Phillips and Peck, would venture to recommend that an appropriation, sufficient for the construction of one of the smaller vessels, be made for this purpose. In

addition to the reasons above mentioned, which have induced us to offer
the foregoing suggestion, is the testimony with which we were presented
to prove that Mr. Phillips has actually constructed a vessel of this kind,
and experimentally tested all parts of the contrivance.[59]

Phillips' use of buoyancy tanks and compressed air was a precursor
of the surfacing and diving methods utilized by submarines during the
First and Second World Wars. His advanced design in all respects was
decades ahead of its time. Late spring and early summer was a busy
time for Davis and his fellow members of the Permanent Commission,
for a veritable blizzard of submarine diagrams poured into the commission's offices. In addition to Hervey's (which was rejected), and Phillips'
and Peck's (which wasn't), the chief engineer for the Pacific Pearl Company, Julius H. Kroehl, sent a letter and pamphlet for scrutinization. "I
received the pamphlet which you were so good as to send to me, which I
read with great interest; and I have also read your letter of the 14th [not
found]," responded Davis on June 15. "If you wish to submit your submarine boat to the examination and report of the Permanent Commission of the Navy Department appointed to investigate such subjects, it is
necessary that you should write to the Secretary of the Navy, transmit-
ting to him your plans and drawings, and ask to have them examined
and reported upon." Kroehl followed Davis' direction, and within a
short time the Secretary of the Navy recommended his submarine plans
be turned over to Chief Naval Engineer W. W. Wood for examination.[60]

◆   ◆   ◆

While the Permanent Commission was being bombarded with submarine
schemes of one variety or another, Halligan's boat was rapidly nearing
completion at the Selma Iron Works in Alabama. The unification of
Catesby Jones (the works' commander) and Halligan had gone off without
a hitch, and work had progressed rapidly. "I enclose a letter [not found]
from Captain Halligan, the constructor of the torpedo boat. I think he will
endeavor to carry out in good faith what he proposes," Jones wrote to
Maury in Mobile on June 16. The submarine, continued Jones, "will be
launched in a few days. It combines a number of ingenious contrivances,

which, if experiments show that they will answer the purposes expected, will render the boat very formidable." Thanks to Jones' communication we now know that Halligan's boat was not only a submarine, but one "propelled by steam (the engine is very compact), though under water by hand. There are also arrangements for raising and descending at will, for attaching the torpedo to the bottom of vessels, etc. Its first field of operation will be off Mobile Bay, and I hope you may soon have evidence of its success."[61]

The unflappable Jones, who had commanded the *CSS Virginia* during her epic fight in Hampton Roads against the *USS Monitor*, was clearly impressed by Halligan's submarine. Little could he have known that six months of bickering between the army and navy would elapse before the boat would be allowed to seek out an enemy warship.

◆   ◆   ◆

C. Williams of the Triton Company was not a happy man. The submarine advocate who had submitted a report to the Confederate Congress entitled "Submarine Vessels" some months earlier, lodged a complaint with Secretary of War James Seddon that one of his inventions was being used by others who claimed it as their own. Mr. Williams' wartime activities were not limited to his involvement with the Triton Company, as evidenced by his four-page dispatch to Seddon. In fact, the Triton Company member was deeply involved in clandestine underwater operations and other Secret Service–type activities. "It is clearly known to you," Williams wrote to Seddon, "that I am involved in designing inventions for the destruction of enemy vessels and property." My two main projects, he continued, were "rendering submarine navigation profitable and safe, and the adoption of the 'clock torpedo' for the destruction of the enemy army's railroads and depots." The "clock torpedo" was an "explosive . . . shipped in a box or bundle of combustible material designated as ordinary freight. The latter I designed soon after the commencement of the war, as also improvements in submarine navigation."[62]

It was the work of a pair of agents operating "within the enemy's lines," however, that upset Williams. He charged that these spies had constructed a device called the "freight torpedo," and that they claimed

CLASS V.—STEAM ENGINES, &c.

No.	Invention.		Patentee.		Residence.		Date.
237	Steam condenser,	-	M. L. Parry,	-	Galveston, Texas,	-	April 2.

CLASS VI.—NAVIGATION.

No.	Invention.		Patentee.		Residence.		Date.
241	Sea-going vessel,	-	F. G. Smith,	-	Columbia, Tenn.,	-	April 18.
258	Sub-marine boat,	-	C. Williams,	-	St. Louis, Mo ,	-	Oct. 6.
261	Sub-marine boat,	-	Do.	-	Do.	-	Oct. 25.

CLASS VII.—MATHEMATICAL INSTRUMENTS.

No.	Invention.		Patentee.	Residence.	Date.
240	Instrument for calculating distances,	-	J. D. Gressit,	Urbana, Va.,	April 15.

CLASS VIII.—CIVIL ENGINEERING, &c.

No.	Invention.	Patentee.	Residence.		Date.
239	Bridge,	J. E. Garlington,	Chambers C. H., Ala,	-	April 9.

CLASS IX.—LAND CONVEYANCE, &c.

No.	Invention.	Patentee.	Residence.	Date.
243	Mode of turning excentrics for railroads, -	J. B. Gayle,	Laurinburg, N. C.,	April 27.

Page from the original book of patents granted by the Confederate government for the year 1864. On October 6 and 25, Mr. C. Williams of the Triton Company received patents for two submarine boats. *Brockenbrough Library, Museum of the Confederacy* the development of the invention as their own. While Williams admitted he could not claim "exclusive rights to the Clock torpedo," he reminded Seddon that patent papers describing his device were on file in the Confederate Patent Office in Richmond. "It may be well to say that the 'Freight Torpedo' is a modification of that which I designed to use in connection with the submarine apparatus."[63]

Inventions such as the "clock torpedo" were known as "infernal machines" in the Victorian Age, and anyone caught planting such a device would have been sent to the gallows. To avoid fatal reprisals at the end of the war, documents dealing with these and similar inventions were burned or otherwise destroyed to keep the names of their designers and builders secret. Unfortunately, this also accounts for the scarcity of Confederate documents relating to submarines developed by the South during the Civil War. Although a few documents have survived, most have not.

The destruction of these historically rich paper archives is the reason Mr. C. Williams vanishes from the historical record. His letter to Seddon is the last wartime communication attributed to Williams. Although his residence was given as St. Louis, Missouri—as stated in Senator Marshall's letter to the Secretary of War in early 1863—there was no one with that initial and surname living there immediately before or during the war. Who he was or even whether he survived the war is unknown.[64]

◆   ◆   ◆

While we know next to nothing about the Triton Company and the elusive C. Williams, more is known about the Singer Submarine Corps during this period of the war. Much of the knowledge of its activities is derived from a detailed communication written to Maj. Gen. John B. Magruder by a member of the Singer group, R. W. Dunn. In what was essentially a letter of introduction, Dunn briefly outlined for Magruder, the commanding officer of the District of Texas, New Mexico, and Arizona, the history of the Singer organization and its engineers. Dunn's letter also outlined the current status of several of the group's projects, which were germinating across the South. Dunn experienced quite an adventure reaching the wilds of the Trans-Mississippi Theater. "In crossing the Mississippi River on the night of [March] 16th, in company with Col. Ward and Col.

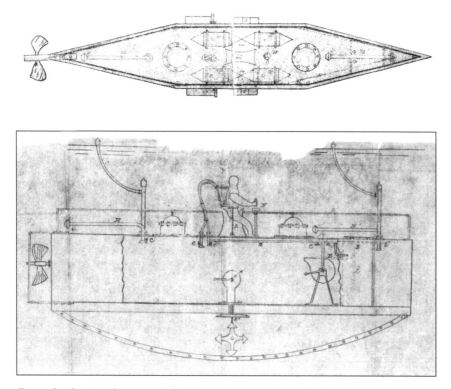

Top and side view diagrams of the Triton Company's second submarine boat that were submitted to the Confederate Engineering Department for approval in late 1863. It's quite possible that members of the Triton group may have been influenced by the *Hunley*'s design, for the two vessels appear strikingly similar. *National Archives*

Clark," wrote Dunn, "I had the misfortune to lose my papers, having been closely pursued by launches from a gunboat, and fired at three times from a small swivel gun on their bow, before reaching the shore." The agent's intent was to "lay before you [Magruder] our propositions for forcing the Enemy's Fleet, lying off our Bars and Harbors, to take some of our medicine."[65]

While "operating" in Charleston, wrote Dunn,

> . . . it was fully demonstrated that torpedoes could be used on the prow, placed on the bow of a boat, without any damage to herself, yet causing

certain destruction to the vessel attacked. On the ninth of November last, I returned again to Richmond, to obtain articles for the construction of such boats as would enable us to operate with safety to our crews, and at the same time strike terror to the enemy. Quite a number of small boats known as 'cigar boats,' for night attacks are now being constructed at Richmond, Wilmington, Charleston and Mobile.

The Sloop-of-War *Housatonic* was destroyed in Charleston Harbor by one of our torpedoes, attached to the prow of a small submarine boat propelled by nine men. In Tennessee we have blown up eight railroad trains.

These successes show conclusively the certainty of explosion of our torpedoes and we would add, that with the use of the safety wire, instead of the trigger [as used on the *Hunley's* torpedo?] we could work such boats as we are building, over a bay where it lacked 4 or 5 feet of water.

After considerable hesitation, we were finally ordered by the Secretary of War to construct one boat at Selma, Alabama and one at Willmington, North Carolina on the following dimensions. 160 feet long, 28ft beam and 11 foot hold, with flat decks—carrying all their machinery below—to be iron sheathed with no capacity for guns, and only showing 2 feet above water when ready for work.

They are to be armed with torpedoes, worked from below decks, and through tubes forward, aft, and on both sides. It is believed by engineers of the highest rank that these boats will be perfectly able to raise the Blockade of all the Harbors in the Confederacy.[66]

Dunn's letter sheds a new light on the Singer group's activities. For example, his claim that "In Tennessee we have blown up eight railroad trains," is the first indication that the submarine organization was also engaged in railroad sabotage—just like the Triton Company and Mr. C. Williams. Dunn's use of the phrase "cigar boats," however, is unfortunately vague, for both the *Hunley* and "David" class of torpedo boats were known interchangeably as "cigar boats." Whether any of the torpedo vessels Dunn claimed were under construction were capable of being entirely submerged will probably never be known.

◆　　◆　　◆

While Dunn was writing his brief history of the Singer Submarine Corps for "Prince John" Magruder, Julius Kroehl and his employers were putting the finishing touches on a privately funded submarine in New York Harbor. Kroehl, the chief engineer of the Pacific Pearl Company, had earlier in the year submitted his plans to the Navy Department, which assigned Chief Naval Engineer W. W. Wood to review them. The military, however, did not take over the project (perhaps it was finally rejected), and Kroehl went forward on his own. The New York–based submarine "could have been used for war purposes, in entering harbors and severing electric wires which led to planted torpedoes," Kroehl later explained.[67]

That the military was not more involved is rather remarkable, for by any standard the *Explorer*, as she would come to be christened, was an advanced underwater boat. For example, she carried large quantities of compressed air for both breathing and equalizing the pressure within the "working chambers" by which divers exited the submarine. When running beneath the surface, explained Kroehl, "The bottom of the boat could be opened or closed, as desired. When exploring in considerable depths the bottom was closed, to save the crew from the heavy pressures." During the summer of 1864, while the land armies were deadlocked in combat around Richmond and Petersburg in the East, and Atlanta in the West, the *Explorer* was towed to the Pearl Islands, near the Bay of Panama, where she proved very successful in the harvesting of pearl-bearing oysters. "The divers employed in the boat enjoyed better health than other pearl divers," claimed Kroehl.[68] The chief engineer of the Pacific Pearl Company was obviously an accomplished submarine designer, but little else about his wartime efforts, if any, are known.

◆   ◆   ◆

Union Admiral David G. Farragut, commander of the West Gulf Blockading Squadron, was a man of action. The 63-year-old sailor had boldly steamed past Forts St. Philip and Jackson two years earlier to lay claim to New Orleans, and he wanted to repeat his performance. His new target lay some 200 miles to the east and was sure to offer a more forceful defense.[69] The admiral had begun planning the capture of Mobile Bay eight months earlier. The bay represented part of the Confederates' outer defenses for the city proper, and if he could capture it, the city would be that much more difficult for the Rebels to hold. With his monitors in the lead and his wooden ships lashed together in pairs behind them, his fleet steamed into the main channel at dawn on August 5. Fort Morgan, the main Southern defensive structure defending the entrance to the bay, spewed forth shot and shell against the attacking Federal vessels in a vain attempt to arrest their progress. The *Tecumseh,* Farragut's leading monitor, struck a submerged Singer contact mine that had been planted some months earlier. As the iron monitor rolled to one side, her huge propeller was seen thrashing air in the last few seconds before she vanished into the depths, taking more than 100 men, including her commanding officer, down with her. A handful of survivors appeared amidst the foam created from the sinking vessel, and Confederates at Fort Morgan held their fire until the men could be rescued by the *USS Manhattan,* which had been following in *Tecumseh's* wake.[70]

From his position high above the deck in the rigging of the *USS Hartford,* Admiral Farragut viewed the disaster with disbelief, for within minutes after the disappearance of the *Tecumseh,* his other attacking vessels began to evidence signs of hesitation. It was during this moment of high drama that Farragut is said to have shouted his immortal words, "Damn the Torpedoes, Four bells Captain, go ahead." As the fleet's wooden vessels pushed forward through the submerged minefield, terrified sailors below decks could hear the steel rods of Singer's contact mines snap against their primers as their ship's hull brushed past. No one knows why none of the torpedoes (except for that which sunk *Tecumseh*) exploded that day. In all likelihood, they had suffered water damage from being submerged since the previous February. Once the fleet was past the guns of Fort Morgan and inside the minefield, Admiral Farragut engaged the formidable ironclad *CSS Tennessee,* which had steamed out from under the fort's guns to meet the enemy. Admiral Franklin Buchanan, the *Tennessee's* brave commander, could not surmount odds of 17 to 1, however, and before long he surrendered. Mobile Bay was in Federal hands.[71]

Soon after the Battle of Mobile Bay, a story began circulating that a Confederate submarine had been captured there. Whether the boat took part in the battle may never be known, for no reports or documents of its actions exist. This historical gap was compounded when everyone on board was killed when the boiler exploded.[72]

A detailed sketch of this mystery boat appeared in the September 24, 1864, edition of *Harper's Weekly*. Judging from its appearance, the submarine pictured was almost certainly the same steam-powered submarine described in General Stephen Hurlbut's April 12, 1864, letter to the Navy Department. The *Harper's* sketch, for example, clearly displays the "small smoke outlet and pilot house" specified in Hurlbut's description of the vessel. Unfortunately, until the "rude sketch" that the general sent with his communication is found, it may never be known for certain whether the submarine he described was the one captured in Mobile Bay, or the boat under construction by Mr. Halligan at the Selma Iron Works.[73]

According to *Harper's Weekly*, the sketch showed a "rebel torpedo boat,"

which was designed to do much injury to Farragut's fleet. Farragut, while outside of the Bay, was in continual expectation of a visit from this boat, of which he had accurate information. She attempted to get out but lost her reckoning, and the adventurers on board becoming frightened, dropped their torpedo, as it impeded their progress, and made their way back into the Bay again.

After that rough weather delayed the proposed expedition, and at last it was found that the boiler was not trustworthy. She was sent to the city for a new one. Returning to Fort Morgan the new boiler exploded, killing the three men who managed her and sinking the vessel. The boat was made of wood, covered with a sheathing of one-fourth inch iron. Her length was 38 feet, and her diameter 7 feet. The boat will be repaired for the use of the Federal fleet.[74]

Was the captured craft a "David" variety torpedo boat, or was she a submarine on the order of the *Hunley?* Thereafter, like so many Confederate underwater machines, nothing more was recorded about the boat. That is, until more than a century later, when a remarkable news story appeared in a Mobile paper. "Was the Union ironclad *Tecumseh* sunk in the Battle of Mobile Bay by a Confederate mine, as history relates, or could the submarine *Captain Pierce* have made the kill?" asked the paper in a provocative headline . . .

Fantastic? Never heard of a submarine taking part in the famed naval battle almost 105 years ago? Neither had we until last week when we received a letter from Wilson N. Rogers a Clearwater, Florida Realtor relating exploits of his grandfather, Captain Albert Pierce and his secret mission to stop Admiral David Farragut's fleet from entering Mobile Bay by a surprise submarine attack.

As related by Rogers, Captain Pierce, who lost a leg in the battle, never claimed to have sunk the *Tecumseh,* and in fact believed his daring mission was a failure. But the interesting speculation that maybe he did sink the Federal monitor without realizing it persists.

Rogers had the story from his Aunt Flora Pierce, Captain Pierce's daughter, now 95 and living in Jacksonville, Florida. Here is a condensed version of the story, as related by Rogers:

The South was cheered by the feat of the submarine *Hunley,* built at Mobile, in sinking the Union sloop-of-war *Housatonic* off Charleston, February 17, 1864, even though the explosive charge that wrecked the Federal vessel also sank the sub.

Captain Pierce and others believed that construction of a fleet of small submarines by the Confederacy could yet turn the tide of defeat into victory for the South. And so the submarine was built in a large barn near Mobile Bay and launched just in time to take part in the great naval battle.

Only President Jefferson Davis and some of his cabinet members, Admiral Franklin Buchanan, commander of the Confederate fleet in Mobile Bay and a few of his trusted officers knew of the building of the secret weapon designed to surprise and repulse Farragut.

Before dawn on the day of the battle, Captain Pierce and two companions, chosen by lot, proceeded down Mobile Bay on the mission. Under cover of darkness, the submarine proceeded to attach a charge of dynamite to an unnamed Federal ship. (Was the unidentified Federal ship that later picked Pierce up, struggling in the water for his life and half delirious with pain, the vessel his sub tried to sink, as he believed? Or could it have been the *Tecumseh* he attacked?)

Harper's Weekly woodcut showing a Confederate submarine captured at the mouth of Mobile Bay, Alabama, in 1864. The boiler within the craft exploded, killing three of the four men aboard her.

To save his life, Captain Pierce underwent the excruciating ordeal of having his shattered leg amputated with a saw and butcher knife aboard the Federal vessel. The only anesthetic available for the crude operation was a copious slug of liquor.

Pierce survived and was taken as a prisoner of war to a prison outside of Mobile, Alabama. The captain's wife, Elizabeth, and two of his brothers, who had fought for the North, persuaded President Lincoln to pardon and release Pierce.

The Pierces later moved to Clearwater, where one of the main streets on which he built his home is named for the heroic captain.

Rogers was recently in Mobile to attempt to document the legend of the submarine *Pierce*. He could find nothing in local archives, nor were there any newspaper files in Mobile for an eight-month period after August 5, 1864 that might have thrown some light on the matter. Rogers believes publications were suspended during the siege of Mobile after Farragut's naval victory explaining absence of news of his grandfather's exploit.

But perhaps even after 105 years, documentation may be found that would add an amazing new chapter to naval history in the battle of Mobile Bay.

Several years ago a sunken object was reported near the *Tecumseh* lying buried in the sand off Fort Morgan. If, in explorations in its efforts to raise the *Tecumseh*, the Smithsonian Institution should run across a submarine, Confederate model—of course, it would have to be the *Captain Pierce*.

We leave this mystery to the future and to history, but regardless of what they find, we thank Mr. Wilson Rogers for his efforts to relate for history the story of Captain Pierce and his participation in the Civil War. He truly was an unsung hero. We have documentation to prove that he built this submarine and participated in the Battle of Mobile Bay. His descendants living in Florida we know are all proud of this great man whose exploits and brave deeds have never been recorded in history.[75]

The story of the *Captain Pierce* collaborates in some details the *Harper's Weekly* account, which also stated that the captured submarine carried a three-man crew. If Pierce lost his leg as a result of the boiler explosion (this is not satisfactorily explained), it would be a simple mistake for the magazine to have claimed that all three men aboard were killed. The captured submarine was one of the clandestine semi-private ventures sanctioned but not funded by the Confederate government. If family records and traditions are correct and only high-ranking members of the government were aware of the submarine's construction, Captain Pierce and his associates may have belonged to the Confederate Secret Service, whose records were destroyed in Richmond at the end of the war. Sadly, nothing more exists about the steam-powered submarine captured at the mouth of Mobile Bay.[76]

Although Admiral Farragut probably rested easier knowing that the Rebel "infernal machine" had been captured, another steam-powered submarine was nearing completion in Selma. Unbeknownst to Farragut, the boat's destination was Mobile.

◆   ◆   ◆

The disastrous explosion of the boiler on the Mobile Bay submarine, coupled with his experiences with the *Hunley* in Charleston, convinced Baxter Watson that another means of propulsion was necessary. On October 10, three weeks after the story of the captured "rebel torpedo boat" appeared in *Harper's Weekly,* the underwater veteran took pen in hand inside the Park and Lyons machine shop in Mobile. The addressee was none other than President Jefferson Davis, and Watson's letter outlined a plan to build a very unusual submarine. "Being the inventor of the Submarine boat that destroyed the Yankee vessel *'Housatonic'* in Charleston harbor in February last," began Watson, "and being unable to build another, I have concluded to lay the matter before you, and ask your assistance and influence in the matter, as I have exhausted all the capital that I had in building and experimenting with that one which was lost in Charleston." His "three years of experience," however, had taught him that a boat like the *Hunley* "can not be used successfully . . . without Electro-Magnetism as power, the air in the boat will not sustain so many men long enough for the time required. I have tried to procure an Electro Magnetic engine, but so far have not accomplished it." Such an engine was available in either "New York or Washington City," continued Watson, "but the amount of five thousand dollars in exchange necessary is more than I can raise." I assure you, he concluded, that such a boat "is of much value to the Confederacy and would like to have the government take the matter in hand. If you desire it, I will be happy to give you a full description, and all the necessary proofs of the utility of the enterprise."[77]

By the time this letter was received in the Southern capital, the Richmond-Petersburg siege was entering its fourth month. General Lee's army was trapped in trenches around the key cities, Atlanta was in the hands of Federal Maj. Gen. William T. Sherman, and the breadbasket of the Confederacy, the Shenandoah Valley, was dominated by Phil Sheridan's Federal Army. The Confederacy was steadily losing the war, and it seemed as though nothing could reverse the tide of defeat. How much attention President Davis paid to Watson's letter, if he even had an opportunity to read it, is unknown.

◆　　◆　　◆

In the middle of October—perhaps as Jefferson Davis was pondering Baxter Watson's intriguing letter—John P. Halligan's Selma-built submarine was ready for sea trials. The War Department had ideas about putting Halligan's boat under army command, and he quickly moved to stop it. "I far prefer to be under the supervision of the Naval Commander of this Department Flag Officer E. Farrand as my enterprise is a naval and not military one," Halligan telegraphed Richmond on October 27. His request was honored, and Special Order No. 259 issued four days later: "Second Lieutenant J. P. Halligan, of a secret service company, will report for temporary duty with Flag-Officer E. Farrand, C.S. Navy, at Mobile, Alabama."[78]

Here again is evidence that many of these men working on underwater projects were members of a "secret service company." As such, Halligan was considered a government agent whose duties could be transferred to whatever branch of service was deemed necessary. This arrangement may have been established at the beginning of the project, when Jefferson Davis granted an exemption to Halligan on January 26, 1864.[79]

John Halligan was an Irish immigrant and just 31 years old in 1864. His ethnic heritage explains why he named his submarine *Saint Patrick*. Although official Confederate documents do not refer to the submarine by this name until December, Halligan had christened his vessel some months earlier. Catesby Jones, the commander of the Selma works where the machine was built, was so impressed with the *Saint Patrick* that he personally accompanied Halligan on two water trials, apparently in the Alabama River at Selma. "I write at the request of Captain Halligan to state that on his invitation I made two trips in the torpedo boat, *Saint Patrick*, one on the 27th of June, and one on the 30th," wrote Jones on July 1, 1864, to Naval Secretary Stephen Mallory. "The boat was under complete control, and made on the 30th about seven knots per hour. The machinery also worked well."[80]

It did not take long for authorities in Washington to learn about the *Saint Patrick*. Indeed, a letter sent to the Washington Naval Yard on November 29, 1864, named John Halligan as both designer and commander of the boat. "I am possessed of certain information which I think will be of use to your Department, and not knowing if you are already in possession of it, take this medium of communicating," an informant named Edward La Croix wrote. At Selma, Alabama, he continued,

. . . has just been built a torpedo boat. Length about 30 feet; has water tight compartments; can be sunk or raised as desired; is propelled by a very small engine, and will just stow in 5 men. It has some arrangements of machinery that times the explosions of torpedoes, to enable the operators to retire to a safe distance. The boat proves to be a good sailor on the river and has gone to Mobile to make last preparations for trying its efficiency on the Federal vessels. Was built and commanded by Halligan. What I have stated you can rely on as strictly true; as to the danger to be anticipated from the boat, you can judge better than I [can].[81]

La Croix's warning was taken to heart by the Navy Department. "By direction of the Secretary of the Navy, I enclose herewith for your information a copy of a letter from Edward La Croix, Detroit, Michigan, relative to a torpedo boat recently finished at Selma, Alabama," Gustavus Fox wrote Farragut six days later on December 5. Gideon Welles was not taking any chances.[82]

Halligan and his staff, meanwhile, were laboring under some misunderstandings with General Dabney Maury's headquarters. The day before Fox sent the warning letter to the victor of Mobile Bay, General Maury was scheming to take the underwater offensive against Farragut—and take Halligan's boat away from him in the process. "Farragut has gone to the North," wrote Mobile's commander to Secretary of War James Seddon on December 4, and "the *Hartford* and other heavy vessels have disappeared from down the bay." After describing the strategic situation confronting him, Maury turned his attention on the Selma submarine. "Halligan, recently appointed Lieutenant, has not yet used his torpedo boat; I do not believe he ever will. His boat is reported a most valuable invention. Many officers, army and navy, are urgent for command of her. May not Commodore Farrand or myself place proper officer in command, to attack enemy at once?"[83]

Maury decided not to wait for a response. The next day, December 5, he dispatched a message to Mobile's naval commander, Capt. Ebenezer Farrand, ordering him to confiscate Halligan's boat:

Every opportunity and facility having been afforded Mr. Halligan to enable him to use his boat against the enemy. Please order a suitable officer of your command to take charge of the *Saint Patrick* at once and attack without unnecessary delay. He may go on the boat with the officer you will appoint to command it; and I presume that pecuniary reward granted by law on account of destruction of enemy's vessels will be secured for Mr. Halligan in case of the successful use of his invention. Pray inform me at once of your decision in the premises, as several officers of my immediate command are urgent applicants for the service we have so long been endeavoring to have accomplished.[84]

Sixty-one-year-old New York–native Ebenezer Farrand, however, the hero of the 1862 land-sea engagement at Drewry's Bluff, refused to snatch Halligan's boat away from him. Farrand had helped Catesby Jones build ships at Selma and was now in command of Mobile's naval forces. Perhaps mindful of Jones' relationship with Halligan, Farrand's refusal may have stemmed from his unwillingness to offend his fellow naval officer. Whatever his reason, Farrand would not act as Maury desired. Clearly the divided command structure in Mobile was not militarily healthy. As the situation between Maury and Farrand steadily deteriorated, Lt. Gen. Richard Taylor, the commander of East Louisiana, Mississippi, and Alabama, cast his eyes about for a solution. Finding none, he sought his superior's assistance. Three days before the war's last Christmas, Taylor wrote Gen. P. G. T. Beauregard, who was now the administrative commander of the massive Military Division of the West. "A conflict exists between land and naval commanders in regard to a torpedo boat," explained Taylor through his aide, George Brent, with "the former ordering it into active service, the latter refusing to obey. What must be done?"[85]

Beauregard was in no mood to deal with another submarine boat. John Bell Hood, who had taken command of the Army of Tennessee from Joe Johnston at the gates of Atlanta that July, had ignored Beauregard's advice and driven north through Alabama into Tennessee. The result was the piecemeal destruction of the South's only viable Western Theater army at Franklin and Nashville. William T. Sherman, meanwhile, had marched three Federal armies through Georgia and was now on the verge of capturing Savannah, one of the last seaports besides Wilmington still open to the Confederacy. General Lee's Army of Northern Virginia, unable to escape U.S. Grant's death hug, was suffering a horrible winter in the cold and muddy trenches before Richmond. A message about commanders squabbling over a torpedo boat may have brought a grim smile to the Creole's face. Even if Halligan's submarine could be used successfully in Mobile, it was too late to turn back the tide of defeat.

The new underwater weapon which had promised so much for so long had delivered so little.

CHAPTER 5

1865:
BEGINNINGS

"Uncle Jim went into the government service for the Confederates—I suppose you know he ran the blockade after Mobile was quarantined. He had a submarine, and passed out of the Bay, passing Fort Morgan frequently, and the Federals in charge of the fort never caught him."

—1930s description of James A. Rice, a submariner attached to the Confederate submersible CSS Saint Patrick

B y January of 1865, the battered Confederacy was tottering on the brink of collapse. In the Eastern Theater, the static strategic situation now favored the Federals. The Shenandoah Valley had been destroyed as a granary for Southern armies, allowing General Grant at Petersburg and Richmond to focus all of his attention on Robert E. Lee's dwindling Army of Northern Virginia, which was wrapped up tightly behind its entrenchments. Each day the Confederates remained in them weakened the army through desertions and casualties. In the Western Theater, the vital Georgia cities of Atlanta and Savannah were in Federal hands, John Bell Hood's campaign to occupy Tennessee had ended in the rout of his army at Nashville in mid-December 1864, and Federal armies were poised to slice through the remaining bits of the Confederacy as soon as weather permitted. Only one major port, Wilmington, was now open to blockade runners, and the Federals were preparing to launch the largest combined operation of the war to seize it.

Even though the war's end was rapidly approaching, submarine construction and operations continued unabated. In fact, the final weeks of the war witnessed another attack by a Confederate submersible.

While Maj. Gen. Dabney Maury and Capt. Ebenezer Farrand bickered in Mobile over who should control John Halligan's new submarine torpedo boat, Baxter Watson, the codesigner of the three ill-fated boats *Pioneer, Pioneer II,* and *Hunley,* was attempting to build yet another underwater boat. He had sought the assistance necessary from President Jefferson Davis the previous October, but was apparently rebuffed. General Beauregard was now his final hope. Watson wrote to the general from Mobile on January 6 and plead for help.

"Being the inventor of the submarine boat that destroyed the *Housatonic* in Charleston in February last, and losing all I had with her," Watson began, "I have concluded to lay the matter before you, and request your assistance in building another for the same place." The *Hunley* itself, claimed the inventor, was a "complete success," and its ultimate failure to sink more ships and raise the blockade around Charleston "came about through mismanagement, a fault over which I had no control, as my supervision of her ceased as soon as she was in the water." Watson proposed to construct another submarine, this one with an "electromagnetic engine to propel a boat of that description, as a boat of that kind is impracticable with any other kind of power. I firmly believe that I can destroy the blockade in Charleston in a short time if I get the assistance."[1] General Beauregard's response to Watson's plea for help, if indeed he responded at all, has not been located.

While Baxter Watson waited, General Maury grew increasingly irritated over the unresolved situation surrounding Halligan's inactive *Saint Patrick.* Although Richard Taylor had sought Beauregard's guidance on the subject, whatever the Creole offered had not settled the issue. The weeks were passing, Mobile was increasingly threatened, and the submarine was sitting idle. On January 13, Mobile's commander telegraphed directly to Jefferson Davis. "Halligan, with torpedo and boat, will not attack enemy," complained Maury, "[and] has been transferred by Commodore Farrand. Please have him and boat placed under my orders, with authority to me to place an officer of the army or navy in command, that the enemy may be attacked at once." The *Saint Patrick,* explained the general, "is said to be the best of the kind. Halligan and five or six men have now been for months exempt from service on account of her. There has never been so good an opportunity for a torpedo boat to operate as is afforded by the fleet off Mobile."[2]

President Davis acted quickly, perhaps because he realized that traditional means were not going to alter the course of the war. On Janu-

Commandant of the Selma
Iron Works, Catesby ap R.
Jones, took a ride in Halli-
gan's submarine *Saint Patrick*
during late June of 1864.
Naval Historical Center

ary 18, he telegraphed Maury in distant Mobile that the "Secretary of the
Navy [Mallory] does not know that his Department has any control over
the boat, but has directed Captain Farrand, if under his control, to turn it
over to you." Although Mallory's order to Farrand has not been found, it
did the trick and the torpedo boat was placed at Maury's disposal.[3]

Maury's January 26 letter to Inspector-General Samuel Cooper in Richmond sheds a substantial amount of light on the acrimony surrounding the
Saint Patrick. "In accordance with instructions from the Navy Department,
communicated to Commodore Farrand, that officer transferred to my command the torpedo boat *Saint Patrick,* built on a contract with the Government by a man named Halligan," Maury explained the submarine was to:

> have been ready for action in July last, and I hoped to use it against
> the enemy's fleet off Fort Morgan. I therefore caused every possible

assistance to be given to Halligan in building her, and urged her early completion. It was not, however, till the month of [left blank in original letter] Halligan arrived here with the boat. I therefore had him supplied with every means to move against the enemy, and notified him that if he did not attack at once I would place an officer in charge of her who would.

Halligan, however, was not about to sit back and have his submarine—which he viewed as private property—stolen out from under him. "In the course of a few days," continued Maury in his letter to Cooper of January 26,

> I found it necessary to supersede Halligan, who then placed his affairs in the hands of a lawyer and procured from Richmond a transfer of his boat to the naval commander of this station. Impressed with the importance of using so formidable a vessel as this is said to be, I have continually and repeatedly urged Commodore Farrand to make Halligan attack or to place the boat in charge of one of the clever young officers of the Navy or Army who have been pressing for the command of her. This, however, he did not do until in consequence, I presume, of my official reports to higher authority, he was ordered to transfer the *Saint Patrick* to me.

Halligan was not about to give up. When his legal attempts to retain control of the *Saint Patrick* failed, the builder utilized another method to keep it out of operation. "I immediately asked [Farrand] to let me have Lieutenant Walker, of the Navy to command her," explained Maury to Cooper,

> And on placing that officer in charge of the vessel, now lying under the guns of the eastern shore, he found that Halligan had been absent from her for two weeks, and had taken off with him several essential parts of her machinery. After some search Halligan was found comfortably established in the Battle House, and Mr. Walker, by energetic and good management, has recovered from him the necessary machinery and thinks he can operate tomorrow night.

The escalating hysteria over control of the submarine strained relations between Maury and Farrand. "I regret to perceive the impression has been made on his mind that a cordial desire to cooperate with each other may not exist here," wrote Maury. "Our relations have always been pleasant and our intercourse free, and I shall not permit any private feelings to interfere with the business before us. When I find the Commodore disagrees with my views of what is required," Maury concluded, "I shall refer the matter to higher authority."[4] Maury won out, and the *Saint Patrick* was put under the command of Lt. John T. Walker, a daring Confederate naval officer who had been requesting command of the submarine for some time.

Of John Halligan and his staff of submariners, nothing more is known. Neither is information available as to why he did not immediately launch an attack against the Federal warships off Mobile. Maury later claimed that Halligan had "shown himself deficient in nerve or capacity to attack the enemy." Perhaps such was the case. Lieutenant Walker, however, possessed the requisite strength of will to give it a go, and he did not waste any time getting the new boat ready for action. On the night of January 27, 1865, just three days after formally taking command, he and a daring crew pushed off after dark to seek out and destroy any blockading vessel that crossed their path.[5]

The method Walker employed to approach enemy ships is not known, for the *Saint Patrick's* log books have never been found. The torpedo boat was designed to operate beneath the surface of the water, and it is difficult to imagine the vessel's smokestack belching a plume of telltale smoke as it weaved its way through a screen of steam-powered Federal picket boats patrolling around Admiral Farragut's fleet. With enemy sentries scanning the surface of the dark water with calcium lights, Lieutenant Walker surely submerged his vessel for at least the initial part of his approach that night.

What we know for sure, however, is that Walker came within a hair's breadth of going down in history as the commanding officer of the second submarine to sink a Federal warship. The attack was made on the dark night of January 27, explained General Maury to Samuel Cooper a week following the attempt. "At 1 a.m. he struck the enemy's flagship *Octorara* aft the wheelhouse. The torpedo missed fire[d]. The greatest consternation and confusion was occasioned on the ship, so that the fire of artillery and musketry, which was directed against the *Saint Patrick*, failed to strike her, and she returned with her crew to the protection of our batteries." The *Octorara* was a 10-gun paddle wheel steamer under the command of Lt. Comdr. W. W. Low, whose report of the incident has not been found. The *Saint Patrick* did not escape completely unscathed. "Some portion of her machinery was damaged during the expedition," continued Maury in his report to Richmond, "but Mr. Walker is confident that he will be ready to go out again by the next dark moon. I take pleasure in reporting to the War Department the fine conduct of Lieutenant Walker and in recommending him through you to the favorable notice of the Navy Department."[6]

It is unclear whether the crew of the *Octorara* fully appreciated that they had been the target of yet another submarine attack. In all likelihood they believed that a David-class torpedo boat had been sent against them—especially since the final leg of the attack was conducted with the smokestack up and operating. *Harper's Weekly* reported on the episode just a few weeks later:

Incident on Board the *Octorara:*

The incident illustrated in the above cut is thus narrated by our correspondent: On the night of the 26th a torpedo-boat came out from Mobile Bay, and made an unsuccessful attack upon the *Octorara*. At about 2 A.M., though the night was very dark, an object was discovered not many yards astern, and making direct for the vessel. The look-out hailed lustily 'Boat ahoy!' The response came 'Ay, ay!' as though from one of our own boats. The officer of the deck immediately sang out to them to 'lie on their oars'; to which they answered 'Ay, ay!' A moment after they rasped along the vessel's side from aft forward to the guards. The knowledge that it was the torpedo-boat of the rebels now flashed upon all. The intrepidity of the captain of the after-guard is worthy of the highest praise. Though all expected momentarily to be blown up, this man, seeing how readily they could gain an advantage over the enemy by prompt action, grasped her smoke-pipe as it came by the guards of the ship, at the same time crying out lustily for a rope to make the devil fast with it. The remaining sailors, acting under different impulses, recoiled to the opposite side of the deck. Several shots were fired at this brave man, and as his exertions were hardly sufficient to retain his hold on the hot pipe, he preferred to let go rather than be dragged overboard.[7]

Lieutenant Walker worked hard to prepare the *Saint Patrick* for another attack against the blockaders, and in early February once more left the protected mooring beneath the heavy guns of the eastern shore batteries and entered Mobile Bay. Instead of being the hunter, however, Walker was ordered to create a diversion in favor of another vessel, the *Red Gauntlet.* For more than six months the blockade runner had been bottled up in Mobile Harbor following Admiral Farragut's stunning naval victory. With her hold bulging with valuable cotton that could be traded for much-needed European supplies, it was decided that an attempt would be made to run the *Red Gauntlet* past the Federal defenders in an effort to reach the open sea.

The key to this desperate plan resided with the *Saint Patrick*, which had to cause enough fuss to open up a lane for the sleek blockade runner to escape through. Although a gap was opened—the exact details of the event are unknown—local commanders decided that the attempt was too hazardous and canceled the operation at the last moment. Thus the *Red Gauntlet* spent the rest of the war waiting beneath the cannons of General Maury's shore batteries for another opportunity that never arrived.[8]

◆   ◆   ◆

During the war's final months, Union headquarters in occupied New Orleans received word that the Rebel "navy" operating in conjunction with Gen. E. Kirby Smith's Trans-Mississippi Army west of the Mississippi River was in possession of as many as five submarine torpedo boats rumored to have been built by a member of the Singer Submarine Corps.

Captain Singer had detailed several members of his submarine corps to one of General Smith's engineering companies as early as mid-September of 1863. The surrender of Vicksburg and its army on July 4 of that year had largely cut off Smith's forces from the eastern section of the Confederacy, and so these activities have remained secret for more than a century. With Western Louisiana, Arkansas, Texas, and the Indian Territories under his command, Kirby Smith fought on, with few dispatches and orders flowing between his Trans-Mississippi command and the distant authorities in Richmond. As Smith labored, so apparently did Southern submarine builders. Confederate naval forces continued to operate out of Shreveport, Louisiana, along the Red River, Houston, Texas, and out of the port city of Galveston, Texas, which was still open to the Gulf of Mexico.[9]

On the same day the Confederate Congress reluctantly voted to allow blacks into the Southern army, March 13, 1865, a remarkable report was prepared by Maj. A. M. Jackson, 10th U.S. Colored Heavy Artillery, and dispatched to the headquarters of the Military Division of West Mississippi in New Orleans. Mysterious activities on the Red River and elsewhere planned with the intent to destroy Federal ships led the major to believe "that there is some such plan on foot, of which the commanders of gunboats should be notified." Several submarines, advised Jackson, "one of which is at Houston and four at Shreveport," were in the hands of the Rebels and ready for operation. Jackson then went on to describe what essentially could have passed for the *Hunley,* an iron hand-cranked submarine boat:

> The following is a description of the torpedo boats. . . . The boat is 40 feet long, 48 inches deep, and 40 inches wide, built entirely of iron, and shaped similar to a steam boiler. The ends are sharp pointed. On the sides are two iron flanges (called fins), for the purpose of raising or lowering the boat in the water. The boat is propelled at a rate of four miles per hour by means of a crank, worked by two men. The wheel is on the propeller principle.
>
> The boat is usually worked seven feet under water and has four dead lights for the purpose of steering or taking observations. Each boat carries two torpedoes, one at the bow, attached to a pole 20 feet long; one on the stern, fastened to a plank 10 or 12 feet long. The explosion of the missile on the bow is caused by coming in contact with the object intended to be destroyed. The one at the stern, on the plank, is intended to explode when the plank strikes the vessel.

The air arrangements are so constructed as to retain sufficient air for four men at work and four idle, two or three hours. The torpedoes are made of sheet iron three-sixteenths of an inch thick, and contain 40 pounds of powder. The shape is something after the pattern of a wooden chum, and about 28 inches long. Jones, the originator and constructor of these boats, also constructed one which attempted to destroy the New ironsides in Charleston, S.C. . . . .[10]

The "Jones" referenced in Major Jackson's report was James Jones of the Singer Submarine Corps. Jones, who together with Captain Singer, R. W. Dunn, and several other members of Singer's group of engineers, had by early 1865 been assigned to Kirby Smith's Trans-Mississippi command. There is some evidence that some of these men had been part of the *Hunley's* inaugural crew. If so, they were knowledgeable men with practical experience beneath their belts.[11]

Other telling evidence exists that R. W. Dunn was leading the effort to construct Confederate submarines in the Trans-Mississippi Theater. In June of 1864, Kirby Smith ordered "Captain H. Lubbock" to strip the iron "off the steamer 'Wave' at Lake Charles," and turn it over to R. W. Dunn "for torpedo service, and report the audit to these headquarters."[12] Several members of the Singer Submarine Corps in addition to Dunn were assigned to Houston, Texas, in early 1865, where one of the alleged submarines discussed in Major Jackson's report was being built. One of the Singer men was Pvt. Timothy Crim of Company B, 2nd Texas Infantry. On March 11, 1865, as the war was winding down to its bitter conclusion, Crim's leave from his unit was "extended for sixty (60) days from expiration of original detail, and he will continue to report to Mr. R. W. Dunn at Houston as a Machinist First Class for special duty." What, exactly was going on in Houston that required Crim to work with Dunn and his associates? The answer, perhaps, was contained in Major Jackson's report.[13]

As implied above, the five submarine boats described by Major Jackson—40' long and 48" deep with tapered ends—must have looked strikingly like the *Hunley*. Even the speed of these machines matched the doomed submarine that was now resting somewhere off the coast of Charleston. Because of the amount of detail supplied by Jackson's source, a Federal spy named "Mr. Hunnicutt," it is worthwhile to examine his statements in light of what we know about the *Hunley* and other Singer Submarine Corps projects. Hunnicutt reported that these Texas and Louisiana boats could be propelled at about four miles per hour, the same speed attributed to the *Hunley* in the postwar memoirs of William Alexander. Perhaps the only difference between these boats and the *Hunley* was in the number of conning towers. According to Jackson, the Trans-Mississippi torpedo boats had "four dead lights (probably mounted in the trunk of the conning tower) for the purpose of steering or taking observations." If true, then these submarines, unlike the *Hunley*, probably had but a single hatch instead of a pair of them.

Hunnicutt's description of the armament of these crafts are also reminiscent of the *Hunley*. According to the testimony he fed Major Jackson, they could either tow their explosive devices at the end of a long rope or mount them on a spar attached to the bow. Although Hunnicutt stated that each boat carried two torpedoes, it seems highly unlikely that explosive devices would be carried off both the bow and stern simultaneously. It seems far more probable that the boats were rigged to utilize either configuration. Both methods (towing and a spar assembly) had been utilized by the *Hunley* earlier in the war. The description of the torpedo itself indicates the explosive device in question was a modified Singer Torpedo. The underwater mines developed by Singer and company had a unique butter-churn appearance that closely matched Hunnicutt's description of the torpedoes used by the Texas-Louisiana torpedo boats.

One portion of Hunnicutt's statement seems at odds with itself, however. When he described the means of propulsion and number of crew members necessary to man the vessel, he initially stated, "The boat is propelled at a rate of four miles an hour by means of a crank, worked by two men." Widespread experience in both Northern and Southern states had conclusively proven that two men could not possibly have cranked a 40' iron submarine anywhere. Hunnicutt then stated: "The air arrangements are so constructed as to retain sufficient air for four men at work and four idle, two or three hours." Given the size of these machines (40'), this second description seems more probable and falls in place with what we know about the *Hunley* and other similar vessels:

these Singer boats were manned by a crew of eight, the same number of shaft turners that had been required to man the *Hunley*. Hunnicutt's statement about the submerged oxygen supply offers one last tantalizing clue evidencing the hand of Singer operatives with these boats. William Alexander was the only surviving crew member with widespread operational experience in the *Hunley*, which had undertaken numerous nocturnal patrols without finding a victim. Vital information as to the boat's performance would have been shared with the surviving members of the Singer Submarine Corps, as well as with other Confederate submariners. Alexander was also the last surviving crew member of the ill-fated *Hunley's* endurance test in the Back Bay behind Battery Marshall at Charleston. The knowledge that a submarine of the *Hunley's* size could sustain life-giving air to a crew of eight for "two or three hours," as Hunnicutt informed Major Jackson, would only be known to someone who had access to that information—someone like James Jones of the Singer Submarine Corps, who had closely worked with Lieutenant Alexander and other engineers of the group.[14]

Unfortunately, any original reports filed on behalf of these western submarines have not come to light, so their existence is open to some question. Although no documentation currently exists regarding these Trans-Mississippi submarine boats, the following lines taken from the Federal spy M. P. Hunnicutt's original report on the subject, indicate that he at least was convinced of their authenticity. "On the stage from Marshall Texas I became acquainted with a man by the name of James Jones who had been sent from Richmond Virginia, where he had been engaged in the torpedo business to destroy the Ram *Tennessee*. I saw his plans and specifications for constructing a boat 40 feet long, 40 inches deep and 48 inches wide for the purpose of destroying that vessel particularly. The hull of the vessel is already at Houston and there are four others at Shreveport. I paid particular attention to his statements and agreed to go into the undertaking with him and invest five thousand dollars in the torpedo association if I did not go to the interior of Mexico. I wrote him from Bagdat that I would go into the interior. The boat is to leave Houston down the Brazos, thence into the Atchafalaya Bayou and through some other Bayou to the Red River. The reason that they did not take one of the boats from Shreveport was because there was so many

Yankee spies around there he was afraid the plot would be discovered. They contemplate starting by the tenth of March and certainly by the twentieth. From all the circumstances connected, I consider that the attempt will be certain."

If Hunnicutt had taken the previous days stage, or had never struck up a conversation with Singer operative James Jones, we would be totally in the dark as to this bold Singer plan. From the way Hunnicutt described his accidental encounter with the talkative Jones, we can assume that Jones had no idea that he was giving away valuable information to an enemy spy, for Hunnicutt, as strange as it may sound, even stated that Jones had invited him to "invest five thousand dollars in the torpedo association" of which James Jones was a member. [15]

◆　　◆　　◆

While Major Jackson and other Union naval officers in New Orleans pondered the new threat posed by the reported Rebel Houston and Shreveport submarines, the war east of the Mississippi River was rapidly drawing to a close. The arrival of spring meant that General Grant's army could now move to break the final rail link supplying Petersburg and Richmond. Meanwhile, Gen. Joseph E. Johnston, recently assigned by Robert E. Lee to coalesce fragments of Confederate units in the Carolinas and stop William T. Sherman's relentless drive northward, attacked his enemy at Bentonville on March 19, 1865. The brief tactical victory turned against the South as more Federals flooded onto the field. After two more days of inconclusive skirmishing and combat, Johnston retreated. By this time Lee realized that his final hope was in maneuver. The Confederate capital at Richmond would have to be abandoned and the remnants of the once-mighty Army of Northern Virginia would attempt to slip away and link up with Johnston's army, then operating near Raleigh, North Carolina. Perhaps together they could defeat Sherman and then turn and meet Grant. It was a plan born of desperation and doomed to failure.

Even during these last dying days of the Confederacy a young Southern diver named A. J. Wilson was putting onto paper a design for a new "Submarine Armor (diving suit)," he hoped could be used against

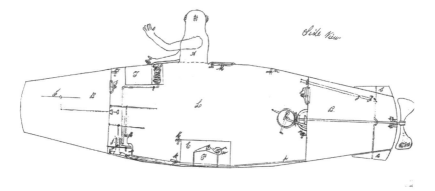

This diagram of a submarine was submitted by a naval officer on blockade duty off Mobile, Alabama, during the early spring of 1865. *National Archives*

the powerful Union fleet operating below Richmond on the James River. The diver, a boatswain on the ironclad *CSS Fredericksburg,* anchored in the James River, sent his suggestion to Navy Secretary Stephen Mallory on March 31, 1865, the day before Maj. Gen. George Pickett was defeated at Five Forks and the Federal floodgates opened upon Lee's beleaguered army. It is doubtful whether Mallory even saw Wilson's intriguing letter.

"I have the honor to lay before you the enclosed diagram of a submarine armor for attaching torpedoes to the bottom of the enemy's ships," began Wilson. His plans, he explained, had been "communicated with officers of the C.S. Navy," who suggested they be forwarded to Mallory for action. "Should you think proper to consider this application, I respectfully request I may be permitted to give a verbal explanation which I can better accomplish than by a written statement." Wilson attached "a diagram with explanation," of the unique and rather complex apparatus:

The lower part of the body is seated on the crutch 'L'. with feet attached to the crank 'K'. 'G'. The lower part of the armor, in form conical, to be made of thin metal so far as the waist band 'N, M'. The jacket to be made of rubber the same as the common armor with hoops on the inside, as at 'B', of thin metal, to keep the dress clear of the body, for ventilation.

The jacket must be covered with canvas on the outside, and coated with oil, to prevent injury, and attached to the metal part 'G', at the waist bolt 'N'. The helmet 'C', to be made of metal as the common armor, with eye lights, as at 'F'. The 'D' air pipe, with valve 'E', to be stopped at any time, when necessary.

The shaft 'I', will go to the clutch 'L', on which the man is seated, with a cog wheel at 'J'. The crank 'K', also with cog wheel, will turn the propeller and give sufficient motion to propel the armor through the water, which can be guided by the hands.

It will be necessary to have shot bags for ballast, so as to give the buoyancy required, which is just to a sinking point, some of which ballast can be detached if necessary, and the slightest motion will propel me to the surface. Provided with this armor I can carry a torpedo of 100 lbs. of the same buoyancy as the armor, secured to the breast of the jacket. The torpedo will have a clamp, and screw, to enable me to secure it to the bottom of a ship. There must be an air chamber in the torpedo for the clock work which can be put in motion on my leaving the boat.

I propose thus equipped to approach the enemy's ships with a boat, conveniently as it can be done with the boat, then put the clock in motion, and getting myself into the armor, propel through the water, with the air pipe above the surface, to the bow of the ship intended to be destroyed. I then close the valves and haul myself by the stern of the ship, under her bottom, secure to the keel the torpedo with the clamps, and return to the boat. At the expiration of the time the clock has been set for it will strike a sensitive tube, which will explode the torpedo.

I have had years of experience with marine armors and feel assured of success.[16]

The day after Wilson wrote his letter Pickett's men were crushed at Five Forks, which resulted in the severing of the Southside Railroad. The following dawn, April 2, Grant launched a massive assault all along the lines and the Petersburg front began to collapse. Instead of overseeing the construction of a new "submarine armor," Mallory issued orders to Adm. Raphael Semmes, the commander of the James River Squadron, to torch his ships (including the *Fredericksburg*) and

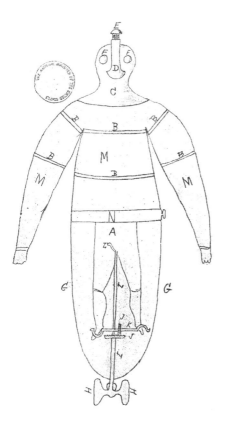

This faded and darkened diagram for "submarine armor" (a diving suit) was submitted to the Confederate Navy Department by diver A. J. Wilson, a boatswain on the ironclad *CSS Fredericksburg*. *National Archives*

join General Lee's retreating remnants en route toward Danville, Virginia. Admiral Semmes left a breathtaking description of the memorable evening of April 2, 1865:

> An explosion, like the shock of an earthquake, took place, and the air was filled with missiles. It was the bowing up of the *Virginia II*, my late flagship. The spectacle was grand beyond description. Her shell room had been full of loaded shells. The explosion of the magazine threw all these shells, with their fuses lighted, into the air. The fuses were of different lengths, and as the shells exploded by twos and threes, and by the dozen, the pyrotechnic effect was very fine.
>
> The explosions shook the houses in Richmond and must have waked the echoes of the night for forty miles around. . . . Owing to a delay [at the bridge], the sun, a glorious unclouded sun, as if to mock

our misfortunes, was now rising over Richmond. Some windows, which fronted the east, were all aglow with the rays, mimicking the real fires that were already breaking out in various parts of the city. In the lower part of the city, the school ship *Patrick Henry* was burning, and some of the houses near the Navy Yard were on fire. But higher up was the principal scene of the conflagration. Entire blocks were on fire here, and a dense canopy of smoke, rising high in the still morning air, was covering the city as with a pall. The rear guard of our army had just crossed as I landed my fleet at Manchester, and the bridges were burning in their rear. The Tredegar Iron Works were on fire, and continual explosions of loaded shells stored there were taking place.[17]

Jefferson Davis and his cabinet officials had commandeered all the trains and departed the city. Luckily, Admiral Semmes and his 500 sailors managed to find an old locomotive with a faulty engine. Somehow they managed to repair it and hurriedly departed the burning city just as Union forces began crossing the James River. As Semmes and his ragged force of sailors moved away from their burning capital, smoke from the burning Mechanic's Institute and other buildings, which housed government documents, choked the morning sky. Those flames consumed most of the secret documents chronicling the Confederate submarine service.

Just as Richmond was doomed, so too was General Lee's army, which staggered westward until April 9, 1865, when it surrendered at Appomattox Courthouse. The fate of "Submarine Armor" designer A. J. Wilson, the former boatswain on the *CSS Fredericksburg*, is unknown. Perhaps he fought with the bulk of Semmes' men in the fiasco at Sayler's Creek on April 6.

◆   ◆   ◆

The Confederate capital was a smouldering ruin and General Lee's Army of Northern Virginia was only days away from surrender when the final chapter of the Mobile-based submarine torpedo boat *Saint Patrick* was written.

Although Mobile Bay had fallen to the powerful Federal navy in August of 1864, the victors had found it impossible to drive the stubborn Confederates from the seaport itself. By mid-March 1865, a large combined operation was planned to take Mobile. The city's primary method of defense, in addition to the motley Confederate flotilla, was centered on two large earthen strongholds. Fort Blakely and Spanish Fort were situated on the eastern shore, the former near the mouth of the Alabama River, and the latter almost directly across from Mobile itself. Together their firepower continued to thwart Admiral Farragut's best efforts to capture the city. The only way to take the place was to lay siege from behind the forts.[18]

During the opening nights of April 1865, the *Saint Patrick* was used to ferry supplies to the isolated garrison at Spanish Fort. Since the boat was nearly ballasted to neutral buoyancy, it would have been necessary to remove her internal ballast and replace the numerous ingots of lead or pig iron with cases of shot and shell or other weighty items. The boat's supply runs lend credence to the fact that 44-year-old James A. Rice, a native of Alabama, was on board at this time. In 1933, Rice's niece wrote a brief family history claiming that her uncle had been involved with running supplies past Farragut's fleet by submarine during the closing days of the Civil War:

> Uncle Jim went into the government service for the Confederates—I suppose you know he ran the blockade after Mobile was quarantined. He had a submarine, and passed out of the Bay (Mobile), passing Fort Morgan frequently, and the Federals in charge of the fort never caught him. He did much in getting supplies into the city, and you may be sure he always sent things to our Grandparents and mama. I have heard my father say, 'Uncle Jim was one of the boldest, bravest men he ever knew.'[19]

Although family histories written so long after the event must be treated with some suspicion as to their accuracy, this one has the ring of truth. Recently discovered evidence confirms that the *Saint Patrick* was indeed a submarine, and that it acted as a supply vessel during the final weeks of the war. In addition Rice's niece utilized an interesting choice of words when she explained that her uncle "went into the government service for the Confederates." Documents kept throughout the war confirm that the phrase "government service" was often tied to submarine experimentation or related underwater activities. James A. Rice may

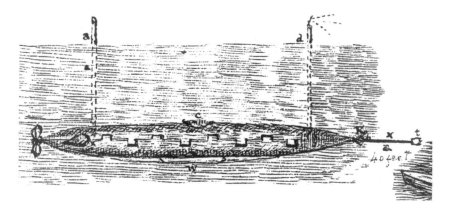

This hand-cranked, cigar-shaped submarine with twin snorkels was drawn by the commander of the Confederate Torpedo Bureau, General Gabriel Rain. No information regarding the construction of this vessel has thus far come to light. *Brockenbrough Library, Museum of the Confederacy*

well have been a member of the Confederate Secret Service, and most Confederate submariners had close ties to that organization. Nothing more of Rice's contributions to the Southern war effort is known, for he drowned in Mobile Bay in early January of 1877, without leaving a record of his "government service."

While the *Saint Patrick* was supplying the garrison of Spanish Fort, an order was being issued from Louisiana appointing a commander for the Galveston, Texas, torpedo boat built by James Jones of the Singer Submarine Corps. The telegram is a testimony of the severed communications between the Trans-Mississippi and the Southern capital, for it was directed to Navy Secretary Mallory in Richmond on April 8— almost a week after the city fell to the Federals. "I have ordered Lieutenant Phillips to Texas to take command of a torpedo boat built near Galveston by the Engineering Department," wrote J. H. Carter, the commander of the naval defenses in western Louisiana in Shreveport. Lieutenant Phillips started his journey to Texas on April 9, 1865, the same day General Lee surrendered at Appomattox Courthouse.[20]

General Lee's surrender had ended the war in Virginia, but fighting continued in other parts of the South. General Joe Johnston did not surrender his army until April 26, 1865, at Durham, North Carolina. In far-

A confederate "David" class submersible is shown at the U.S. Naval Academy in this postwar photograph. *Naval History Center*

off Texas and Louisiana, Kirby Smith's forces remained active until the final days of May. Their last official engagement near Brownsville, Texas, ironically, ended in a Confederate victory. Smith's surrender documents were not executed until June 2, 1865.

◆   ◆   ◆

Some weeks later a Union naval force was sent far up the muddy and twisting Red River north of Shreveport, Louisiana, to demand the surrender of the ironclad *CSS Missouri* and a small Confederate naval squadron that remained on station there. Although warned in advance of the dangers of a torpedo attack, none materialized. By that time the mysterious Shreveport Singer-built submarines were undoubtedly sinking into the silty bottom, scuttled by their inventors when the end arrived.[21]

The capitulation of that tiny Southern armada anchored in the head waters of the Red River marked the last official act of the American Civil War.

CONCLUSION

Although tons of Southern documents were burned or otherwise destroyed at the end of the war, and Federal manuscript material on the subject is incomplete and fragmented, enough contemporary evidence remains to reach several conclusions about the early development of underwater "infernal machines."

There is now no doubt that the birth of the modern submarine took place during the American Civil War. The *Hunley*, for all of the justifiable attention she has received, was but one of perhaps two dozen underwater boats constructed during the conflict by both sides. With the strangling capacity of the Federal blockade tightening around it, and without a strong navy to raise it, the agrarian Confederacy was forced to experiment with more radical means to turn the tide of the war, including the wholesale construction of submarine "torpedo boats." The fact that the South did so early and often was largely the result of Stephen Mallory's farsightedness and the dedication and ingenuity of a number of private individuals and organizations. That the South was unable to accomplish more with so many enemy ships anchored off her coasts is understandable: builders and designers like Baxter Watson and Horace Hunley could imagine the possibilities, but underwater submarine technology was unable to keep pace with their dreams.

The Federals had far fewer opportunities to utilize the submarine as an offensive weapon. Instead, naval planners viewed it more as a means of destroying underwater obstructions in Southern harbors and rivers. Indeed, as we have seen, at least one submarine expedition was launched up the James River in 1862 with the intent of ripping apart obstructions. Still, given the possibilities of this new technology and the widespread industry in the Northern states, it is surprising that more was not done to perfect this new machine.[1]

In April of 1866, three years after her keel had been laid down in a Newark, New Jersey, shipyard, the *Intelligent Whale* (briefly discussed in Chapter 3 and also known as "Disastrous Jonah") was finally launched by the United States Navy. Unfortunately for the neophyte

Confederate underwater explosives expert E. C. Singer built the explosive device that destroyed the *Housatonic*. When he was in his mid-90s, this article appeared in the *San Antonio Express*.

This strange vessel was found in Charleston Harbor in 1865. It looks identical to Lodner Phillips's 1851 submarine vessel pictured at the top of page 258. *Washington Navy Yard, Navy Historical Center*

American underwater arm, the vessel was a disaster and killed by some accounts over thirty men during her various trials. She was dry docked soon after her catastrophic tests and is now on display at the Washington Navy Yard not far from where Brutus de Villeroi's *Alligator* underwent her propulsion modifications during the winter of 1863.[2]

The tragic consequences associated with the ill-fated *Intelligent Whale* unfortunately put an end to American military submarine development for over thirty years. It was not until 1897 that the United States Navy again witnessed a submarine vessel amongst its fleet. Europeans, however, continued experimenting with submarine boats of every size and propulsion system imaginable.[3]

In an effort to catch up with rival nations across the Atlantic, the United States Navy commissioned the *Plunger* into her fleet during the summer of 1897. Although the boat was slow and never met her designer's expectations, it was clear to the navy that the submarine could no longer be ignored. Over the last century, several wars and decades of peacetime trials have evolved the underwater boats into today's nuclear-powered submarines.

This unidentified Confederate submersible was photographed at the Washington Navy Yard in 1865. *Navy Historical Center*

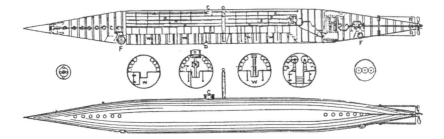

Lodner Phillips' 1851 submarine was written of extensively in English papers during the 1850s. Did Irish immigrant and Confederate submarine designer John Halligan base his *Saint Patrick* on this boat, which was described and pictured in an 1859 issue of *The London Illustrated News?* Surviving descriptions of Halligan's Mobile-based boat and Phillips' vessel (both of which were steam powered with retractable smokestacks), are virtually identical.

The response of the Civil War–era media—especially from French newspapers of the 1860s—also makes for some interesting discussion. Both Union and Confederate submarines were sketched and described in newspapers and magazines early and often. Frenchman Brutus de Villeroi's pre-*Alligator* submarine boat—which was chased down and captured at the beginning of the war in the Delaware River—was diagramed in an 1861 edition of *Frank Leslie's Illustrated Newspaper.* The Confederate submarine captured in Mobile Bay in 1864 was discussed and shown in the September 24, 1864, edition of *Harper's Weekly.* These American news coups were skillfully lifted throughout the war by the French and presented to an insatiable audience overseas. French illustrators, however, had a tendency to grossly exaggerate the size of the boats. Those seen by the French public were depicted as being over 100 feet long. The influence of this embellishment may have been more profound than anyone realized.

Frenchman Jules Verne's monumental undersea epic novel *20,000 Leagues Under the Sea* was first published only four years after the end of the American Civil War. Since Verne was researching and writing his novel during and after the war, it seems highly unlikely that French depictions of huge American submarine boats would have gone unnoticed. Was Captain Nemo's *Nautilus* based on one of those gigantic underwater

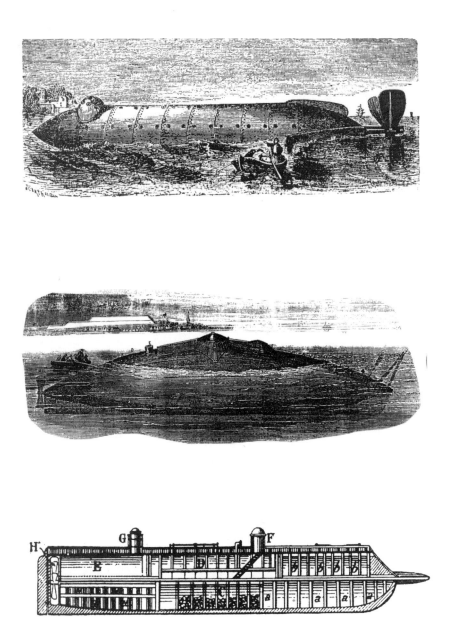

All three of these American subs appeared in French newspapers during the Civil War. Could Jules Verne have based his *Nautilus* on one of these woodcuts?

monstrosities pictured in his country's illustrated newspapers? Evidence suggests that it was. For example, in the novel Captain Nemo is relentlessly pursued through the summer of 1866 (the year after the Civil War ended). His pursuer is an American captain named Farragut (after Admiral David Farragut?) Farragut's ship is the *USS Abraham Lincoln*. These similarities validate that Jules Verne was well aware of Civil War naval history, and perhaps borrowed his concept of undersea vehicles from events that took place on the other side of the Atlantic during the Civil War.

EPILOGUE

The Recovery & Excavation
of the *H.L. Hunley*

The intact recovery of the Confederate submarine *H.L. Hunley* during the summer of 2000 is perhaps the greatest accomplishment in underwater archeology ever to take place in the western hemisphere. For nearly five years following her discovery by the adventure novelist and underwater explorer Clive Cussler in 1995, an international team of marine archeologists and engineers studied the wreck site in great detail. They debated various plans on how best to recover this history-making vessel. It was during this period of preliminary investigation that the author first became involved with the recovery operation by taking part in a series of dives to ascertain the current condition of the *Hunley's* victim, the sloop-of-war *USS Housatonic*.[1]

During the summer of 1999, underwater archeologists from the National Park Service, United States Navy, and the South Carolina Institute of Anthropology and Archaeology spent several weeks digging into the wreck site to assess what damage the *Hunley* had caused on the night of the attack in 1864. In 1909, what then remained of the *Housatonic's* boilers had been demolished and hauled away because the relatively shallow wreck had been a hazard to Charleston navigation since Reconstruction.[2] From a late 1864 report on the vessel's condition it was known that several feet of her hull had settled into the sediment soon after her loss, and everyone hoped that these buried portions remained intact.[3]

If enough of the *Housatonic*'s hull were still in existence, it was thought that it might be possible to determine the extent of the original damage inflicted during the attack, as well as to gain valuable information about the sub-bottom conditions that might be encountered while excavating the hull of the nearby *Hunley*. With two 6-inch diameter dredges constantly throbbing, a total of three 15-foot diameter test pits

During the summer of 2000 the crane barge *Karlissa B* was towed to Charleston and anchored near the *Hunley.* Her huge crane hoisted the Confederate submarine from her watery grave on August 8, 2000. *Photo by Mark Ragan*

were excavated during the weeks that followed. The diving conditions within these excavated holes (ranging from about 10 to 15 feet deep and in roughly 30 feet of water) were the worst that could be encountered, because the *Housatonic* had been resupplied with coal shortly before her sinking, and the coal-laden sediments that were dredged up caused the water in the test pits to turn pitch black and take on the consistency of crude oil. In an often heavy sea, we labored in teams of two under these sightless conditions day after day.

Numerous artifacts ranging from shoes and musket parts to a single-shot pistol and various pieces of naval ordnance were recovered from deep within the wreckage. The experience gained during excavations proved to be invaluable to those of us who would ultimately take part in the attempted recovery of the *Hunley*. In the late spring of 2000, with a team of over fifty experts gathered from around the globe, Project Director Dr. Robert Neyland commenced the history-making recovery of the world's first successful combat submarine.

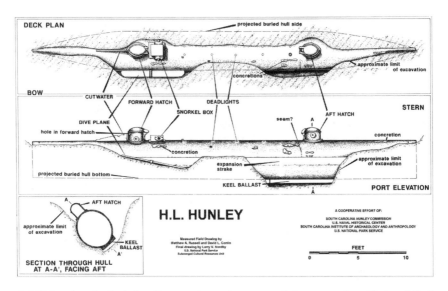

A 1996 archaeological site diagram shows the extent of the excavation. *National Park Service*

With the little submarine buried under 3 to 4 feet of sediment, it was decided that the excavation would first uncover the upper third of the submarine so that her overall condition could be assessed. Prior to the summer of 2000, portions of the upper-hull structure had twice before been partially uncovered to collect small samples of hull material, as well as to take core samples of the surrounding sediments that encased the vessel. Ensuing tests of the retrieved materials proved that the metal was sound enough to be recovered. From the deck of the crane barge *Karlissa B* (a huge work platform that had been towed to Charleston and anchored over the site), dredging operations around the *Hunley* continued night and day until the exposed upper hull of the vessel lay in the middle of a huge excavated depression in the ocean floor that measured 40 feet wide by 130 feet long.

While underwater archeologists excavated around the hull, oceaneering divers dredged out two huge pits about 10 feet distant from both the *Hunley*'s bow and stern. When these holes had been dredged to a sufficient depth, two gigantic steel cylinders measuring 12-by-18 feet

A diver examines the *Hunley's* forward conning tower prior to recovery. *Photograph courtesy of the Friends of the Hunley*

The author prepares for his 2:30 a.m. work shift on the *Hunley*. Project divers and archeologists usually worked in shifts ranging from two and a half to four hours. *Photograph taken by an unnamed oceaneering diver*

were lowered into them and anchored, acting as support for a large truss, or cage, that would soon be positioned over the entire length of the submarine. With the truss lowered and secured some days later, round-the-clock operations to expose and sling the *Hunley*'s encrusted hull began.

Based on past experiences with similar operations, it was decided that helmeted divers fitted with two-way communications and supplied with air from the surface would be the only underwater personnel allowed on site after the truss had been anchored into place. To get lost or snagged in zero visibility within the confines of this huge cage could prove deadly to a scuba diver, so every diver who worked the site after the truss had been secured had to have prior surface supply training. These helmets weighed in excess of 30 pounds each and were quite cumbersome on the surface. Whenever I found myself in near-zero visibility, somewhere within the metal framework of the truss that surrounded the *Hunley*—usually at two or three o'clock in the morning—communicating with a friendly voice from the surface or my unseen partner working in the darkness on the far side of the wreck, any discomforts associated with wearing the tight-fitting helmet quickly faded away.[4]

With the truss in place and the hull of the submarine continually being dredged, thick nylon slings injected with hardening foam designed to contour to the *Hunley*'s hull were slung beneath the vessel's keel and secured to the metal frame that loomed a few feet above the wreck. In this manner, between two and three slings could be secured in a twelve-hour work period. At about 8:30 a.m. on the morning of August 8, 2000, the Confederate submarine *H.L. Hunley* was hoisted from her murky resting place by the huge crane of the *Karlissa B*, and within seconds after the history-making submarine had broken the surface (shown live on CNN), deafening cheers from the 200 or so pleasure boats that had come to the site and anchored before dawn echoed across the water.

After being gently lowered onto a waiting barge, the *Hunley*, in an almost carnival atmosphere, was escorted by hundreds of pleasure craft into Charleston Harbor while low flying military jets streaked overhead in salute to the submarine's return after 137 years at sea. To everyone's great surprise, we found the harbor lined with thousands of cheering well-wishers who had taken time off from work on a Tuesday morning

The *Hunley* was placed aboard a huge barge and towed to the Warren Lasch Conservation Center in North Charleston. *Photograph courtesy of the Friends of the Hunley*

The *Hunley* at rest in a custom-built holding tank at the Warren Lasch Conservation Center. *Photograph courtesy of the Friends of the Hunley*

just to catch a glimpse of the returning *Hunley*. By early afternoon, the historic vessel had completed her journey to the Warren Lasch Conservation Center and was safely transferred to a custom-built holding tank.

In order to enter safely and examine the *Hunley*'s interior, a careful study and mapping of the hull had to be conducted. Utilizing a revolutionary new technology called 3-D laser scanning, Dr. Neyland and his international team of archaeologists and conservators were able to map the entire exterior of the *Hunley* to within 2 millimeters during the months that followed. Using the digital model created from the scan, the group determined the best point of entry that would not cause undue damage to the submarine or to the valuable artifacts she presumably held. As *Hunley* Project Historian, I had little or no involvement with this phase of the operation, and for the most part stood in awe of what the professional archaeologists were attempting to do.

By mid-January of 2001, it was decided that an existing hole in the aft ballast tank provided an excellent point of entry for a preliminary investigation of the interior, so with trowels, assorted dental tools, and custom-made implements on hand, the excavation commenced. This phase of the delicate operation revealed to us how the submarine's iron hull plates were attached and how much the sediment within had built up since her sinking in the winter of 1864. With the valuable knowledge gained during this phase of the excavation, three upper hull plates were removed from the center section of the vessel in the weeks that followed.

To everyone's great surprise, thick steel rings (known as ring stiffeners on modern submarines) were found within the vessel's interior at intervals of every 3 feet or so. (My own 12-foot K–250 submarine has ring stiffeners every 10 inches.) No known historical diagrams of the *Hunley* show these support rings within the hull, and their discovery only reinforced the assumption that the Singer group built an extremely solid and advanced submarine for its time.

With the *Hunley*'s entire hull packed from top to bottom with a dark, clay-like material, the monumental task of digging into it began. All sediments from within the *Hunley*'s hull were deposited into five-gallon buckets and sieved through three wet screens. Materials found (mostly small sea shells and marine-related items) were sorted by size and composition for future study.

To gain access to the inner hull the water level was lowered and several plates from the *Hunley* were removed. At the end of each workday the water level was once again raised. *Photograph courtesy of the Friends of the Hunley*

After meticulously digging into the sediment for several days, the upper part of the crew's wooden bench came into view, and within hours after that, a Confederate-issue artillery button and swatch of uniform cloth was recovered. By late March, additional uniform cloth, human rib bones, and a sailor's leather shoe—as well as the upper part of the propeller's crankshaft—were visible. At that point we became confident that the *Hunley* would continue to yield a great quantity of historically significant artifacts.

Throughout this period of excavation, I traveled back and forth from my home near Annapolis, Maryland, to Charleston. Although my educational background includes a bachelor's degree in anthropology/archaeology and a two-month archaeological dig in lower Egypt with Boston University, my credentials were inadequate to take part in the

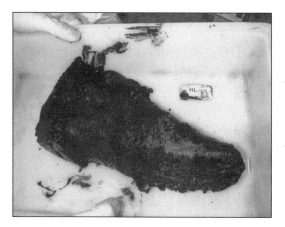

This well-preserved sailor's shoe is one of sixteen found within the *Hunley's* cramped interior. *Photograph courtesy of the Friends of the Hunley*

excavation process. Instead I was allowed to help occasionally with internal measurements, artifact transfers, and the hauling and screening of bucketed sediments recovered from the submarine's interior. Although I never actually excavated with a trowel in the *Hunley*'s hull, I was able to recover and catalog from the bucketed sediments several small artifacts, ranging from two finger bones and numerous strands of human hair to a couple of uniform buttons and swatches of cloth and leather.

The discovery of the first skulls had a sobering effect on me, for suddenly it became possible to gaze into the empty eye sockets of the various crewmembers whom I had studied over the years, and knew literally by name. As more and more human remains were uncovered, so too were the personal articles they had carried with them into the submarine on the evening of February 17, 1864. Over the weeks that followed, smoking pipes, shoes, additional pieces of clothing, and a wallet were recovered from the stern area of the submarine, as well as the remains of a slouch hat, a sewing kit (including a thimble and six buttons), and what appeared to be a sailor's silk bandana.

On April 27, perhaps the most unexpected artifact in the vessel was found: a Union soldier's identification disk inscribed "Ezra Chamberland, Company K, 7th Regiment Connecticut Volunteers." As strange as it might sound, it would appear that the disk was worn by one of the crew—it was recovered from the neck area of one of the skeletons. The local Charleston press speculated about a Union spy aboard the *Hunley*, but research at the National Archives determined that Ezra Chamberland had been killed in action at the Battle of Fort Wagner, which guarded Charleston harbor, and that the identification disk in all likelihood was a war souvenir worn by one of the *Hunley* crewmen.[5]

With the stern and center sections of the *Hunley* excavated, a fourth hull plate that supported the snorkel assembly and internal leather bellows (located just behind the forward conning tower) was removed in early May, allowing access to the submarine's most important area—the commander's forward compartment, where the submarine's diving controls were located. Within days after first digging into the sediments that filled Dixon's station, his remains slowly were uncovered, and the first artifact found in association with his bones was a small signal lantern. The same lantern that in all likelihood was used to signal shore after his crew and submarine had successfully sunk the *Housatonic*.

If I could not be on site, I made telephone calls for updates. From day to day it was never known what delays might be encountered and it was hit or miss as to whether or not I would be on site during a period of great discovery. One of my more memorable days during the excavation was in late May when, quite by accident, I found myself sifting buckets of sediment on the same day that head archaeologist Maria Jacobsen was going to excavate around Dixon's torso and lower legs. I knelt in the chilled clammy submarine next to Maria early in the day, and she pointed out to me the heels of Dixon's shoes protruding from the sediments, and in a serious voice told me to keep a sharp eye because small swatches of Dixon's uniform cloth would more than likely end up in the sediment buckets I was to examine.

As the hours wore on, several sediment-filled buckets were given to me for examination, and as Maria had predicted, several swatches of textile were discovered within. At the end of the day, I was once more invited into the submarine's forward area, where Maria showed me Dixon's fully exposed shoes and lower shin bones draped in what remained of his trousers. As Maria crawled out of the *Hunley*'s cold interior I paused for several moments and gazed on the dimly lit, sediment-filled area where the rest of Dixon's body lay, and I pondered

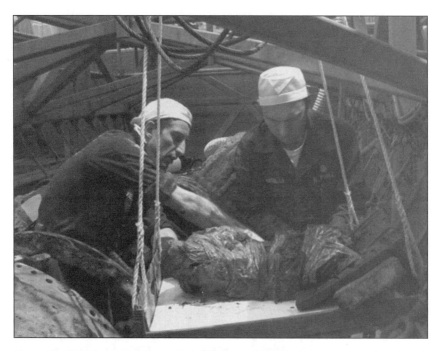

Part of Lt. Dixon's remains were block lifted out of the *Hunley* and removed to the lab for further study. *Photograph courtesy of the Friends of the Hunley*

what wonderful discoveries would be made during the days and weeks that followed.

With Dixon's upper torso and lower extremities so abundantly rich with uniform fabric, it was decided that all his remains would be block lifted and removed to the laboratory for further study. It was while preparing one of these block lifts that the most extraordinary artifact from the *Hunley* was discovered—a twenty-dollar gold piece carried by Dixon at the Battle of Shiloh that had stopped a Federal bullet. According to an article about Dixon that appeared in a 1904 edition of the *Mobile Daily Herald*, the coin had been given to him as a good luck charm by his sweetheart prior to his regiment's departure from Mobile. At Shiloh, the good luck charm was reported to have stopped a bullet, and sure enough, just as the article had stated almost a century before,

Senior archaeologist Maria Jacobsen holds a dented twenty-dollar gold piece recovered from Lt. Dixon's torso. The coin had been given to the young soldier by his sweetheart prior to his going to war, and had stopped a Union bullet at the Battle of Shiloh in 1862. *Photograph courtesy of the Friends of the Hunley*

there was Dixon's dented coin bearing the postbattle inscription, "Shiloh April 6th 1862, My Life Preserver G.E.D."[6]

The X-rays of the block lifts that contained Dixon's remains revealed among other small artifacts a large watch and a pair of small binoculars. In the weeks that followed the removal of Dixon's remains, a large brass compass and its wooden housing were recovered, as well as small shards of glass tubing that had once made up the submarine's mercury-filled depth gauge.

In all, eight skeletons were eventually recovered from the *Hunley* and examined by forensic experts prior to their burial, with military honors, at Charleston Magnolia Cemetery—next to the graves of the two previous submarine crews that had perished during training operations.

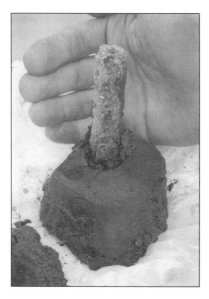

The *Hunley*'s candle was still in its wooden holder when it was recovered from the forward area of the submarine. *Photograph courtesy of the Friends of the Hunley*

O ver the past century several stories have circulated around New Orleans regarding the originator of the mysterious New Orleans submarine, which is on display in front of the Louisiana State Museum in Jackson Square. One of the more fanciful appeared in Simon Lake's 1918 book, *The Submarine in War and Peace:*

The New Orleans submarine boat was also built by the Confederates during the Civil war. A friend of mine who took the photographs of this vessel told me the following story as related to him by a southern gentleman who was familiar with the history of the boat. It appears that the submarine was the conception of a wealthy planter who owned a number of slaves. He thought that it would add considerable interest to the occasion of her launching if, when the vessel left the ways, she would disappear beneath the waves and make a short run beneath the surface before coming up. So he took two of his most intelligent slaves and instructed them how to hold the tiller when the vessel slid down the ways, and in which way to turn the propeller for a time when she began to lose her launched speed. He told them when they got ready to come up they should push the tiller down and the vessel would come to the surface to be towed ashore.

A great crowd assembled to see the novel launching, 'when things were all ready,' said the southern gentleman, 'sure enough, them two slaves got into the boat and shut down the hatches; and do you know, suh, that at that time them negroes was worth a thousand dollars apiece.' Well, it seems that the boat slid down the ways and disappeared under the water just as had been planned. The crowd waited expectantly, but the vessel did not reappear. Eventually they got into boats and put out hooks and grappling lines, but she could not be found. The designer of the craft stated as his opinion that 'he might have known better than to trust them pesky slaves anyway,' and he was willing to bet that they had taken the opportunity to steal the vessel and run away. He asserted that very likely they would take the boat up north and give it to the Yankees, and that they could expect to hear of the Yanks' using it to blow up some of their own (Confederate) ships.

Her disappearance remained a mystery for a great many years, until long after the war closed, in fact, and the incident had been forgotten. Years afterward, during some dredging operation to deepen the harbor, the dredge bucket one day got hold of something they could not lift. A diver was sent down to investigate, and he reported that there was some metal object buried in the mud that looked like a steam boiler. They set to work to raise this, and putting chains around it they lifted it onto the wharf. The old gentleman, in closing his narrative, remarked, 'And do you know, suh, that when they opened the hatch them two blame negroes was still in there, but they warn't worth a damn cent.'

While entertaining, the story is almost certainly a tall tale with little or no historical relevance.

NOTES

CHAPTER 1

1. Frank Busby, "Manned Submersibles" (Office of the Oceanographer of the Navy, 1976), p.1.
2. T. Roscoe, *Picture History of the U.S. Navy* (New York, 1956), plate 118.
3. C. Lawliss, *The Submarine Book* (Houston, 1991), p. 33.
4. Ibid., p. 34.
5. Roscoe, *Picture History of the U.S. Navy*, plate 350.
6. Ibid.
7. W. M. Robinson, Jr., *The Confederate Privateers* (New Haven, 1928).
8. G. W. Baird, "Submarine Torpedo Boats," *Journal of American Societies of Naval Engineers*, vol. 14, no. 3 (1902), p. 852.
9. Ibid.
10. Statement of Isaac Bell, July 26, 1919, as to Civil War Activities of Franklin G. Smith, copy in possession of William C. Schmidt, Jr., Columbia, S.C., Sidney H. Schell, Mobile, Alabama, and the author.
11. Ibid. The last known copy of Reverend Smith's pamphlet on "Submarine Warfare" was reported to have been in the collection of a Mr. P. Hunter of Nashville, Tennessee, in 1919. Evidence supporting the existence of Reverend Smith's Mobile-based submarine is presented in the following chapter.
12. E. P. Doer Letter, June 25, 1861, in Letters Received by the Secretary of the Navy, Record Group 45, National Archives.
13. James E. Kloeppel, *Danger Beneath the Waves: A History of the Confederate Submarine H. L. Hunley* (Orangeburg, S.C., 1987), p. 11.
14. S. Lake, *The Submarine in War and Peace: Its Development and its Possibilities* (Philadelphia, 1918), p. 39. For years many have thought that this mysterious submarine was the *Pioneer*, another small early-war submersible built in New Orleans during the autumn months of 1861. Recent archival research discussed elsewhere in this study, however, eliminates that possibility. A photograph and brief summary of Lt. Frances J. Wehner's involvement with the New Orleans submarine is located in the "Hunley File" at the Alabama Archives in Montgomery, Alabama. Copies of this article are also in the authors collection.
15. "First Torpedo Boat," *New Orleans Picayune*, April 2, 1909.
16. *Philadelphia Evening Bulletin*, May 17, 1861.
17. *New York Herald*, May 17, 1861.
18. *Philadelphia Evening Bulletin*, May 18, 1861.
19. Lines from an undated news clipping that accompanied Brutus de Villeroi's September 4, 1861, letter to President Abraham Lincoln, in Misc. Letters Received by the Secretary of the Navy, September 1861, Record Group 45, National Archives.
20. Burke Davis, *The Civil War: Strange and Fascinating Facts* (New York, 1982), p. 176.
21. Louis H. Bolander, "The Alligator, First Federal Submarine of the Civil War," U.S. Naval Institute Proceedings (June 1938), p. 848.

22. Navy Department Bureau Letters, September–December 1861, Record Group 45, Vol. 3, #77, National Archives.

23. Brutus de Villeroi, Misc. Letters Received by the Secretary of the Navy, National Archives.

24. Ibid., clipping attached to September letter from de Villeroi.

25. Allan Pinkerton, *The Spy of the Rebellion: A True History of the Spy System of the United States Army During the Late Rebellion* (Kansas City, 1883), p. 395.

26. Ibid.

27. Submarine diagrams, Letters Received by the Navy Dept., Record Group 45, Entry M–517, Box 23, # 312, National Archives.

28. William Cheeney Propeller Diagram pictured in the "Archer Account Book," Virginia Historical Society, Richmond, Virginia; Tredegar Iron Works Records, October 1861 Order Books, p. 1166, Virginia State Library. Evidence that Cheeney's vessel may well have been in the design stages several months earlier can be ascertained from the following account found in the June 24, 1861, edition of the *Charleston Mercury* "From our Richmond Correspondent. . . War brings out talent and genius. Some individuals here [Richmond] are endeavoring to establish the efficacy of a marine infernal machine, and propose to test its powers as soon as a company of capitalists can be formed who will guarantee a sufficient sum to put the exterminator in operation. I have taken some pains to inquire into its nature. It is a submarine battery which can be affixed to the keel of any vessel by means of water pressure. The operator has armor by which means he may be sustained underwater for twenty-four hours, having sufficient time to attach the machine; when that is done, he retires beyond the sphere of explosion, attaches a fulminating cap to his conducting tube, and the blockading ship is blown to atoms. . . The appeal of the inventor to the patriotism of capitalists is well enough, but there are very few persons who are willing to invest their money without ocular proof of the efficiency of the invention." Evidence that William Cheeney may have presented his submarine plans to the Confederate Navy Department during the summer of 1861, can be found in the following entry taken from the wartime diaries of naval officer John Brooke "August 17, 1861. Two or three days ago Mr. Mallory [Secretary of the Navy] directed me to examine or consider a plan proposed by Mr. William G. Cheeney for the destruction of blockading ships. The plan I believe practical and effective, reported accordingly."

29. Pinkerton, *The Spy of the Rebellion*, pp. 402–404. A variety of terminology was employed to describe the new technology both sides were attempting to deploy. Pinkerton, for example, used "submarine batteries" generically to include submersibles, while Gideon Welles usually used it to mean submerged torpedoes attached to galvanized wire and set off with electricity.

30. *New York Herald*, October 15, 1861.

31. *The War of the Rebellion: A Compilation of the Official Records of the Union and Confederate Navies*, 31 vols. (Washington, D.C.: U.S. Government Printing Office, 1901), series 1, vol. 6, p. 363. Hereinafter cited as *ORN*.

32. Leavitt, Charles P., "Compiled Service Records of Confederate Soldiers Who Served in Organizations From the State of Virginia," Record Group 109, National Archives.

33. Leavitt, Charles P., letter dated October 21, 1861. Letters Received by the Confederate Secretary of War 1861–1865, Record Group 109, National Archives.

34. Letters Sent by the Confederate Secretary of War, October 28, 1861, Record Group 109, National Archives.

35. Busby, "Manned Submersibles," p. 421; Leavitt letter, October 21, 1861.

36. *Harper's Weekly*, September 24, 1864.

37. Leavitt letter, February 4, 1862, Letters Received by the Confederate Secretary of War 1861–1865, Record Group 109, National Archives.

38. Leavitt, Charles P., CSR, Record Group 109, National Archives.

39. Leavitt letter, February 4, 1862.

40. Navy Department Bureau Letters, September–December 1861, Record Group 45, #76, National Archives.

41. *Harper's Weekly*, November 2, 1861.

42. Bolander, "The Alligator: First Federal Submarine of the Civil War," p. 850.

43. Commodore Joseph Smith Document found in Navy Subject File, Section "AV," Box 119, Record Group 45, National Archives; William C. Davis, *Duel Between the First Ironclads* (New York, 1975), pp. 20–22.

44. *ORN* 6, p. 392; Davis, *Duel Between the First Ironclads*, pp. 107–109.

45. *Harper's Weekly*, November 2, 1861.

46. *New York Herald*, October 19, 1861.

47. Tredegar Iron Works Record Books, October 1861 Order Books, p. 1212, Virginia State Library.

48. Roscoe, *Picture History of the U.S. Navy*, plate 816.

49. Milton F. Perry, *Infernal Machines: A History of Confederate Submarine and Mine Warfare* (Baton Rouge, 1965), p. 138.

50. Pinkerton, *The Spy of the Rebellion*, p. 403. Although Pinkerton mentions that contemporary newspapers discussed the submarines, I have been unable to locate any such references.

51. Letter from Goldsborough to Welles, "Navy Area File," Record Group 45, entry 81, National Archives.

52. Listing of Ship's Logs in Collection with corresponding dates, Record Group 45, National Archives.

53. William Cheeney note, December 15, 1861, "Confederate Navy Subject File," Record Group 109, Entry "BM" (Misc. Torpedoes), National Archives.

54. James McClintock letter to Matthew Maury, vol. 46 of the Matthew Maury Papers, Items 9087–9094, Manuscript Division, Library of Congress, Washington. D.C.; See the preface, generally, for a discussion of Southern submarine effort, in Kloeppel, *Danger Beneath the Waves*.

55. Commodore Joseph Smith Document, Box 119, Record Group 45, National Archives; Bolander, "The Alligator: First Federal Submarine of the Civil War," p. 850.

56. Biedermann letter, Misc. Letters Received by the Secretary of the Navy, January 1862, Record Group 45, National Archives.

57. Ibid.

CHAPTER 2

1. Sidney H. Schell, "Submarine Weapons Tested at Mobile During the Civil War," *Alabama Review* (July 1992), p, 164; Charles H. Poolen letter to General Leadbetter, January 5, 1862, McMillan Collection, Mobile City Museum, Alabama. It is interesting to note that General Braxton Bragg performed an inspection tour of Mobile during this period

41. *ORN* 7, pp. 545–546.

42. Ibid.

43. *OR* Series 2, 7, pp. 316, 343–344.

44. *ORN* 7, p. 477.

45. Ibid., p. 480.

46. Ibid., p. 488.

47. Letter of October 25, 1911, found in the *Alligator* File "Z" Files, Naval Historical Center, Bldg. 54, Washington Navy Yard, Washington, D.C.; ibid., letter of June 18, 1862.

48. *ORN* 7, p. 477.

49. Ibid., pp. 494–495.

50. Letter of June 21, 1862, found in the *Alligator* File, "Z" Files, Naval Historical Center, Blgd. 54, Washington Navy Yard, Washington, D.C.

51. *ORN* 7, p. 496.

52. Ibid., p. 497.

53. Ibid., p. 499.

54. Ibid., p. 499, 501.

55. Ibid., p. 501. Fort Darling was a powerful fortification on the heights of Drewry's Bluff overlooking the James River about eight miles below Richmond.

56. Bolander, "The Alligator: First Federal Submarine in the Civil War," p 852.

57. Ibid.; *ORN* 7, p. 500.

58. Ibid., p. 503.

59. Ibid., p. 500, 513.

60. Ibid., p. 523.

61. Ibid.

62. Ibid.

63. Surprisingly, there is no outstanding treatment yet in existence detailing the titanic struggle on the Virginia Peninsula. The best single book on the subject is Stephen W. Sears, *To the Gates of Richmond: The Peninsula Campaign* (New York, 1992). An excellent modern 3-volume set of original essays on the campaign is also available in William J. Miller, ed., *The Peninsula Campaign of 1862: Yorktown to the Seven Days*, 3 vols. (Savas Publishing Co., 1994–1998). Five of the thousands of Southerners who charged the summit that day were uncles of the author's great grandfather. All of them served in Company A, "Roxboro Grays," 24th North Carolina Infantry, Brig. Gen. Robert Ransom's Brigade. Two of the five would never return to duty: one was severely wounded and discharged, while the other was captured and died of typhoid fever on a Union prison barge several weeks later.

64. *ORN* 7, p. 526.

65. Ibid., p. 537.

66. Ibid., p. 540.

67. Goldsborough letter to Welles, July 5, 1862, in Letters Received by the Secretary of the Navy From Commanding Officers of Squadrons, 1841–1886, Record Group 45, Entry M89, National Archives.

68. Ibid.

69. W. A. Alexander, "The True Stories of the Confederate Submarine Boats," *New Orleans Picayune*, June 29, 1902; J. A. McClintock letter to Matthew E Maury, Maury Papers, Library of Congress, Washington, D.C.

70. Baxter Watson letter of October 10, 1864, in Letters Received by the Confederate Secretary of War, 1861–1865, Record Group 109, Entry M437, National Archives.

71. F. Buchanan, Letter book, entry of February 14, 1863, Southern Historical Collection, University of North Carolina at Chapel Hill, Chapel Hill, North Carolina.

72. Alexander Speech delivered to the Iberville Historical Society on December 15, 1902. A transcript is on file at the Mobile City Museum, Mobile, Alabama.

73. Buchanan Letter book, February 14, 1863, Southern Historical Collection

74. Perry, *Infernal Machines*, p. 18.

75. Philip Van Doren Stern, *The Confederate Navy: A Pictorial History* (New York, 1962), p. 109; *Harper's Weekly.*

76. Thomas O. Selfridge, *What Finer Tradition: The Memoirs of Thomas O. Selfridge, Jr., Rear Admiral, U.S.N* (Columbia, 1987), introduction, and p. 68.

77. Ibid., p. 69.

78. Ibid.; J. L. Christley, "Rest Your Oars." *All Hands Magazine* (March 1982), p. 15.

79. Selfridge, *What Finer Tradition*, p. 69.

80. Ibid. Samuel Eakins first appears in the Navy Yard's payroll book, at a monthly salary of $125, on July 9, 1862. See also, Eakins letter August 7, 1862, in Letters Received by the Secretary of the Navy from Officers Below the Rank of Commander, 1802–1884, Record Group 45, Entry M148, National Archives. On July 9, 1862, just five days after the *Alligator* left for the Washington Navy Yard, Secretary Welles decided to clean up some unfinished business: the *Alligator's* original crew still needed to be paid. "You will pay off and discharge the following men now attached to the submarine propeller," the secretary wrote to John A. Dahlgren, commander of the Washington Navy Yard: "C. Wordington, P. C. McCraven, Berry Claypool, P. C. Miller, Frank Snow, Henry Mc-Kenger, George C. Gorden, and Henry Maser." Welles to Dahlgren, July 9, 1862, in Letters Sent by the Secretary of the Navy to Officers, 1798–1868, Record Group 45, Entry M149, National Archives.

81. Selfridge, *What Finer Tradition*, p. 69.

82. Ibid., p. 70.

83. Eakins letter to Welles, August 7, 1862, in Letters Received by the Secretary of the Navy from Officers Below the Rank of Commander, 1802–1884, Record Group 45, Entry M148, National Archives.

84. Ibid., Thomas O. Selfridge letter, August 8, 1862.

85. Welles to Harwood, August 12, 1862, in Letters Sent by the Secretary of the Navy to Officers, 1798–1868, Record Group 45, Entry M149, National Archives; Selfridge, *What Finer Tradition.* p. 71; Perry, *Infernal Machines*, pp. 32–34. The *Cairo* was discovered in the 1950s and salvaged. It is now on display at the Vicksburg National Military Park. Edwin C. Bearss, *Hardluck Ironclad: The Sinking and Salvage of the Cairo* (Baton Rouge, 1966), details the search and raising of this magnificent ship.

86. Commander Smith to Eakins, August 18, 1862, in "Alligator File,"—"Z" Files, Naval Historical Center, Blgd 54, Washington Navy Yard, Washington, D.C.

87. *Philadelphia Evening Bulletin*, May 17, 1861.

88. Confederate Patent Office Records, Museum of the Confederacy, Richmond, Virginia.

89. Burke Davis, *The Civil War: Strange and Fascinating Facts* (New York, 1982), pp. 89–90, 176. Although Davis' book is not footnoted and is unreliable in several instances, the story discussed is consistent with recently unearthed documentation

concerning various weapons projects and undersea experimentation being conducted by Welles and company.

90. Ibid.

CHAPTER 3

1. Franklin Buchanan letter to Stephen Mallory, February 14, 1863, in Letter Book, Southern Historical Collection, University of North Carolina at Chapel Hill, Chapel Hill, N.C.; James McClintock letter to Matthew F. Maury, Maury Papers, Library of Congress, Washington, D.C.
2. William A. Alexander, "The True Stories of the Confederate Submarine Boats," *New Orleans Picayune*, June 29, 1902.
3. Buchanan letter, February 14, 1863.
4. *ORN* 19, p. 628.
5. William A. Alexander, "The True Stories of the Confederate Submarine Boats," *New Orleans Picayune*, June 29, 1902; S. H. Schell, "Submarine Weapons Tested at Mobile During the Civil War," *Alabama Review*, p. 168. Seaman James Carr's claim that the Mobile submarine was "in charge of the Frenchman who invented it," suggests an obvious question: was the Frenchman Brutus de Villeroi? Although de Villeroi breached his contract with the government and all but vanishes from the historical record, Seaman Carr was not discussing the Nantes, France, native. Evidence has been found that de Villeroi remained in Pennsylvania during this period.
6. Buchanan letter to Mallory (undated), Buchanan Letter Book.
7. H. L. Hunley letter of September 19, 1963, in Confederate Papers Relating to Citizens or Business Firms, Record Group 109, Entry M346, National Archives.
8. Telegram dated February 10, 1863, in "Alligator File," "Z" Files, Naval Historical Center, Blgd. 54, Washington Navy Yard, Washington, D.C.
9. Letter of February 29, 1940, outlining history of the Permanent Commission, in Navy Subject File 1175–1910, Record Group 45, Box 48, National Archives; Patricia Faust, *Historical Times Illustrated Encyclopedia of the Civil War* (New York, 1986), p. 206.
10. Victor Von Sheliha, *A Treatise on Coast Defence* (New York, 1868).
11. Welles to Harwood of February 12, 1863, in Letters Sent by the Secretary of the Navy to Officers, 1798–1868, Record Group 45, Entry M149, National Archives; Letter dated July 13, 1932, found in "Alligator File," "Z" Files, Naval Historical Center, Blgd 54, Washington Navy Yard, Washington, D.C.
12. Bolander, "The Alligator: First Federal Submarine of the Civil War," p. 854; Miscellaneous Letters sent by the Secretary of the Navy, 1798–1886, Entry M209, p. 469, Record Group 45, National Archives.
13. Letters Sent by the Secretary of the Navy to Officers, 1798–1868. Record Group 45. Entry M149, March 20, 1863; Acting Appointments, October 31, 1862 to July 30, 1863, No. 3, pp. 155, 165, 199, Record Group 45, National Archives.
14. Harwood to Fox, March 25, 1863, in Commandants Letters, Washington Navy Yard, January–March 1863, Record Group 45, National Archives; March 26, 1863 entry, Orders to Volunteer Officers, October 1862–July 1863, Record Group 45, National Archives.

15. Stern, *The Confederate Navy*, p. 55.

16. Roscoe, *Picture History of the U.S. Navy*, Plate 805; *ORN* 8, p. 636.

17. Eakins letter of May 11, 1863, in Letters Received by the Secretary of the Navy, Miscellaneous Letters, 1801–1884, Record Group 45, Entry M124, National Archives.

18. Winchester report, April 9, 1863, in Letters Received by the Secretary of the Navy from Officers Below the Rank of Commander, 1802–1884, Record Group 45, Entry M148, National Archives.

19. Ibid., letter from Eakins to Welles, April 9, 1863.

20. Brutus de Villeroi letter of January 29, 1870, Navy Subject Files, Record Group 45, Entry "AV-Alligator File," Box 119, National Archives.

21. Roscoe, *Picture History of the U.S. Navy*, Plate 805; Stephen R. Wise, *Gate of Hell: Campaign for Charleston Harbor, 1863* (Columbia, 1994), pp. 25–32. Wise's account of the myriad of activities surrounding 1863 Charleston is the best available on this subject.

22. On the same day (April 9) that Acting Master Samuel Eakins was writing his report to the Navy Department concerning the loss of the *Alligator*, a Confederate agent operating in Monterey, Mexico, notified his own War Department of an underwater invention docked in Barcelona that could be of great service to the Confederacy. "Narciso Monturiol, a scientific Catalonian, has invented a vessel for submarine navigation. She is called 'Ictineo' (fish like vessel)," explained John A. Quintero, a "confidential agent of the [War] Department." Quintero went to explain to Judah Benjamin:"As a man-of-war she can prevent not only the bombardment of the ports, but also the landing of the enemy, If the services of Mr. Monturiol are secured and the necessary number of vessels built, no federal squadrons would dare to approach our coasts, since an unseen enemy can leave our harbors and destroy their ships. The 'Ictineos' have guns which fire underwater and also rams and torpedoes. They can navigate in a depth of about twenty-five fathoms.The want of atmosphere to support animal life in the depth of the seas, which has been the great drawback to submarine navigation, has been obviated. The inventor creates an artificial atmosphere and shutting himself up, like a larva, carries with him the elements of existence. Several of the Spaniards here are well acquainted with Mr. Monturiol and are satisfied that he is not an idle talker. He has lately made experiments at Barcelona which prove his success." See John A. Quintero to Judah Benjamin, April 9, 1863, in Letters Received by the Confederate Secretary of War 1861–1865, Record Group 109, National Archives. It is unknown whether agents of the Confederate government ever contacted Monturiol in his Barcelona boarding house, or what became of his version of an "infernal machine."

23. H. N. Hill, "Texan Gave World First Successful Submarine Torpedo," *San Antonio Express*, July 30, 1916.

24. R. H. Duncan, *The Captain and Submarine CSS H. L. Hunley* (Memphis, 1965), pp. 63–64.

25. Alexander, "The True Stories of the Confederate Submarine Boats," *New Orleans Picayune*, June 29, 1902; Alexander, "Work of Submarine Boats," *SHSP*, 30, pp. 164–168.

26. "Dixon, Builder of the Submarine *Hunley*, Went to Death in the Deep," *Mobile Daily Herald*, November 15, 1904.

27. A. J. Marshall letter dated April 1863, Letters Received by the Confederate Secretary of War 1861–1865, Record Group 109, National Archives.

28. Ibid.
29. Confederate Patent Office Records, Museum of the Confederacy, Richmond, Virginia. I am grateful to John M. Coski, former historian and now librarian with the Museum of the Confederacy, for bringing this letter to my attention. In the accompanying cover letter, Dr. Coski wrote, "The reference in the second letter to secret files is certainly tantalizing." Tantalizing indeed. One can only guess as to what "infernal machine" diagrams once existed in that secret Confederate archive. From a drawing of the Triton Company vessel it would appear that the submarine was powered by two sets of oars.
30. Schell, "Submarine Weapons Tested at Mobile During the Civil War," p. 172.
31. Ibid.
32. Ibid., p. 173.
33. Ibid. Colonel E. H. Angamar may not have perished in Mobile Bay. According to a September 28, 1863, letter sent by Maj. Gen. Dabney H. Maury, the commander of Mobile, to Gen. Samuel Cooper in Richmond, a man simply referenced as "Angamar" was "captured by my pickets near Pascagoula while endeavoring to go to the enemy." OR 52, pt. 2, p. 552. The surname is highly uncommon and the letter was written by the commander of the city in which Colonel Angamar was operating only two months after he disappears from the record. Those two factors alone suggest this was the same individual associated with the rocket torpedo boat. But as is often the case with these matters, the record is too incomplete to make a definitive judgment.
34. Professor Horstford letter and diagram, Cambridge, Massachusetts, July 1863, in Letters Referred to Permanent Commission, Record Group 45, Entry 363, National Archives; Lawliss, The Submarine Book, p. 39.
35. Horstford Letter, July 1863
36. Baird, "Submarine Torpedo Boats," p. 848.
37. Horstford Letter, July 1863
38. Extract from Eustace Williams Collection, Mobile Public Library, Mobile, Alabama.
39. Ibid.; Alexander, "The True Stories of the Confederate Submarine Boats," New Orleans Picayune, June 29, 1902; Alexander, "Work of Submarine Boats," SHSP, 30, pp. 164–174.
40. Charles Davis Letter to Professor Horstford, July 27, 1863, in Reports of the Permanent Commission, Record Group 45, Entry 193, National Archives. The Permanent Commission and Professor Horstford were by no means strangers. Horstford's name appears in the record books and he regularly attended their monthly meetings. It seems safe to speculate that he knew the commission members personally and they knew him, and his ideas and opinions were respected by all. Reports of the Permanent Commission, Record Group 45, National Archives.
41. Buchanan Letter book, August 1, 1863, Southern Historical Collection.
42. James Slaughter postwar letter from file ADM 1/6236/39455, "Submarine Warfare," on file at the British Admiralty, London, England.
43. There may have been other reasons at work for the transfer of the base of operations to Charleston. Although Horace Hunley may have, as claimed in one contemporary report, "admired Genl. Beauregard above all men . . ." one historian claims money was the primary reason for the move. John Frazer and Company in Charleston offered $100,000 to anyone who could sink the New Ironsides or the Wabash, and $50,000 for any monitor sent to the bottom. Perry, Infernal Machines, p. 99. Perry is probably in er-

ror, since the original offer was not communicated to McClintock and company until August 15, 1863, several days *after* they arrived in Charleston. *OR* 28, pt. 2, p. 285. Alexander, in his postwar account "Work of Submarine Boats," *SHSP*, 30, pp. 164–174, makes no mention of the reward money as a reason for transferring to Charleston.

44. General James E. Slaughter file, Compiled Service Records of Confederate General and Staff Officers, and Non-Regimental Enlisted Men, Record Group 109, National Archives.

45. Buchanan Letter book, August 1, 1863, Southern Historical Collection.

46. Telegrams Sent, August 7, 1863, Department of South Carolina, Georgia, and Florida, 1863–1864, Record Group 109, National Archives, Washington, D.C.

47. Alexander, "The True Stories of the Confederate Submarine Boats," *New Orleans Picayune*, June 29, 1902; Alexander, "Work of Submarine Boats," *SHSP*, 30, pp. 167–168; *ORN* 15, p. 229, contains an account from a deserter, wherein the boat is called "the American Diver"; John Kent Folmar, *From that Terrible Field* (University of Alabama Press, 1986), pp. 117–118.

48. Gift letter, August 8, 1863, in the Ellen Shackelford Gift Papers, Southern Historical Collection, University of North Carolina.

49. Dahlgren letter, August 11, 1863, in Letters Received by the Secretary of the Navy from Squadron Commanders, Record Group 45, Entry 89, Reel 144, Number 121, National Archives.

50. Telegrams Sent, August 11, 1863, Department of South Carolina, Georgia, and Florida, 1863–1864, Record Group 109, National Archives; B.A. Whitney, Unfiled Papers and Slips Belonging in Confederate Compiled Service Records, Record Group 109, Entry M347, National Archives.

51. Letters Sent, Department of South Carolina, Georgia, and Florida, 1863–1864. Record Group 109, National Archives. It is possible that at the same time the Singer Submarine Corps was preparing the *Hunley* for action against the Union fleet off Charleston, members of the Triton Company of Richmond, Virginia, were also in Charleston preparing a submarine of their own. Senator A. J. Marshall, in a letter sent to the Confederate War Department some months earlier, stated that Charleston was the city in which he planned to operate. This Richmond group of adventurers were planning to utilize the same sort of craft that had been used in the James River in 1861, and the submarine in question was also to incorporate the services of a diver stationed in a false bow. The Charleston Engineering Department had a less than favorable opinion of the company's submarine diagrams, and would later suggest that no government funding be granted to the project. See Jeremy F. Gilmer letter dated October 15, 1863, in Letters Received by the Confederate Secretary of War, 1861–1865, Record Group 109, Entry M437. Further evidence suggests that the Confederate War Department released Thomas Smith—the machinist/engineer working for the Navy Department in Selma, Alabama, whose services were requested by Senator Marshall—from his duties so he could lend his unique knowledge of submarine boats to the Triton Company. See statement of Isaac Bell, July 26, 1919, as to Civil War Activities of Franklin G. Smith, copy in possession of the author.

52. *OR* 28, pt. 2, p. 670. Dispatches or telegrams written in August 1863 by the commander of Sullivan's Island refer to Whitney's vessel as the "torpedo-boat," and imply this

command relationship between McClintock and Whitney. Evidence on this point is admittedly thin.

53. Jordan to Whitney, August 154, 1863, in Letters Sent, Department of South Carolina, Georgia, and Florida, 1863–1864, Record Group 109, Entry 71. This is reprinted in *OR* 29, pt. 2, p. 285.

54. Letters Sent, Department of South Carolina, Georgia, and Florida, 1863–1864, Record Group 109, Entry 71, National Archives.

55. S. G. Haynes, Letters Received by the Secretary of the Navy: Miscellaneous Letters, August–September 1863, Record Group 45, Entry M124, National Archives.

56. Document/Diagram found in Navy Subject File 1775–1910, Record Group 45, Section "AD," Box 48, National Archives.

57. Ibid. Of all the nautical inventions reviewed by the Permanent Commission, Ensign Hartshorn's submarine plans were among the only diagrams submitted to the Navy Department that did not end up in the commission's large scrapbook of fanciful inventions (now in the collection of the National Archives). The diagram and description of Hartshorn's submersible can instead be found cataloged in its own folder in the Navy Subject File. Unfortunately, the record books kept by the Permanent Commission are fragmented, and it may never be known just how much consideration was given to his unique undersea invention. Careful examination of Ensign Hartshorn's diagram and letter suggest he had designed something closer to a small research submarine rather than a combat vessel to be used against enemy ships. At about 12' long, it is not unlike this author's own mini-sub, and if her iron hull were properly reinforced, I have no doubt that the little vessel would have been quite capable of diving to a significant depth. With her side and downward facing "flint glass" view ports, she would have been well suited for undersea exploration. Perhaps this is the use Ensign Hartshorn had in mind all along for his boat.

58. H. L. Hunley, August 21, 1863, in Unfiled Papers and Slips Belonging in Confederate Compiled Service Records, Record Group 109, Entry M347, National Archives.

59. Faust, *Historical Times Illustrated Encyclopedia of the Civil War*, p. 738.

60. Thomas Clingman report of August 23, 1863, in Letters Received, Department of South Carolina, Georgia, and Florida, 1862–1864, Record Group 109, Entry 72. National Archives.

61. *OR* 28, pt. 1, p. 670.

62. *ORN* 14, p. 513.

63. Theodore Honour letter to Wife Beckie, August 30, 1863, Honour File, South Carolina Library, Columbia, South Carolina; H. N. Hill, "Texan Gave World First Successful Submarine Torpedo," *San Antonio Express*, July 30, 1916.

64. Letters Sent, Department of South Carolina, Georgia, and Florida, 1863–1864, Record Group 109, National Archives; Hill, "Texan Gave World First Successful Submarine Torpedo," *San Antonio Express*, July 30, 1916; D. Wilkinson, "Peripatetic Coffin," *Oceans* (No. 4, 1978).

65. C. L. Stanton, "Submarines and Torpedo Boats," *Confederate Veteran*, 40 vols. (1914), vol. 22, pp. 398–399. Stanton, a friend of Payne's and fellow member of the *CSS Chicora*, wrote after the war that "Lieutenant Payne, although a willing volunteer for this dangerous enterprise, never at any time had faith in the success of the enterprise." Ibid., p. 398. Lieutenant Stanton had volunteered for duty aboard the *Hunley*, but was instead assigned to watch duty aboard the ironclad *Chicora*.

66. James McClintock's letter to Matthew Maury, Vol. 46 of the Matthew Maury Papers, Items 9087–9094, Manuscript Division, Library of Congress, Washington, D.C.

67. Lake, *The Submarine in War and Peace*, pp. 40–41. Lake is considered by many historians to be the father of the modern submarine.

68. McClintock letter to Matthew Maury, Matthew Maury Papers; Honour letter to Wife Beckie, Honour File, South Carolina Library.

69. *Charleston Post and Courier*, August 30, 1863. The *CSS Palmetto State* was another ironclad of the Charleston squadron. Augustine Smythe letters, South Carolina Historical Society, Charleston, S.C. Augustine Smythe was a Charlestonian who was attached to the *CSS Palmetto State* during the summer of 1863.

70. Beauregard to Ripley, September 1, 1863, Telegrams Sent, and Orders, Department of South Carolina, Georgia, and Florida, 1863–1864, Record Group 109; Smith and Broadfoot File, Confederate Papers Relating to Citizens or Business Firms, Record Group 109, Entry M346, National Archives.

71. Ripley to Bearegard, September 14, 1863, Letters Received, Department of South Carolina, Georgia, and Florida, 1862–1864, Record Group 109, National Archives.

72. *ORN* 14, p. 643.

73. H. L. Hunley letter to Beauregard, September 19, 1863, in Confederate Papers Relating to Citizens or Business Firms, Record Group 109, Entry M346, National Archives. Hunley's letter seems to substantiate that the *Pioneer* was lost during an attack.

74. Jordan to Trezevant, September 22, 1863, in Letters Sent, Department of South Carolina, Georgia, and Florida, 1863–1864, Record Group 109, National Archives; Alexander, "The True Stories of the Confederate Submarine Boats," *New Orleans Picayune*, June 29, 1902. Milton Perry incorrectly states that Beauregard summoned Hunley to come to Charleston and take command of the submarine. Perry, *Infernal Machines*, p. 100.

75. "The Heroes of the *Hunley*," *Munsey Magazine* (August 1903); Alexander, "The True Stories of the Confederate Submarine Boats," *New Orleans Picayune*, June 29, 1902. Since the names of the first Mobile crew have not come to light, I can only speculate as to the possibility of this theory.

76. Captain Edward B. Hunt, Civil War Pension File, National Archives. The April 17, 1862, letter to Hunt from the Adjutant General's Office in Washington reads as follows: "Captain E.B. Hunt, U.S. Engineers, Washington, D.C. Sir: The Secretary of War assents to a request made by the Honorable Secretary of the Navy, March 29, to cooperate with such authorities as his Department may designate to prepare certain plans for the destruction of vessels by submarine agency. You will report to the Secretary of the Navy accordingly. Respectfully, E.D. Townsend, Assistant Adjutant General." Ibid.

77. Ibid., Certificate of Death, Maj. Edward B. Hunt; Hunt's pension file also contains a report filed several months later with the United States Army Pension Commission concerning Major Hunt's detached duty: "The late Major Edward B. Hunt, Corp of Engineers, U.S. Army, was placed on duty under the direction of the Secretary of the Navy for the purpose of aiding in the preparation of certain plans for the destruction of vessels by submarine."

78. "Death of Major Hunt," *New York Times*, October 3, 1863.

79. Captain Edward B. Hunt, Civil War Pension File, National Archives. Judging from letters found in Hunt's pension file, several of his descendants were seeking information about their Civil War ancestor more than 70 years after his death.

80. Alexander, "The True Stories of the Confederate Submarine Boats," *New Orleans Picayune*, June 29, 1902; Hoehling, *Damn The Torpedoes! Naval Incidents of the Civil War* (Winston-Salem, 1989), pp. 77–87; Alexander, "Work of Submarine Boats," *SHSP*, 30, pp. 164–168.

81. Journal of Operations in Charleston Harbor, Sept 1, 1863–Jan. 21, 1864, Chapter 2, Volume 192, pp. 103, 105, Record Group 109, National Archives.

82. Ibid. After the *Charleston Mercury* article regarding the loss of the submarine *Alligator* had appeared, it would seem that military officials in the city expected similar attempts, for on March 11, 1863, the following unsubstantiated article regarding the loss of additional Union submarines appeared in the same paper. "Gone to the Bottom – Four submarine contrivances, intended for work in Charleston Harbor, were recently sent form New York in tow of the schooner *Ericsson.* After fourteen days passage the steamer arrived at Port Royal with only one of the machines, the others having broken loose and gone to the bottom." The source of this information was not revealed.

83. Rowan to Dahlgren, October 6, 1863, Area File of Naval Records Collection, Record Group 45, Entry M625, Area 8, National Archives.

84. Faust, *Encyclopedia of the Civil War*, p. 205; *Perry, Infernal Machines*, p. 84.

85. Ibid.; Dahlgren letter of February 19, 1864, Letters Received by the Secretary of the Navy From Commanding Officers of Squadrons, 1841–1886, Record Group 45, Entry M89, National Archives.

86. Perry, *Infernal Machines*, p. 85; Rowan to Dahlgren, November 28, 1863, in Letters Received by the Secretary of the Navy From Commanding Officers of Squadrons, 1841–1886, Record Group 45, Entry M89, National Archives. Several historians have referred to the "David" class of semi-submersible torpedo boats as submarines, although this classification in not correct. These were torpedo boats incapable of entirely submerging, and could only be ballasted to allow the vessel's narrow smokestack to remain above the surface. The photographs of these vessels (one of which appears in this book) confirms they were not submarines.

87. Journal of Operations in Charleston Harbor, Sept 1, 1863–Jan. 21, 1864, Chapter 2, vol. 2.

88. P. G. T. Beauregard, "Torpedo Service in the Harbor and Water Defenses of Charleston," *SHSP* 5 (1878), pp. 145–165.

89. Roswell Ripley, October 16, 1863, in Letters Sent, Department of South Carolina, Georgia, and Florida, 1863–1864, Record Group 109, National Archives.

90. Jeremy Gilmer letter, October 15, 1863, in Letters and Telegrams Sent and Endorsements on Letters Received by the Engineer Office, Department of South Carolina, Georgia, and Florida, 1863–1864, Chapter III, Vol. 9, Record Group 109, National Archives. Since it is obvious members of the Triton Company were in Charleston at this time lobbying for the construction of their boat, it is logical to assume they were familiar with Singer's group of ill-fated adventurers from Alabama. Indeed, it can be assumed they followed the *Hunley's* sea trials with some interest. On October 27, C. Williams sent General Gilmer a response to his October 15 letter in which were included detailed diagrams of both the Triton Company submarines that had been designed by the group. The letter refuted much of what General Gimer had concluded and is an irreplaceable reservoir of Triton Company-related information. Original copies filed in Engineer Bureau Miscellaneous Papers, Record Group 109, Entry 27, Box 1, National Archives.

91. Letter and Captured Submarine Diagrams, Letters Received by the Navy Dept., Record Group 45, Entry M–517, Box 23, #312, National Archives. Perhaps abandoning hope of getting the boat constructed east of the Mississippi River, the Triton members headed west. Two of its members hailed from that part of the country (E. Allen from Texas and C. Williams from Missouri), so it is logical they would exhaust all avenues for possible success.

92. Handwriting matches C. Williams' letter of June 30, 1864, on file in Letters Received by the Confederate Secretary of War 1861–1865, Record Group 109, National Archives.

93. Letter and Captured Submarine Diagrams, Letters Received by the Navy Dept., Record Group 45, Entry M–517, Box 23, #312, National Archives.

94. Isaac Bell letter, July 26, 1918, pertaining to the Civil War and submarine activities of Franklin G. Smith, Author's Collection. As shall be demonstrated shortly, C. Williams— the drafter of the captured submarine diagrams and member of the Triton Company— was a true submarine advocate who regularly petitioned the Confederate Congress and Engineering Department regarding the construction of submarine vessels.

95. Journal of Operations in Charleston Harbor, Sept 1, 1863–Jan, 21, 1864 (October 18, 1863), Record Group 109, Chapter 2, vol. 192, National Archives.

96. Alexander, "The True Stories of the Confederate Submarine Boats," *New Orleans Picayune*, June 29, 1902; Smith and Broadfoot File, Confederate Papers Relating to Citizens or Business Firms, Record Group 109, Entry M346, National Archives.

97. Beauregard, "Torpedo Service in the Harbor and Water Defenses of Charleston," *SHSP*, p. 159.

98. Alexander, "The True Stories of the Confederate Submarine Boats," *New Orleans Picayune*, June 29, 1902.

99. Letters Sent, Department of South Carolina, Georgia, and Florida, 1863–1864, Record Group 109, National Archives; *Charleston Mercury*, November 9, 1863. The last letter, mentioned in the newspaper articles, has not been located.

100. The day after the loss of the *Hunley*, Lt. George Dixon and Dillingham were immediately given transportation to Mobile "on business connected with the Submarine Torpedo Boat." Ripley letter of October 16, 1863, in Letters Sent, Department of South Carolina, Georgia, and Florida. Although not specified, this "business" included recruiting others familiar with how the boat operated. As Dixon had proven over the past several weeks, the *Hunley* was well-designed and could be operated without any problems in the hands of a capable pilot and well-practiced crew. The orders sent them to Mobile to recruit anyone still alive who had any experience in the machine. After relating the tragic accident that had taken place in Charleston, Dixon would presumably have reported to General Dabney Maury with an account of the sinking and with a request for permission to extend his detached duty in South Carolina. Whatever documents, letters, or orders he may have carried with him from the besieged South Carolina city have not come to light.

101. Contracts found in Navy Subject File, 1775–1910, Record Group 45, Section "AY," Box 132, National Archives.

102. Beauregard to Dixon, November 5, 1863, in Telegrams Sent, Department of South Carolina, Georgia, and Florida, 1863–1864, Record Group 109, National Archives.

103. Orders and Circular (Quartermaster, January 10, 1864), Department of South Carolina, Georgia, and Florida. September 1863–March 1864, Record Group 109, National Archives.

104. J. I. Hartwell, "An Alabama Hero," *Montgomery Advisor Journal*, March 11, 1900; Beauregard, "Torpedo Service in the Harbor and Water Defenses of Charleston," *SHSP*, p. 160; Alexander, "The True Stories of the Confederate Submarine Boats," *New Orleans Picayune*, June 29, 1902. Whether or not Henry Dillingham returned to the city with Dixon and Alexander is not known. Either General Beauregard's memory is faulty, or his order that the *Hunley* not submerge was flagrantly disobeyed or cancelled. It is well documented that the *Hunley* not only continued to dive, but that she and her new volunteer crew, under the command of Lieutenants Dixon and Alexander, did so with greater vigor and determination then ever before.

105. Dixon to Jordan, November 14, 1863, in Letters Received, Department of South Carolina, Georgia, and Florida, 1862–1864, Record Group 109. National Archives.

106. C. Williams letter of November 27, 1863, in Index to Letters Received by the Department of South Carolina, Georgia, and Florida, Record group 109, National Archives; Charleston Military Headquarters Register of Letters Received, autumn 1863, letter of November 27, 1863. An intriguing letter from the Confederate Patent Office to Mr. Williams, dated September 5, 1863, discusses his attempts to obtain a patent "for additional improvements in submarine boats . . ." The letter does not discuss the specifics of these improvements. Instead, it focuses on bureaucratic red tape regarding the payment of fees. It seems logical, though, that Williams shared these "additional improvements," whatever they were, with Dixon and his associates in Charleston. Confederate Patent Records, Letter Book, September 5, 1863, Museum of the Confederacy, Richmond.

107. Alexander, "The True Stories of the Confederate Submarine Boats," *New Orleans Picayune*, June 29, 1902. The question of why Dixon and Alexander selected but five men from the *Indian Chief* was a mystery for some time. A letter dated January 10, 1864, to the Chief Quartermaster answered the question. The correspondence directed that officer to: "cause Lt. G.E. Dixon to be refunded his actual expenses for lodging and subsisting for four men in Charleston attached to the Sub-marine Torpedo Boat or Engine of War, from the 12th of November to the 16th of December 1863, being the sum of six hundred and thirty one (631) dollars." Orders and Circular, Department of South Carolina, Georgia, and Florida, September 1863–March 1864 (January 10, 1864, Order #73), Record Group 109, National Archives. The four men were Lieutenants Dixon and Alexander, and two unidentified associates, all of whom had been given accommodations in a Charleston hotel or boarding house.

108. Ibid.

109. *ORN* 15, p. 337. The accident at the Fort Johnson dock claimed five lives, and mishap near the mouth of the Cooper River killed eight men, including Horace Hunley.

110. December 16, 1863, in Letters Sent by the Confederate Engineering Department, 1861–1865, Record Group 109, Entry M–628, National Archives. The term "submarine batteries" was used interchangeably with both underwater mines and submarine boats.

111. Ibid.

112. Captain Henry Bolton, Compiled Service Records of Confederate Engineers, Record Group 109, National Archives.

113. Letter dated March 4, 1864, found in Confederate Navy Subject File, 1861–1865, Record Group 109, Entry "M," National Archives. Although nothing is currently known regarding the alleged submarine vessel built in Wilmington, late 1930's news

articles transcribed from the *Wilmington Morning Star News* state the following "The Confederate government built a small submarine patented after that built in Charleston, S.C. that sank a Yankee vessel. One submarine was built at Ben and Bill Beery's shipyard across the river where now R.R. Stone has a shipyard. It was launched the day before the Yanks came into Wilmington and was burned the same day to prevent it from falling into the hands of the Yanks. . ." Rev. Andrew Howell was told by John S. Barnes that he had helped build the submarine at Beery's shipyard. "It was not put into service," Howell wrote, "but it was a reality." Originally researched by Chris Fonvielle, Jr. Documentation in authors collection.

114. Alexander, "The True Stories of the Confederate Submarine Boats," *New Orleans Picayune*, June 29, 1902; Smythe letter, February 21, 1864, in Smythe Letters, South Carolina Historical Society, Charleston, S.C.

115. Orders and Circular, Department of South Carolina, Georgia, and Florida, September 1863–March 1864, December 14, 1863, Gen. P. G. T. Beauregard Special Orders No. 271, Record Group 109, National Archives. From the dates previously cited, supra, note 107, on Lieutenant George Dixon's lodging refund from the Chief Quartermaster (November 12 through December, 16, 1863), it can be claimed with some certainty that within 48 hours after General Beauregard ordered the *Hunley* back into action, Dixon, Alexander, and their two unnamed associates moved from their Charleston hotel to join their crew on the Mount Pleasant side of the harbor. Orders and Circular, Department of South Carolina, Georgia, and Florida, September 1863–March 1864 (January 10, 1864, Order #73), Record Group 109, National Archives.

116. Alexander, "The True Stories of the Confederate Submarine Boats," *New Orleans Picayune*, June 29, 1902.

117. Notes from the papers of Engineer James Tombs, January 186[5], *ORN* 15, p. 334.

118. Ibid.

119. Ibid.

120. Letters Sent by the Confederate Engineering Department, 1861–1865, Record Group 109, Entry M–628, National Archives.

CHAPTER 4

1. Testimony of Shipp and Belton, January 5, 1864, in Area File of Naval Records Collection, Record Group 45, Entry M625, Area 8, National Archives.

2. Ibid.

3. Admiral Dahlgren Circular, January 7, 1864, in Area File of Naval Records Collection, Record Group 45, Entry M625, Area 8, National Archives.

4. Alexander, "The True Stories of the Confederate Submarine Boats," *New Orleans Picayune*, June 29, 1902. It was about this time that an interesting entry was made in the record books kept by the Confederate Congress in Richmond. Within the index book of resolutions and departmental reports is a notation dated January 11, 1864, describing a report submitted by the Confederate Navy Department entitled "Torpedo Boats." Journal of the Congress of the Confederate States of America, 1861–1865, (Catch Book), Record Group 109, National Archives. This report and thousands of other government documents was likely consumed in the fires that raged through the

44. Barnes letter to Gideon Welles, National Archives. Professor Horstford's submarine was being built at this time as well, and the Permanent Commission was aware of its fabrication. Barnes' and Horstford's boats were almost certainly one in the same. *Harper's Monthly Magazine* (June 1916), published an article entitled "The Submarine and Torpedo in the Blockade of the Confederacy," that substantiates the connection between Barnes and Horstford: "During these months [summer of 1864], there was also experimenting with a submarine devised by Professor Horstford, as there had been trials with Mr. Villeroi's diving-boat in 1861." Professor Horstford was from Cambridge, Massachusetts, and was presumably building his submarine vessel within the borders of his native state; Barnes' submarine was being constructed in Springfield, Massachusetts, at the same time. What is the likelihood that two Massachusetts-based submarine boats were being completed and launched simultaneously?

45. Ibid., Barnes to Fox.

46. Ibid., Welles to Barnes, March 2, 1864.

47. Ibid., Barnes to Welles, April 23, 1864; Ibid., Welles to Barnes, April 26, 1863.

48. Ibid., Barnes to Welles, August 5, 1864; Ibid., Welles to Barnes, August 12, 1863.

49. "Submarine Engines," *Army & Navy Journal*, March 19, 1864.

50. *ORN* 15, p. 882.

51. Stephen A. Hurlbut letter of April 12, 1864, in Letters Received by the Secretary of the Navy, Miscellaneous Letters, 1801–1884, Record Group 45, Entry M124, National Archives.

52. Stephen A. Hurlbut letter of April 12, 1864, in Letters Received by the Secretary of the Navy, Miscellaneous Letters, 1801–1884, Record Group 45, Entry M124, National Archives. Although the "rude sketch" which once accompanied this communication has not been located, it seems unlikely Hurlbut's letter was discussing Halligan's submarine project. Halligan's work was just getting underway, he was not working in Mobile but Selma, and there was nothing to sketch. It is more likely that Hurlbut's informants had information about another submarine, one that was steam-powered and definitely operating in Mobile Bay. In fact it was captured later that summer. Since the sketch accompanying Hurlbut's letter cannot be found, it may never be known with certainty which submarine was being described. The sketch would have answered the question since the captured Mobile boat (to be discussed shortly) was depicted as "Rebel Torpedo Boat" on the cover of the September 24, 1864, edition of *Harper's Weekly*.

53. Journal of the Congress of the Confederate States of America, 1861–1865 (Catch Book), "Bills and Resolutions of the Confederate Congress," Record Group 109, National Archives. Fortunately, Confederate patent records help fill in a few of the blanks. Williams, it seems, submitted diagrams on at least two of the vessels discussed in the report filed with Congress. January 1865 patent documents hold that on October 6 and 25, 1864, he was granted patent numbers 258 and 261 for two "Submarine boats" of his own design. Confederate Patent Office Records, Museum of the Confederacy, Richmond, Virginia. Reverend Franklin G. Smith was also busy that year, for on April 18, 1864, he received patent number 241 for "a sea-going vessel." Ibid. Unfortunately no other details were filed.

54. Letter/Diagram, Lt. Horace L. Hervey, 11th Connecticut Volunteers camped near Bermuda Hundred, May 12, 1864, in Letters Referred to Permanent Commission, Record Group 45, Entry 363, National Archives.

55. Ibid.
56. Adm. Charles H. Davis to Gideon Welles, July 18, 1864, in Letter Book of the Permanent Commission, Record Group 45, Entry 366, No. 2 of 2, p. 126, National Archives.
57. Letter/Diagram by "Phillips and Peck," dated June 9, 1864, in Letters Referred to Permanent Commission, Record Group 45, Entry 363, National Archives; Patricia A. Harris, *Great Lakes' First Submarine* (Michigan City Historical Society, 1982) p. 20.
58. Ibid., p. 24. Phillips and Peck letter, June 9, 1864.
59. Admiral Davis Report, June 28, 1864, in Letter book of the Permanent Commission, Record Group 45, Entry 366, National Archives; Ibid., Entry 193.
60. Ibid., Davis letter of June 15, 1864.
61. Jones to Maury, June 16, 1864.
62. Williams letter, June 30, 1864, in Letters Received by the Confederate Secretary of War, 1861–1865, Record Group 109, National Archives.
63. Ibid.
64. Perry, *Infernal Machines*, pp. vii, 138.
65. R. W. Dunn file, letter of April 9, 1864, in Confederate Papers Relating to Citizens or Business Firms, Record Group 109, Entry M346, National Archives.
66. Ibid. It is not known whether work had actually begun on the enormous vessel described by R. W. Dunn, from which torpedoes could be delivered "through tubes forward, aft and on both sides," before the war brought about an end to the effort. One thing is fairly certain: no such vessel was ever launched in the Confederacy.
67. Baird, "Submarine Torpedo Boats," *Journal of American Societies of Naval Engineers*, p. 854.
68. Ibid.
69. Faust, *Historical Times Illustrated Encyclopedia*, p. 504.
70. Ibid.; Perry, *Infernal Machines*, p. 161.
71. Ibid. See also, Farragut Report, in *ORN*.
72. "The Rebel Torpedo Boat," *Harper's Weekly*, September 24, 1864.
73. Ibid.
74. Ibid.
75. W. N. Rogers, "The Unsung Hero of the Civil War," Clearwater, 1973.
76. There is a substantial likelihood that James McClintock and Baxter Watson, the two Louisiana steam gauge manufacturers who had built both the *Pioneer* and *Pioneer II* with the late Horace Hunley, had a hand in developing the boat captured by Farragut. McClintock and Baxter had for some months been mining Mobile Bay with other members of the Singer Submarine Corps. Both names appear on a Singer Group roster (it is unusual that one was kept at all) for early spring of 1864; McClintock is listed as 39, and Watson as 34. See Letters Received by the Confederate Secretary of War, 1861–1865, Record Group 109, National Archives. Since the two partners had at one point attempted to power their second vessel (*Pioneer II*) with steam, and since both were recognized as early submarine pioneers, it is unlikely that their services would not have been sought out. At the least, they surely were aware of the Mobile submarine's fabrication prior to her capture. Wartime records from Mobile, Alabama, are very incomplete, but it is difficult to imagine McClintock and Watson not being in involved in some capacity.
77. Baxter Watson to Jefferson Davis, October 10, 1864, in Letters Received by the Confederate Secretary of War, 1861–1865, Record Group 109, Entry M437, National Archives.

78. John Halligan to Samuel Cooper, in Letters Received by the Confederate Adjutant and Inspector General, 1861–1865, Record Group 109, Entry H–3032, National Archives; Special Order Number 259, Paragraph 10, Adjutant and Inspector General's Office, Record Group 109, National Archives.

79. *ORN* 22, p. 268. Thanks to the efforts of John Hunley, a fellow Civil War submarine enthusiast from Louisiana, I was able to correspond with John Halligan's great granddaughter, who lives near Houston, Texas. After explaining my research she graciously supplied me with several documents she had acquired herself while investigating her Civil War grandfather. Some of them were new to me, and filled important holes in the John Halligan story. It is largely due to her research that I am able to explain the history of this late war submarine with greater accuracy and detail.

80. Letter Book of Catesby Jones, July 1, 1864, Commandant of the Selma Cannon Foundry, Selma, Alabama, Record Group 109, p. 301, National Archives.

81. *ORN* 21, p. 748.

82. Ibid.

83. Dabney Maury letter, December 4, 1864, received December 10, 1864, in Letters Received by the Confederate Secretary of War, 1861–1865, Record Group 109, Entry M437, National Archives.

84. *ORN* 21, p. 931.

85. Ibid.

CHAPTER 5

1. Baxter Watson letter dated January 6, 1865, to General P. G. T. Beauregard, Hunley File, Mobile Historic Preservation Society, Mobile, Alabama.

2. Halligan File, National Archives. It is interesting to note that Milton Perry, in his fine book *Infernal Machines*, p. 183, refers to the "St. Patrick" [sic] as a "torpedo boat." Perry, however, is not using the term interchangeably, as did the Confederates, to mean "submarine." Perry instead believed the boat was of the "David" class. Judging from his bibliography and endnotes, it is apparent he did not have access to the documentation I have discovered. There is no doubt that Halligan's *Saint Patrick* was in fact a steam-powered submarine capable of running both on and beneath the surface—even though she may have resembled a David in many respects. The method of attack against the *USS Octorara* (on the surface with her smokestack showing) has confused many students of the war as to the true nature of her construction and abilities.

3. Ibid.

4. *ORN* 22, pp 267, 268. General Cooper's office endorsed the letter with the following summary and passed it along to the Secretary of War on February 18, 1865. "The person in the written communication, John P. Halligan, was exempted January 26, 1864, upon recommendation of the Secretary of the Navy and by direction of the President, until July 1, 1864, to construct a submarine torpedo boat. The exemption was at the expiration of said time extended while the boat should be bona fide engaged in operating against the enemy. Every facility was afforded him to complete his work; he failed to avail himself of any of them. Upon application of General Maury he was removed,

when he carried off several essential parts of the machinery. After some search these were recovered. H.L. Clay, Assistant Adjutant-General." Ibid.

5. Ibid., p. 269.

6. Ibid., pp. 25, 269.

7. *Harper's Weekly*, "Incident on Board the *Octorara*," February 25, 1865. Thomas Keys, a Confederate soldier stationed in Mobile, kept a diary during this period. An entry on February 6, 1865, provides an excellent description of a steam

8. Schell, "Submarine Weapons Tested at Mobile During the Civil War," *Alabama Review*, p. 181. Schell does not elaborate as to exactly what the *Saint Patrick's* diversion consisted of.

9. Letters Sent by the Confederate Engineering Department, 1861–1865, Record Group 109, Entry M–628, p. 549, National Archives.

10. *ORN* 22, pp. 103–104. Major Jackson's information was obtained through a spy network of some sort and a captured letter, and thus its complete reliability is to some degree suspect. Jackson credits much of his evidence to the word of "Mr. Hunnicutt," who was a union spy. In any case, Hunnicutt's testimony that members of the Singer Submarine Corps were involved—James Jones, for example—lends credence to the account, for we know they were operating with General Smith in the Trans-Mississippi Theater at this time. See, for example, Singer, E. C., Breaman, J. D. and Dunn, R. W, Parole Papers, Kirby Smith's Army, in Un-filed Papers and Slips Belonging in Confederate Compiled Service Records, Record Group 109, Entry M347, National Archives. James Jones is mentioned in a letter in Naval Receipts, vol 22, p. 104. Other evidence found in Jackson's report substantiates the veracity of his entire account. For example, Jackson's information discusses an "Ike Hutchinson," from Lavaca, Texas, "who has charge of the torpedoes in Red River." This Hutchinson was almost surely Pvt. J. R. Hutchinson, a member of the 8th Texas Cavalry who was assigned on May 20, 1864, for duty with R. W. Dunn and the Singer Submarine Corps at Shreveport, Louisiana. See Special Orders for Texas, New Mexico, and Arizona, 1864, Special Orders No. 22, May 20, 1864, Record Group 109, Chapter 2, National Archives.

11. Singer, Breaman, and Dunn Parole Papers, National Archives.

12. Special Orders for Texas, New Mexico, and Arizona, 1864, Special Orders No. 22, June 21, 1864, Record Group 109, Chapter 2, National Archives. Since the order called for Captain Lubbock to "report the audit (of the quantity of metal issued)," it seems logical to assume that a large amount of the metal was turned over to Dunn. Singer contact mines, however, required only small amounts of internal ballast to submerge them. In light of the heretofore discussed reports, including Major Jackson's concerning the five submarine boats, it seems logical to assume that the iron in question may have been used by Dunn on these boats.

13. Special Orders number 70, March 11, 1865, for Texas, New Mexico, and Arizona, March–May 1865, Record Group 109, Chapter 2, Volume 103, National Archives.

14. Hill, "Texan Gave World First Successful Submarine Torpedo." *San Antonio Express*, July 30, 1916.

15. Report submitted by M. P. Hunnicutt dated March 13, 1865. Letters Received Office of the Chief Signal Officer District of the Gulf and Mississippi, Box 4, Number 1407, National Archives.

16. A. J. Wilson, Letter/Diagram dated March 31, 1865, in Confederate Navy Subject File, Record Group 109, Entry "BM" (Misc. Torpedoes), National Archives.

17. Coski, *Capital Navy*, p. 220.

18. For a good account of Mobile during the war and its defensive efforts in 1865, see Arthur W. Bergeron, Jr., *Confederate Mobile* (Baton Rouge, 1991). Bergeron also treats the *Saint Patrick* as nothing more than a "David," even though he includes a quote from Catesby Jones, the commandant at Selma, that "it is to be propelled by steam . . . though underwater by hand." Ibid., p. 169. The additional documentation unearthed regarding this submarine (and cited above) corroborates that the vessel was a true submersible and not simply a David-type torpedo boat as commonly believed.

19. Schell, "Submarine Weapons Tested at Mobile During the Civil War," *Alabama Review*, p. 182. The information on James A. Rice is taken from a 14-page letter penned by his niece in 1933. A descendant of hers graciously supplied me with this information, which is now in my possession. The Alabama family wishes to remain anonymous. Genealogical records accompanied the family history confirming James A. Rice's age as at least 44 years in 1865, rather old for a common sailor. A search of Confederate military and civilian records turned up several individuals named James A. Rice; unfortunately, none of them recorded any involvement with a submarine boat, which was to be expected.

20. Letter book of J. H. Carter, entry dated April 8, 1865, Commanding Naval Defenses in Western Louisiana, Record Group 109, National Archives. It's known from surviving Department of Texas, New Mexico, and Arizona order books that a huge ironclad torpedo boat, built by the Singer group, was then nearing completion in Galveston, and it could have been that vessel to which Phillips was being assigned.

21. *ORN* 27, pp. 228, 230.

CONCLUSION

1. Welles to Goldsborough, June 19, 1862, *OR* 7, p. 77.

2. Roscoe, *Picture History of the U.S. Navy*, Plate 929; C. Lawliss, *The Submarine Books* (New York, 1991), p. 38.

3. Ibid., p. 48.

EPILOGUE

1. Mark Ragan was granted volunteer diver status on the Housatonic Project after accepting an invitation from the South Carolina Underwater Archeologist, Christopher Amer. Dr. David Conlin, Dr. Robert Neyland, and Dr. Christopher Amer oversaw overall operations.

2. "Diving for the *Housatonic*," *Charleston News and Courier*, Charleston, S.C., July 12, 1908.

3. *Official Records of the Union and Confederate Navies in the War of the Rebellion*, Series 1, volume 15, page 334.

4. During March of 2000, all the Underwater Archeologists as well as Project Historian Mark Ragan, went through a five-day, forty-hour surface supply training seminar in Charleston, S.C. After the large metal truss had been placed over the *Hunley*, only those who had gone through such training were allowed on site.

5. Information obtained from Private Ezra Chamberland's War Record at the National Archives.

6. "Dixon, Builder of the Submarine *Hunley*, Went to Death in the Deep," The *Mobile Daily Herald*, Mobile, AL, November 15, 1904. The text in question reads "When the Twenty-first Alabama left Mobile the ladies of Mobile came out in full force to bid the boys adieu and say their loving farewells [for some would never return]. Among those present was the sweetheart of George Dixon. Just before the departure of the train she handed him a $20 gold piece, bidding him to keep it for her sake. In a hot corner of the fight not long after [the battle of Shiloh], he was shot down by a most painful wound in the groin. It was in a vital part and would have been mortal had not the ball first struck the gold piece and carried it into the flesh. When removed it was found that the coin was doubled up into such a shape as to form a bell, the bullet being firmly imbedded in the metal." [Dixon's war record on file at the National Archives notes that he was "severely wounded in the left thigh" at Shiloh, and was not "shot down by a most painful wound in the groin."] Compiled Service Records of Soldiers who Served in Organizations from the State of Alabama, Record Group 109, National Archives. Since the story of the bullet stopping gold coin originated in a Mobile newspaper, it's fair to assume that the author of the article obtained the tale from someone who had been close to Dixon, perhaps someone like William Alexander, who is known to have lived in Mobile at the time the story was written.

BIBLIOGRAPHY

MANUSCRIPTS

Charleston Historical Society, Charleston, SC
_____Smythe, Letters.
_____H. L. Hunley File
Library of Congress, Manuscript Division, Washington, DC
_____Matthew Maury Papers
_____E. Willis, "Torpedoes and Torpedo Boats"
Mobile Historic Preservation Society, Mobile, AL
_____*Hunley* File
Mobile Museum Archives, Mobile, AL
_____William Alexander Speech given to the Iberville Historical Society on December 15, 1902
_____Horace L. Hunley File
Mobile Public Library, Mobile, AL
_____Eustace Williams Collection
Museum of the Confederacy, Eleanor S. Brockenbrough Library, Richmond, VA
_____Annual Reports of the Confederate Commissioner of Patents, 1861–1865
National Archives, Washington, DC
_____Acting Appointments, October 31, 1862 to July 30, 1863, No. 3, Record Group 45
_____Commandants Letters, Washington Navy Yard, January–March 1863, Record Group 45
_____Compiled Service Records of Confederate Engineers, Record Group 109 (File of Captain Henry Bolton)
_____Compiled Service Records of Confederate Generals and Staff Officers, and Non-Regimental Enlisted Men, Record Group 109, Entry M331
_____Compiled Service Records of Confederate Soldiers Who Served in Organizations From the State of Alabama, Record Group 109, Entry M311
_____Compiled Service Records of Confederate Soldiers Who Served in Organizations From the State of South Carolina, Record Group 109, Entry 267
_____Confederate Navy Subject File, Record Group 109, Entry "BM" (Misc. Torpedoes)
_____Confederate Papers Relating to Citizens or Business Firms, Record Group 109, Entry M346
_____Endorsements on Letters Received, Department of Alabama, Mississippi, and Louisiana, November 1863–May 1865, Record Group 109 (Ch. II, Vols. 3, 4, 5)

_____Endorsements on Letters Received, Department of South Carolina, Georgia, and Florida, November 1862–February 1864, Record Group 109 (Ch. II, Vols. 23–27, 29, 30, 36, 187; Ch. VIII, Vols. 351, 352)

_____General Orders, Department of South Carolina, Georgia, and Florida, July 1862–January 1864, Record Group 109 (Ch. II, Vols. 41, 43)

_____General and Special Orders of Sub-Commands, Department of South Carolina, Georgia, and Florida, 1863–1864, Record Group 109 (Ch. II, Vols. 258 1/2)

_____Gillmore Papers (Department of the South). Record Group 393, Volume 1

_____Index to the Letters Received by the Confederate Adjutant and Inspector General and by the Confederate Quartermaster General, 1861–1865, Record Group 109, Entry M410

_____Index to the Letters Received by the Confederate Secretary of War, 1861–1865, Record Group 109, Entry M409

_____Inspection Reports, Department of South Carolina, Georgia, and Florida, 1863–1864, Record Group 109, Entry 76

_____Journal of the Congress of the Confederate States of America 1861–1865 (Catch Book), Record Group 109

_____Journal of Operations in Charleston Harbor Sept 1, 1863–Jan. 21, 1864, Record Group 109, Chapter 2, Vol. 192

_____Letter Book of J. H. Carter, Record Group 109

_____Letter Book of C. R. Jones, Commandant of the Selma Cannon Foundry, Selma, Alabama, Record Group 109

_____Letter book of the Permanent Commission, Record Group 45, Entry 366

_____Letters Received by the Confederate Adjutant and Inspector General, 1861–1865, Record Group 109, Entry M474

_____Letters Received by the Confederate Secretary of War, 1861–1865, Record Group 109, Entry M437

_____Letters Received by the Navy Department, Record Group 45, Entry M–517

_____Letters Received, Department of South Carolina, Georgia, and Florida, 1862–1864, Record Group 109, Entry 72

_____Letters Received by the Secretary of the Navy From Commanding Officers of Squadrons, 1841–1886, Record Group 45, Entry M89

_____Letters Received by the Secretary of the Navy: Miscellaneous Letters, 1801–1884, Record Group 45, Entry M124

_____Letters Received by the Secretary of the Navy From Officers Below the Rank of Commander, 1802–1884, Record Group 45, Entry M148

_____Letters Referred to the Permanent Commission-Unfinished Business, Record Group 45, Entry 363

_____Letters Sent by the Confederate Engineering Department, 1861–1865, Record Group 109, Entry M–628

_____Letters Sent by the Confederate Inspector General's Office, 1861–1865, Record Group 109, Entry M–627

_____Letters Sent by the Confederate Secretary of War, 1861–1865, Record Group 109, Entry M–522

_____Letters Sent by the Confederate Quartermasters Department, 1861–1865, Record Group 109, Entry 900

_____Letters Sent by the Chief of Artillery, Department of Alabama, Mississippi, and Louisiana, 1864–1865, Record Group 109 (Ch. II, Vol. 9)

_____Letters Sent, Department of Alabama, Mississippi, and Louisiana, 1864–1865, Record Group 109 (Ch. II, Vols. 8 1/2, 8 3/4, 14)

_____Letters Sent, Department of South Carolina, Georgia, and Florida, July 1862–April 1864, Record Group 109 (Ch. II, Vols. 22, 31, 32, 183, 184)

_____Letters Sent, Department of South Carolina, Georgia, and Florida, 1863–1864, Record Group 109, Entry 71

_____Letters Sent, Engineer Office, District of the Gulf, 1863–1865, Record Group 109 (Ch. III, Vols. 12, 13, 16)

_____Letters Sent by the Confederate Engineering Department, 1861–1865, Record Group 109, Entry M–628

_____Letters Sent by the Naval Commandants Office Shreveport, Louisiana, Jan–May 1865 (J. H. Carter), Record Group 109

_____Letters Sent by the Secretary of the Navy to Officers, 1798–1868, Record Group 45, Entry M149

_____Letters, Telegrams, and Orders, Department of South Carolina, Georgia, and Florida, March 1864, Record Group 109 (Ch. II, Vol. 195)

_____Letters and Telegrams Received, Department of Alabama, Mississippi, and East Louisiana, 1862–1865, Record Group 109, Entry 93

_____Letters and Telegrams Sent and Endorsements on Letters Received by the Engineer Office, Department of South Carolina, Georgia, and Florida, 1863–1864, Record Group 109 (Ch. III, Vol. 9)

_____Miscellaneous Letters Sent by the Secretary of the Navy, 1798–1886, Record Group 45, Entry M209

_____Miscellaneous Papers, Department of South Carolina, Georgia, and Florida, 1861–1862, 1864, Record Group 109, Entry 79

_____Navy Department Bureau Letters, September–December 1861, Record Group 45

_____Naval Records Subject File, 1775–1911, Record Group 45

_____Navy Area Files Record Group 45, Entry 81

_____Navy Subject File, Record Group 45

_____Orders, District of the Gulf, 1862–1865, Record Group 109, Entry 92

_____Orders and Circular, Department of Alabama, Mississippi, and Louisiana, 1862–865, Record Group 109, Entry 94

_____Orders and Circular, Department of South Carolina, Georgia, and Florida, September 1863–March 1864, Record Group 109 (Ch. II, Vol. 150 1/2)

_____Orders and Circular, 1st. Military District, Department of South Carolina, Georgia, and Florida, 1862–1863, Record Group 109 (Ch. II, Vol 37)

_____Orders for Texas, New Mexico, and Arizona, March–May 1865, Record Group 109, Chapter 2, Volume 103

_____Orders to Volunteer Officers, October 1862–July 1863, Record Group 45

_____Papers Pertaining to Vessels of or Involved With the Confederate States of America: "Vessel Papers," Record Group 109, Entry M909

_____Payments Made by the Assistant Quartermaster at Charleston, May–November 1863, Record Group 109, Chapter 5, Volume 237

_____Pension File of Major Edward B. Hunt, Civil War Pensions on File Proceedings of the Naval Court of Inquiry, Case #4345, Record Group 45

_____Receipts for General Orders, Department of South Carolina, Georgia, and Florida, Record Group 109, Entry 81

_____Records of Civilian Employment, Department of South Carolina, Georgia, and Florida, 1863, Record Group 109, Entry 78

_____Records Relating to Confederate Naval and Marine Personnel, Record Group 109, Entry M260

_____Register of Letters and Telegrams Received, Department of Alabama, Mississippi, and Louisiana, 1862–1865, Record Group 109 (Ch. II, Vol. 7 1/2)

_____Registers of Letters Received, Department of South Carolina, Georgia, and Florida, October 1862–November 1864, Record Group 109 (Ch. II, Vols. 19, 20, 33, 34)

_____Reports, Department of South Carolina, Georgia, and Florida, 1863–1864, Record Group 109, Entry 74

_____Reports of the Permanent Commission 1864–1865, Record Group 45, Entry 193

_____Special Orders and Circular, Department of South Carolina, Georgia, and Florida, September 1862–December 1863, Record Group 109 (Ch. II, Vol. 40)

_____Special Orders for Texas, New Mexico, and Arizona, March–May 1865, Record Group 109, Chapter 2, Volume 103

_____Telegrams Sent by the Confederate Inspector General's Office, 1861–1865, Record Group 109, Entry 618

_____Telegrams Sent, by the Confederate Secretary of War, 1861–1865, Record Group 109, Entry M524

_____Telegrams Sent, District Headquarters Houston, Texas (January 28, 1864–May 3, 1865), Record Group 109, Chapter 2, Number 137

_____Telegrams Sent, Department of Alabama, Mississippi, and Louisiana, January 1864–April 1865, Record Group 109 (Ch. II, Vols. 6, 10, 11, 196, 236 1/4)

_____Telegrams Sent, and Orders, Department of South Carolina, Georgia, and Florida, 1863–1864, Record Group 109 (Ch. II, Vols. 45, 48, 50)

_____Un-filed Papers and Slips Belonging in Confederate Compiled Service Records, Record Group 109, Entry M347

National Archives, Southeast Region, East Point, Georgia

_____Miscellaneous Wrecks, 1871–1888, Record Group 77 (#1125)

Naval Archives, Washington Navy Yard, Washington, DC

_____Holmes, J. G., Letters Received by the Naval Archives Concerning the
Confederate Submarine H. L. Hunley. "Z" File
_____*Alligator* File, "Z" files
_____*Hunley* File, "Z" Files
_____*Housatonic* File, "Z" Files
_____*Intelligent Whale* File, "Z" Files
Mark K. Ragan Collection
_____Isaac Bell Statements, July 26, 1919, pertaining to the Civil War activities
of Franklin G. Smith
_____James A. Rice Letter
South Carolina Historical Society, Charleston, SC
_____Augustine Smythe Letters
_____Captain Henry W. Feilden Papers
_____Records of the 1st Military District of South Carolina, 1861–1865
_____Records of Major H. Lee, Charleston Quartermaster, South Carolina,
South Carolina Library, Columbia, SC.
_____T. A. Honour Letters
University of North Carolina at Chapel Hill, South Historical Collection
_____Ellen Shackelford Gift Papers
_____Franklin Buchanan Letter Book
Virginia State Library, Richmond, VA
_____Tredegar Iron Works Record Books (October 1861 Order Books)

NEWSPAPERS

San Antonio Express
Charleston Daily Republican
Charleston Mercury
Charleston News and Courier
Chicago Tribune
Mobile Daily Herald
Mobile Register
Montgomery Advisor Journal
Montgomery Alabama Advertiser
New Orleans Times-Picayune
New York Herald
New York Times
Philadelphia Evening Bulletin
Philadelphia Inquirer
Philadelphia Public Ledger
St. Louis Post Dispatch
Savannah Daily Morning News

Busby, Frank. *Manned Submersibles.* Office of the Oceanographer of the Navy, 1976.

Christley, J. L. "Rest Your Oars," *All Hands Magazine* (March 1982).

Cornelius, George. "Surfacing *Hunley,*" *U. S. Naval Institute Proceedings* (August 1996).

Coski, John. *Capital Navy: The Men, Ships, and Operations of the James River Squadron.* Savas Publishing Co., 1996.

_____. "The Great Submarine Mystery," *The Museum of the Confederacy Newsletter* (Fall 1995).

Craighead, E. *The Hunley From Mobile's Past.* Mobile, AL, 1925.

Cussler, Clive. *The Sea Hunters.* NY, 1996.

Davis, Burke. *The Civil War: Strange and Fascinating Facts.* NY, 1982.

Delaney, Caldwell. *Confederate Mobile: A Pictorial History.* Mobile, AL, 1971.

Delpeuch, M. *La Navigation Sous-Marine.* Paris, 1902.

Dew, Charles B. *Joseph R. Anderson: Ironmaker to the Confederacy.* New Haven, CT, 1966.

Doran, Charles. "Daring Method of Destroying Enemy Ships," *Confederate Veteran,* vol. 16 (1908a).

_____. "First Submarine Boat in Actual Warfare," *Confederate Veteran,* vol. 16 (1908b).

Dorset, P. F. "*CSS Pioneer,*" *Historic Ships Afloat.* New York, 1967.

Duncan, R. H. *The Captain and Submarine CSS H.L. Hunley.* Memphis, TN, 1965.

Durkin, Joseph. *Stephen R. Mallory: Confederate Navy Chief.* Chapel Hill, NC, 1954.

Faust, Patricia. *Historical Times Illustrated Encyclopedia of the Civil War.* New York, 1986.

"Fighting *Hunley:* Made in Mobile," NA. Mobile, AL (December 1973).

Flato, Charles. *The American Heritage Picture History of the Civil War.* New York, 1961.

Ford, A. P. "The First Submarine Boat," *Confederate Veteran,* vol. 16 (1908).

Forest, F., and Noalhat, N. *Les Bateaux Sous-Marins Historique.* Paris, 1900.

Fort, W. B. "The First Submarine in the Confederate Navy," *Confederate Veteran,* vol. 26 (1918).

Fyfe, H. C. *Submarine Warfare: Past and Present.* New York, 1907.

Gunston, B. *Submarines.* Dorset, England, 1976.

Hagerman, G. "Confederate Submarines," *U.S. Naval Institute Proceedings* (September 1977).

Hanks, C. C. "They Called Her a Coffin." *Our Navy* (March 1944).

Harris, Patricia A. *Great Lakes' First Submarine.* Michigan City, MI, 1982.

"H. L. Hunley," NA. *The Retired Officer Magazine* (May 1997).

Hoehling, A. A. *Damn The Torpedoes! Naval Incidents of the Civil War.* Winston-Salem, 1989.

Holmes, E. *The Diary of Miss Emma Holmes 1861–1866*. Baton Rouge, LA, 1979.

Horton, E. *The Illustrated History of the Submarine*. London, England, 1974.

Hovgaard, G. W. *Submarine Boats*. London, England, 1887.

Hoyt, Edwin P. *From the Turtle to the Nautilus: The Story of Submarines*. Boston, MA, 1963.

"Hunley: A Very Curious Machine," NA. *The Confederate Naval Historical Society Newsletter* No. 16 (July 1995).

"The Iron Witch," NA. *True Magazine* (June 1960).

Johnson, John. *The Defense of Charleston Harbor*. Charleston, SC, 1890.

Keatts, Henry C., and Farr, George C. *U.S. Submarines*. Houston, TX, 1991.

Kelln, A. L. "Confederate Submarines," *Virginia Magazine of History and Biography* (July 1953).

_____. "Confederate Submarines and PT Boats," *All Hands* (April 1956).

Kloeppel, James E. *Danger Beneath the Waves: A History of the Confederate Submarine H.L. Hunley*. Orangeburg, SC, 1987.

Kolnitz, H. Von. "The Confederate Submarine," *U.S. Naval Institute Proceedings* (October 1937).

Lawliss, Chuck. *The Submarine Book*. New York, NY, 1991.

Levy, G. S. "Torpedo Boat at Louisiana Soldiers' Home," *Confederate Veteran*, vol. 17 (1909).

Lipscomb, F. W. *Historic Submarines*. London, England, 1970.

Mazet, H. S. "Tragedy and the Confederate Submarines," *U.S. Naval Institute Proceedings* (May 1942).

Melton, Maurice. *The Confederate Ironclads*. South Brunswick, NJ, 1968.

Middleton, D. *Submarine: The Ultimate Naval Weapon, Its Past, Present & Future*. Chicago, 1976.

Miller, Francis. *The Photographic History of the Civil War*. New York, NY, 1957.

Morris, D. R. "The Rebels and the Pig Boat," *Argosy* (October 1954).

Nichols, James L. *Confederate Engineers*. Tuscaloosa, AL, 1957.

Norlin, F. E. *A Short History of Undersea Craft*. Newport, RI, 1960.

Ortzen, L. *Stories of Famous Submarines*. London, England, 1973.

Orvin, Maxwell C. *In South Carolina Waters, 1861–1865*. Charleston, SC, 1961.

Perry, Milton F. *Infernal Machines: The Story of Confederate Submarine and Mine Warfare*. Baton Rouge, LA, 1965.

Pesce, G. L. *La Navigation Sous-Marine*. Paris, 1906.

Peterson, Curtiss. *"CSS Pioneer," American Association for State and Local History* (October, 1987).

Powles, J. M. *"Hunley Sinks the Housatonic!" Navy Magazine* (January 1965).

Preston, A. *Submarines: The History and Evolution of Underwater Fighting Vessels*. London, England, 1975.

Robinson, William M., Jr. *The Confederate Privateers*. New Haven, CT, 1928.

Rogers, W. N. *The Unsung Hero of the Civil War*. Clearwater, FL, 1973.

Roland, A. *Underwater Warfare in the Age of the Sail*. Bloomington, IN, 1978.

Roscoe, T. *Picture History of the U.S. Navy*. New York, NY, 1956.

Scharf, John T. *History of the Confederate States Navy*. Albany, NY, 1894.

Schell, S. H. "Submarine Weapons Tested at Mobile During the Civil War," *Alabama Review* (July 1992).

Shugg, W. "Profit of the Deep: The *H.L. Hunley*," *Civil War Times Illustrated* (February 1973).

Sims, L. "The Submarine That Wouldn't Come Up," *American Heritage* (July 1958).

"South Carolina Confederate Twins," NA. *Confederate Veteran*, vol. 33 (1925).

Stanton, C. L. "Submarines and Torpedo Boats," *Confederate Veteran*, vol. 22 (1914).

Stern, Philip Van Doren. *The Confederate Navy*. New York, 1962.

Stevens, W. R. *Campbell County, Kentucky: History and Genealogy*. Ft. Thomas, KY, 1985.

Still, William N., Jr. "Confederate Naval Strategy," *Journal of Southern History* (August 1961).

_____. *Confederate Shipbuilding*. Columbia, SC, 1987.

_____. *Iron Afloat: The Story of the Confederate Armorclads*. Nashville, TN, 1971.

Thomson, D. W. "Three Confederate Submarines," *U.S. Naval Institute Proceedings* (January 1941).

Tomb, J. H. "Submarines and Torpedo Boats, C.S.N," *Confederate Veteran*, vol. 22 (1914).

"Treasury of Early Submarines (1775–1903)," NA. *U.S. Naval Institute Proceedings* (May 1967).

van der Vat, Dan. *Stealth at Sea: The History of the Submarine*. Boston, MA, 1995.

Verne, Jules. *Twenty Thousand Leagues Under the Sea*. New York, NY, 1956.

Villard, O. S. "The Submarine and the Torpedo in the Blockade of the Confederacy," *Harper's Monthly* (June 1916).

Warner, Ezra J. *Generals in Blue*. Baton Rouge, LA, 1964.

_____. *Generals in Gray*. Baton Rouge, LA, 1959.

Wells, Thomas H. *The Confederate Navy: A Study in Organization*. University, AL, 1971.

Wilkinson, D. "Peripatetic Coffin," *Oceans*, no. 4 (1978).

Wills, Richard K. "The Confederate Privateer Pioneer and the Development of American Submersible Watercraft," *The Institute of Nautical Archaeology Quarterly*, vol. 21 (1994).

Wise, Stephen. *Gate of Hell: Campaign for Charleston Harbor, 1863*. Columbia, 1994.

Wright, Stuart T. *Historical Sketch of Person County*. Danville, NC, 1974.

INDEX